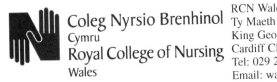

CLINICAL GUIDELINES: LAW, POLICY AND PRACTICE

Cavendish
Publishing
Limited

London • Sydney

CLINICAL GUIDELINES: LAW, POLICY AND PRACTICE

Edited by
John Tingle, BA Law (Hons)
Cert Ed, M Ed, Barrister, Reader in Health Care Law
Director of the Centre for Health Law
Nottingham Law School
The Nottingham Trent University
and
Charles Foster, Barrister
6 Pump Court, Temple, London EC4

Cavendish
Publishing
Limited

London • Sydney

First published in Great Britain 2002 by Cavendish Publishing Limited,
The Glass House, Wharton Street, London WC1X 9PX, United Kingdom
Telephone: +44 (0)20 7278 8000   Facsimile: +44 (0)20 7278 8080
Email: info@cavendishpublishing.com
Website: www.cavendishpublishing.com

© Tingle, J and Foster, C   2002

British Library Cataloguing in Publication Data

Tingle, John, 1954–
Clinical guidelines: law, policy and practice
1 Medical laws and legislation 2 Clinical medicine
I Title II Foster, Charles
344'.01

ISBN 1 85941 692 6

Printed and bound in Great Britain

LIST OF CONTRIBUTORS

Chapter 1

Jo H Wilson, MSc (Dist), PGDip, BSc (Hons), FCIPD, AIRM, MHSM, RGN, RSCN, RM, European Director of Healthcare Services, Marsh Ltd.

Chapter 2

DJ Tuffnell, Consultant Obstetrician and Gynaecologist, Bradford Hospitals NHS Trust.

Chapter 3

DJ Tuffnell, Consultant Obstetrician and Gynaecologist, Bradford Hospitals NHS Trust and Dr John Wright, Associate Medical Director, Consultant in Epidemiology and Public Health Medicine, Bradford Hospitals NHS Trust.

Chapter 4

Dr John Wright, Associate Medical Director, Consultant in Epidemiology and Public Health Medicine, Bradford Hospitals, NHS Trust and DJ Tuffnell, Consultant Obstetrician and Gynaecologist, Bradford Hospitals, NHS Trust.

Chapter 5

AJ O'Rourke, MBChB, MSc, Lecturer, Wisdom Centre for Network Learning, Institute of General Practice, Northern General Hospital, University of Sheffield.

Chapter 6

John Tingle, BA Law (Hons), Cert Ed (Dist), M Ed, Barrister, Reader in Health Care Law, Nottingham Law School, Director of the Centre for Health Law, Nottingham Law School, The Nottingham Trent University.

Chapter 7

Charles Foster, Barrister, 6 Pump Court, London EC4.

Chapter 8

Nicholas A Peacock, Barrister, 6 Pump Court, London EC4.

Chapter 9

Ronni P Solomon, Vice President, Legal Affairs and Risk Management Services, ECRI, Plymouth Meeting, Pennsylvania 19462, USA.

Chapter 10

Ole Frithjof Norheim, Associate Professor, Section for Medical Ethics and the Philosophy of Science, Department of Public Health and Primary Health Care, University of Bergen, Norway.

Chapter 11

Stephen Heasell, Senior Lecturer, Health Economics, Faculty of Economics and Social Sciences, The Nottingham Trent University.

CONTENTS

CHAPTER 1

WHY CLINICAL GUIDELINES?
A NURSING PERSPECTIVE

JH Wilson

SYNOPSIS

Clinical guidelines and Multidisciplinary Pathways of Care© are rapidly becoming an established and essential feature of modern day healthcare practice. There is increasing interest in the potential of clinical practice guidelines to promote the appropriateness, effectiveness and efficiency of healthcare delivery. They can be seen in a wide variety of clinical settings ranging across the primary, secondary and tertiary health and social care spectra. The 1997 White Paper[1] has a strong emphasis on quality and consistency of care delivery with assurances of performance measurements, integrated care[2] and clinical governance. It suggests making it a local responsibility to deliver healthcare which is compliant with national standards, making quality of care the driving force for decision-making at every level of the service, to ensure excellence for patients no matter where the care is provided. A number of controversial issues surround the use of guidelines. Some argue that guidelines are a fetter on clinical discretion and clinical freedom and can lead to the practice of 'cookbook medicine'. They fear guidelines being used against clinicians by serving to define a rigid or unrealistic standard or expectation of care delivery. Others maintain that clinical guidelines are an essential aid to providing safe and appropriate medical and nursing care. They see them as an opportunity to reduce unnecessary variation in treatment processes, enhance interdisciplinary co-ordination, and improve the overall quality of care. There are arguments both for and against the use of clinical practice guidelines which will be discussed in this chapter.

Clinical guidelines are:

Systematically developed statements which assist clinicians and patients in making decisions about appropriate treatment of specific clinical conditions.[3]

---

1   Department of Health, *The New NHS: Modern, Dependable*, 1997, Cmnd 3807, London: HMSO.

2   Wilson, JH, *Integrated Care Management: The Path to Success*, 1996, Oxford: Butterworth-Heinemann.

3   NHS Executive, *Clinical Guidelines*, July 1996, Department of Health.

They originate through professional organisations, evidence-based practices and locally tailored interdisciplinary agreements based on local research. Clinical guidelines should be used reflectively. They are meant to be a guide to share best practice, but are no substitute for professional judgment or individual accountability. Knowledge, education, skills and competencies must be used in order to apply them appropriately: they should not be applied slavishly or automatically. Practitioners are still responsible and accountable for the practices they deliver. Clinical guidelines are broad statements of principle giving practical guidance and consensus agreement, which assist in deciding which path to follow in order to achieve acceptable outcomes. Clinical practice guidelines usually suggest a course of action with elements, which are both optional and mandatory, and they assist in the maintenance of patient and staff safety. Used effectively, they have the potential to reduce the level of complaints and litigation in healthcare by improving the communication processes and the quality of care.

APPLICATION TO NURSING PRACTICE

Nurses increasingly need to base decisions and actions on the best possible evidence and appropriateness in order to contribute to improvements in patient care and maintain professional accountability. Clinical guidelines are an important tool for enhancing and informing this process. The setting of clinical guidelines is becoming an increasingly important aspect of nursing and healthcare strategies to ensure quality and in the utilisation of good risk management practices. Nurses provide 80% of hands-on care to patients and clients, so they are uniquely placed to make a difference to the day-to-day care delivery. This places nurses in the key position to develop evidence-based nursing care and to collaborate with other professionals and organisations to achieve more effective care.

NURSING ACCOUNTABILITY

A nurse is responsible for providing individual patient care of high quality and being able to demonstrate this by setting and monitoring acceptable standards and evaluating patient outcomes.

As registered practitioners, nurses hold a position of responsibility and accountability. Other people, including patients, relatives and other healthcare team members, rely upon the nurse. Nurses are professionally accountable to the United Kingdom Central Council (UKCC),[4] contractually accountable to employers and legally accountable to the law for their actions. The UKCC Code of Professional Conduct sets out to whom nurses, in the context of professional disciplinary regulation, must answer and how. It begins with the statement that:

> Each registered nurse, midwife and health visitor shall act, at all times, in such a manner as to: safeguard and promote the interests of individual patients and clients; serve the interests of society; justify public trust and confidence and uphold and enhance the good standing and reputation of the professionals.

The first four clauses of the code reinforce the professional and personal accountability, ensuring that nurses put the interest of patients, clients and the public before their own interests and those of their colleagues. They are as follows:

> As a registered nurse, midwife or health visitor, you are personally accountable for your practice and, in the exercise of your professional accountability you must ...

- act always in such a manner as to promote and safeguard the interests and well-being of patients and clients;
- ensure that no action or omission on your part, or within your sphere of responsibility, is detrimental to the interests, condition or safety of patients and clients;
- maintain and improve your professional knowledge and competence;
- acknowledge any limitations in your knowledge and competence and decline any duties or responsibilities unless able to perform them in a safe and skilled manner.

Nurses are accountable and responsible for their practice. No one else can answer for them. The code incorporates important themes and principles for nurses which apply to all areas of their work. Nursing practice is constantly changing and nurses can often find it difficult to keep up to date with the best available evidence on which patient-based care is based. Two million clinical research articles are published globally each year, and as nursing research increases exponentially, practising clinicians can find it difficult to keep up to date in current best practice. Without a way of critically appraising the information they receive, nurses can be relatively helpless in deciding what new information to incorporate into their practice. Evidence-based practice involves an ability to assess the validity and importance of evidence before applying it to day-to-day care delivery. Evidence-based practice requires new skills of the nurse, including efficient literature-searching review, and critical evaluation of the clinical literature. Whatever the source of evidence, the primary requisites of evidence-based practice are skills of critical appraisal

---

4   UKCC, *Code of Professional Conduct and Scope of Professional Practice*, 1992, London: United Kingdom Central Council.

and discrimination, as well as the ability to apply the evidence to the current problem. There are three vital sources of information:

(a) past experience and reflective practice;

(b) the patient, his carers and family; and

(c) robust research with new and improved information and techniques.

By formulating nursing guidelines incorporating up-to-date evidence, the huge task of keeping practising nurses informed about best practice becomes more manageable.

Clinical effectiveness is the process of addressing the information management of evidence-based practice and ensuring that the right care is provided to the right person in the right way and at the right time. It has been defined as 'the extent to which specific clinical interventions, when deployed in the field for a particular patient or population, do what they are intended to do, that is maintain and improve the health and secure the greatest health gain'.[5] The measure on its own is useful, but it is enhanced by considering whether the intervention is appropriate by reference to other criteria and whether it represents value for money. Nursing practice needs to be refined in the light of emerging evidence of effectiveness and appropriateness,[5a] but also has to consider other aspects of efficiency (see Figure 1.1) and safety from the perspective of the individual patient, their carers and the wider community in terms of outcomes of care. Adapting clinical effectiveness as a criterion of good practice will help nurses to demonstrate that the care given is the best possible through the following:

• having information about best clinical practice, for example, in the form of national and local clinical guidelines and systematic reviews of research findings;

• being able to put that knowledge into practice through education, clinical audit and change management;

• evaluating the effect on patients through clear audit criteria, monitoring outcomes and patient feedback.

Several national initiatives have been established to improve access to information about best clinical practice and to promote the uptake of evidence into practice. These include the Commission for Health Improvement (CHI), National Institute for Clinical Excellence (NICE), Health Care Evaluation Unit, Centre for Health Services Research, Cochrane Collaboration, the NHS Centre for Reviews and Dissemination and the Centre for Evidence-based Nursing.

---

5   NHS Executive, *Promoting Clinical Effectiveness: A Framework for Action in and through the NHS Source*, 1996, Department of Health.

5a   Wilson, JH and Tingle, JH, *Clinical Risk Modification: A Route to Clinical Governance*, 1998, Oxford: Butterworth-Heinemann.

CLINICAL RISK MODIFICATION – A NURSING IMPROVEMENT MODEL

This model pulls together the basic principles of good clinical risk management.

Figure 1.1: Clinical Risk Modification – A Nursing Care Improvement Model[6]

APPROPRIATENESS	EFFICIENCY	EFFECTIVENESS
CLINICAL GUIDELINES, REFLECTIVE PRACTICE and INTEGRATED CARE	MULTIDISCIPLINARY PATHWAYS CARE, COMMUNICATION AND GOOD RECORD KEEPING	CLINICAL STANDARDS, SUPERVISION and OUTCOME MEASUREMENT
Should it be done?	How to do it?	Did it work?

Appropriateness of care must be based upon having evidence-based research/practice to ensure that there are well justified criteria with which to determine what amounts to best practice. This will enable processes and systems involved to be defended most effectively if things do go wrong, and will provide the quality assurance standards necessary for a controlled environment of care. This must be achieved in line with clinical and cost effectiveness, to ensure that we are using our scarce resources to achieve the balance and not practising defensive medicine to cover our backs and for fear of litigation. Nurses can demonstrate how they provide the care by using Multidisciplinary Pathways of Care, effective communication and good record keeping. Then they can demonstrate the outcomes achieved and show that their practices work for the patient and their family as well as amounting to success within the terms of the guideline's own criteria of success. Not having models of good nursing practices, quality improvements and ways of demonstrating appropriateness, clinical effectiveness and efficiency can result in unnecessary risk exposure through lack of recognition, poor team working, and the inability to apply ongoing risk assessments and modification of high-risk exposures.

---

6   Wilson, JH and Tingle, JH, *Clinical Risk Modification: A Route to Clinical Governance*, 1998, Oxford: Butterworth-Heinemann.

APPROPRIATENESS OF CARE

All three UK White Papers[7] discuss appropriateness of care and how this must become a major focus of quality and clinical governance. None of the papers gives a clear definition of appropriateness of care, but it really means the optimum point of balance between liability and quality which is in line with having the best defensibility in terms of processes and systems if things do go wrong. It also entails quality assurance standards which demonstrate a controlled environment of care. Appropriateness (see Figure 1.2) is dependent on having the best quality improvement systems to guarantee high standards (clinical guidelines), must take into account both patient and staff perceptions in meeting these and must have adequate performance measurements to enable demonstration of the clinical governance criteria. This must be achieved in line with clinical and cost effectiveness to ensure scarce resources are used responsibly.

Figure 1.2:   Appropriateness of care in healthcare risk management

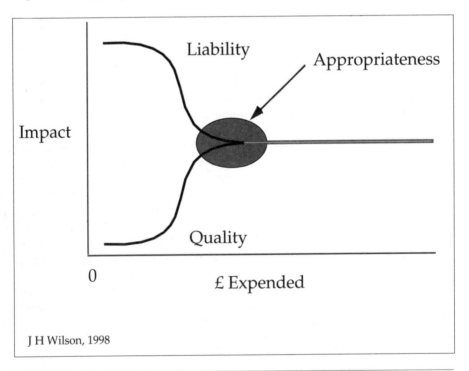

J H Wilson, 1998

---

7   Department of Health, *The New NHS: Modern, Dependable*, 1997, Cmnd 3807, London: HMSO; The Scottish Office Department of Health, *Designed to Care*, 1997, Cmnd 3811, Edinburgh: HMSO; The Welsh Office Department of Health, *Putting Patient First*, 1997, London: HMSO.

However, the preliminary data suggest that quality goes zooming up to meet patient's perceived expectations/softer aspects of quality, and appropriateness declines as it is not clearly defined and accepted (see Figure 1.3). There needs to be more balance of appropriateness in line with evidence-based research/practice and clinical effectiveness. Appropriateness should be at the centre of discussions about whether any clinical practice should be undertaken. Clinical practice guidelines based on research and evidence-based practice can help all Trusts to demonstrate a controlled and high quality environment of care.

Figure 1.3: Preliminary data suggests ...

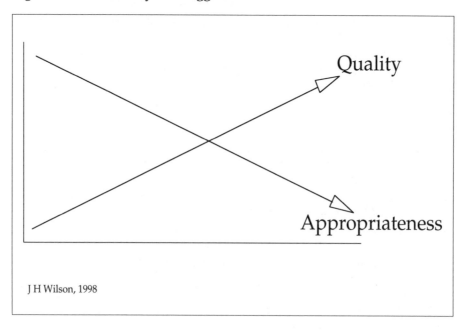

J H Wilson, 1998

DEPARTMENT OF HEALTH SUPPORT

The Department of Health (DOH) is actively encouraging the development and use of best practice guidelines. Winyard states:

Clinical guidelines provide a key vehicle for promoting evidence based practice and a basis for systematic audit. That is why they are so important. The NHS ... with the active participation of the professions, has developed a strategy which aims for evidence based clinical guidelines not just being used by clinicians, but also other partners in care – patients, purchasers, providers, indeed everyone who is involved to some degree in the decision making process.[8]

The NHS Executive good practice booklet on *Clinical Guidelines*[9] establishes criteria by which guidelines should be appraised:

- valid – the guideline recommendations are based on all currently available evidence, which has been correctly interpreted and reported;

- reproducible – given the same evidence and methods of guideline development, another group of developers will come up with the same recommendations and results;

- reliable – given the same clinical circumstances different health professionals interpret and apply the guidelines in the same way;

- cost effective – the guideline is leading to improvements in health at acceptable costs;

- representative – with representatives of all those affected by the guidelines, including patients having been involved in developing the clinical guidelines;

- clinical applicability – patient populations or services affected are unambiguously defined and areas not covered by the clinical guidelines are clearly stated;

- flexible – by identifying exceptions to the clinical guidelines recommendations as well as the patient preferences to be considered in decision making;

- clear – unambiguous language is used, readily understood by clinicians and patients and they are user friendly;

- reviewable – the date and process of review are stated and the guidelines are updated in light of new research or changing professional consensus;

- documentation – the procedures used in developing the clinical guidelines should be carefully described;

- amenable to clinical audit – the guidelines include information on ways adherence may be monitored. This information should be capable of translation into explicit audit criteria.

CLINICAL GUIDELINE AND MULTIDISCIPLINARY PATHWAYS OF CARE© SELECTION

Guidelines cannot cover every area of nursing practice. The following might be relevant in deciding whether or not a guideline would be useful:

---

8 Winyard, G, 'Improving clinical effectiveness: a co-ordinated approach', in Hitch, S and Hitch, M (eds), *Clinical Effectiveness from Guidelines to Cost Effective Practice*, 1995, Essex: Earlybrave.

9 NHS Executive, *Clinical Guidelines*, July 1996, Department of Health.

- common nursing problems/high volume/high cost;
- variations in clinical practice and nursing outcomes;
- general clinical uncertainty or controversy;
- potential rationing or resource issues;
- diagnosis/Healthcare Resource Group/Diagnostic Related Group/Healthcare Benefit Group;
- high risk/risk management issue potential for adverse events;
- clinical and/or nursing audit is well established;
- introduction of new diagnostic tests, therapeutic procedures or medications;
- frequency of complaints;
- quality of care issues perceived by patients, clinicians or managers;
- staff and patient satisfaction surveys to implement changes.

CLINICAL RISK MANAGEMENT: DEVELOPING BEST PRACTICE GUIDELINES

Figure 1.4: Developing best clinical practice guidelines

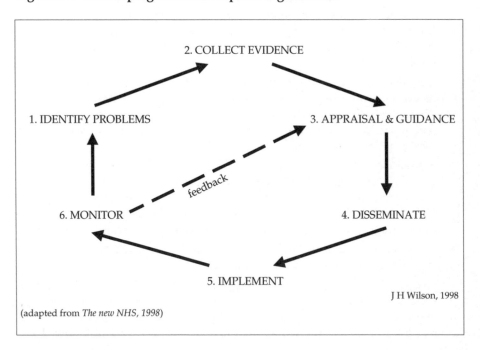

2. COLLECT EVIDENCE

1. IDENTIFY PROBLEMS

3. APPRAISAL & GUIDANCE

feedback

6. MONITOR

4. DISSEMINATE

5. IMPLEMENT

J H Wilson, 1998

(adapted from *The new NHS, 1998*)

- *identify the rationale and the need for a guideline*: what is the risk issue? State the reasoning for the concern and any potential or known problems due to this risk exposure. If the nurse is not able to give a rationale he/she should seriously consider whether an action is appropriate. Are there already clinical guidelines available for this particular topic? If so, can they be adapted and implemented into nursing practice? Guidelines should be based on the latest research and evidence and updated every 1–3 years;

- *make clear the aims and objectives of implementation and communication*: state who is the target group for usage of the guideline. Consider the four main stakeholders: the patient, professionals, commissioners and the general public. Will the guideline have a significant impact on patient care in terms of reducing morbidity and/or mortality? All developments should be supported and endorsed by all clinicians and senior management;

- *devise in the light of current research and evidence-based practice*: ensure all references are provided. Will the guideline answer an area of 'uncertainty' evidenced by a wide variation in clinical practice or outcome? When there are different treatment/care approaches the alternatives should be clearly indicated. Ensure the guideline is in accordance with national and professional policies;

- *screening/clinical procedures should be referred to in brief*: any legal or statutory responsibilities should be outlined. Guidelines cannot anticipate every clinical circumstance, and users should be encouraged to follow their clinical judgment in exceptional cases. Nurses should be told to document their rationale for not following the guideline, for example, 'Risk of procedure/treatment likely to outweigh the benefits, in light of patient condition';

- *the follow-up and recall system should be included*: ensure that the clinical guidelines take into consideration the local circumstances. Identify obstacles and indicate how they can be surmounted. Translate recommendations into local practice. Take into account resource levels and local population requirements;

- *outline methods of evaluation/audit to review the outcomes of the clinical guidelines*: these should be based on quality and not cost containment. Cost can be considered but should be accorded a lower priority than clinical effectiveness. The evaluation procedures should be backed up with an appropriate education programme and use of patient-specific reminders;

- *specify any equipment that will be required and the necessary training and usage*: checks and fail-safes need to be built into the system;

- *specify the necessary ongoing education, training and skills based competence updates and assessments*: outline the practical steps necessary to make sure that there is full implementation. Guidelines are working documents used by busy nurses and therefore they must be easy to read and follow. They need to be developed and owned by, rather than imposed upon, practising clinical nurses;

• *state the professional requirements, procedures/interventions to be undertaken, indications, the patients to be included, the patients to be excluded, and the education, training and expertise required*: the guideline could have a disclaimer stating that it is an educational tool to aid clinical decision-making and does not define the only acceptable practice. Such a guideline should make it clear that the nurse should deviate from the guideline when clinical judgment so indicates. The guideline developer should request a critical review of the drafts of the guidelines and, where appropriate, amend them accordingly.

APPRAISAL OF CLINICAL GUIDELINES

The use of clinical guidelines by nurses has provided an excellent approach for linking nursing research into clinical practice. Clinical guidelines can describe different processes of patient care delivery, and when linked into care pathways their compliance can be measured and linked to standards of care; outcomes and variations can also be recorded. The Health Care Evaluation Unit at St George's Hospital Medical School, using the work of Cluzeau *et al*,[10] has developed an appraisal instrument for clinical guidelines:

> The purpose of the instrument is to encourage the systematic development of clinical guidelines in the UK and to provide a structured and transparent approach to their appraisal. It is designed to assess the extent to which known predictors of good guidelines have been addressed during their development. It can be used by independent appraisers to assess existing guidelines or by guideline developers as an *aide memoire*.

The instrument is a very useful tool for nurses and nursing to ensure the robustness of the guidelines and the clinical application in ensuring that the guidelines work. The instrument contains 37 questions based upon the rigour of development, the context and content and the application, including implementation and dissemination strategies and monitoring.

CLINICAL GOVERNANCE

Clinical governance within healthcare organisations provides a clear framework for the achievement of quality improvement. Quality in this

---

10 Cluzeau, F *et al*, *Appraisal Instrument for Clinical Guidelines*, May 1997, London: St George's Medical School.

context means clinical care as well as customer care, and getting things right first time and every time. It also entails risk management (avoiding the potential for unwanted outcomes and again getting things right every time). Clinical governance encompasses all the processes needed to achieve the highest quality clinical practice possible, within available resources. Clinical governance represents a major opportunity for nurses as it gives them the authority they need to make the health service work more effectively. Nurses have a major role to play in the full range of activities and delivery of the processes of clinical governance.

With the full implementation of the 1997 White Papers,[11] new statutory duties have been imposed on all healthcare providers to participate in the local health plans and health improvement programmes (HIPS) through consultation, partnership, co-operation, communication and integrated care management.[12] NHS organisations also have, for the first time, a statutory responsibility to work in partnership and to maintain and improve the quality of care they provide, by processes which are subject to external scrutiny, review and accountability: s 18 of the Health Act 1999. Since April 1999, all healthcare providers have had to produce an annual report, the aim being to encourage compliance with Clinical Governance objectives. This has incorporated a number of processes, which are detailed below. Clinical Governance places a duty of responsibility on the Chief Executive, Trust Board and all healthcare professionals to ensure that care is 'satisfactory, consistent and responsive. Each individual will be responsible for the quality of their clinical practice as part of professional self-regulation'.

Clinical Governance puts each nurse's individual accountability into the broader concept of corporate responsibility for professional practice. Every nurse has a duty, responsibility and accountability for the quality of his/her clinical practice and the overall quality of care. For nurses, this means that no longer can they rely on myth and tradition to guide their nursing practices: instead they must support practices based upon research and evidence, in order to be confident that they are up to date and providing the best standards of care. This will involve developing partnerships with patients and involving them in the decisions about their care and will include using clinical guidelines. Nurses need to be involved in consulting patients to find out what is appropriate and important to their patients in terms of quality of care, and to obtain feedback on the service in terms of what works and what needs to change. These are all areas which need to be considered in the development of clinical guidelines.

---

11 *Op cit*, fn 7.
12 Wilson, JH, *Integrated Care Management: The Path to Success*, 1996, Oxford: Butterworth-Heinemann.

PRINCIPLES OF CLINICAL GOVERNANCE

All clinicians are expected to participate fully in audit programmes, including specialty and subspecialty national external audit programmes endorsed by the Commission for Health Improvement. Clinical Governance places a duty of responsibility on all healthcare professionals to ensure that care is satisfactory, consistent and responsive. It emphasises that each individual is responsible for the quality of their clinical practice as part of professional self-regulation. It will strengthen the current systems of quality assurance based on evaluation of clinical standards, better utilisation of evidence-based practice and learning the lessons from poor performance (see Figure 1.5, which outlines the continuous process for monitoring best practice and delineates the areas where clinical governance has an essential monitoring role). The clinical governance framework builds upon professional self-regulation and performance review. It takes account of existing systems of quality control and aims to include all relevant information. It is based upon partnership and driven by performance based on efficiency, effectiveness and excellence.

Figure 1.5: Monitoring best practice

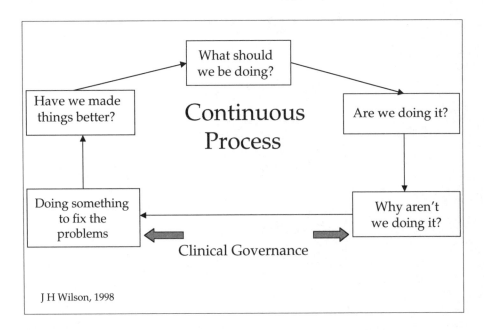

J H Wilson, 1998

Any mechanism designed to improve clinical quality must be compliant with the wider policies of the healthcare provider, and it must be possible to show that it works (see Figure 1.6). An excellent way to achieve this is through Integrated Care Management (ICM) and the full utilisation of Multidisciplinary Pathways of Care© (MPCs©)[13] which have included clinical guidelines, standards, outcomes and variance analysis. MPCs can incorporate components of effective care, including evidence-based practice, clinical audit, change management, multidisciplinary working and performance management. Multidisciplinary means that all members of the team should have an equal say and, although teams require a leader, there is little doubt that effective teams allow individuals to take leadership for particular objectives or responsibilities of that team's performance. Effective teams, which are self managed, self directed and accountable, will identify problems and variations from their targets, and will take responsibility for correcting those problems.

Figure 1.6: Integrated care using best practice

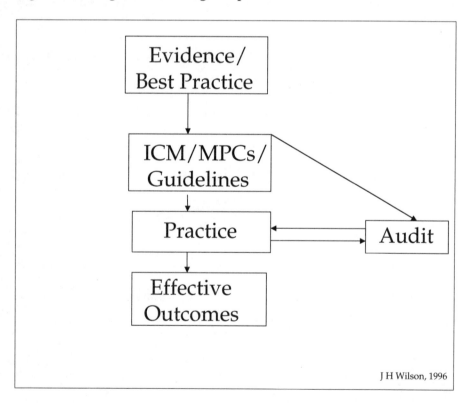

J H Wilson, 1996

---

13   *Op cit*, Wilson, fn 12.

CLINICAL GOVERNANCE PROCESSES

- Clinical quality improvements integrated with the overall organisational continuous quality improvement programmes to identify and build on good practice.
- Good practice systematically disseminated.
- Clinical risk reduction programmes in place.
- Professional self-regulation/assessment, including the development of clinical leadership skills.
- Evidence-based practice systems in place.
- Adverse events, near misses and incidents detected, openly investigated and lessons learned.
- Complaints dealt with positively and the information used to improve the organisation and care delivery.
- High quality performance measurement data collected to monitor clinical care and support professionals in delivering quality care.
- Poor clinical performance dealt with appropriately to minimise harm to patients and other staff.
- Staff supported in their duty to report concerns about colleague's professional conduct and performance and procedures developed for early action to support the individual to remedy the situation.
- Continuing professional development through lifelong learning aligned with clinical governance principles.

SCOPE OF PROFESSIONAL PRACTICE

The number of activities undertaken by nurses is continuing to increase due to a number of factors, such as reduction in junior doctors' hours and nurses being entrusted with wider responsibilities as a recognition of their expanding roles as specialist nurses and nurse consultants.

To maintain high standards of care and service, it is necessary to ensure that all nursing, midwifery and health-visiting staff only provide the care they are qualified to provide. The activities and procedures undertaken should be based upon education, experience and demonstrated competence, in addition to initial qualifications. Initial employment should be based upon a complete review of qualifications, skills and competencies. The clinical competence of all staff members should be documented regularly through individual job plans. There should be evidence of continuing nursing education, professional recognition and clinical audit. In the case of specialist and nurse consultants, it is also appropriate to outline which operations/procedures they may perform with or without supervision.

In 1992, the UKCC 4 published a document, 'The Scope of Professional Practice',[14] which stated that:

- practice must be sensitive, relevant and responsive to patients' needs ... nurses must have the capacity to adjust ... to changing circumstances;
- the range of responsibilities which fall to individual nurses;
- should be related to their personal education, experience and skill;
- nurses must maintain levels of competence and acknowledge any limitation.

The nurse should always act as the patient's advocate. The nurse is not merely a delegatee of the doctor but he/she owes the patient an individual duty of care. If the nurse knows that the doctor is going to make a mistake which will harm the patient, the nurse has to act in the best interest of the patient

A 'Scope of Professional Practice' framework should be developed within each healthcare organisation to ensure that the expansions of professional roles are based upon skills, education and competencies to reduce unnecessary risk exposure.

The organisation should have consistent frameworks and a formal approach to evaluate the scope of practice in a particular area. These should include:

- appraising the evidence supporting the proposed area of role expansion;
- determining who will decide whether a particular activity is appropriate for the clinical group to undertake and how this will be determined;
- evaluating the impact this may have on other clinical groups;
- evaluating the continuing education activities required to support training in the new skill;
- evaluating competence, how this will be assessed and by whom, and what will be the frequency of reassessment.

There should be clear lines of accountability. It must be clear who is in charge of the patient's care at all times.

Safe practice, and therefore safe patient care, can be achieved if:

- staff work to agreed levels of skills and competency as outlined within their individual job plans;
- supervision and support systems are used;
- the care and treatment given are based, where possible, on research and evidence;

---

14 UKCC, 'Scope of Professional Practice', 1992, London: United Kingdom Central Council.

- workload and service demands are not exhausting;
- rotation of staff to develop expertise and skills.

There is a need for an ongoing structured education and training programme for all grades and disciplines of staff linked to topic selection and training needs analysis. Medico-legal education, support and advice should be included through the use of seminars and workshops. Case scenarios can be used to show how to deal with and understand the processes.

Before a nurse's role is expanded consider the following:

- Trust/PCG approval of enhancement;
- provision of relevant education and training;
- ratification of clinical guidelines;
- regular updates and training – specified in terms of frequency and mandatory;
- audit, evaluation and outcome measures – ongoing performance review;
- is basic nursing care being reduced?

SPECIALIST NURSES AND NURSE CONSULTANTS

Taking on specialist and enhanced roles means that nurses are expected to deliver a higher standard of care, which reflects:

- additional training and regular updates;
- additional competency and expertise;
- skills required for the activity;
- guidelines/protocols which guide the current accepted practice.

Guidelines can be very useful in role expansion. Considerations in drafting these guidelines include:

- description of and limitations to the activity being performed;
- the degree of supervision required;
- audit, evaluation and outcome data;
- making the status of the treating nurse known to patient;
- obtaining the patient's consent;
- regular education/training updates.

SUMMARY

There is a growing recognition of the value of clinical guidelines in bringing research evidence into practice. They are here to stay and all relevant professional and higher education organisations should consider how best to promote the use of guidelines for individual specialties in basic and continuing education programmes. Within the broader context of nursing education and training, there has been an important enabling role in implementing published guidelines into routine practice through reflective practice and clinical supervision. Time is an important resource and needs to be made available to enable nurses and other clinicians to be involved in the development of local guidelines and in training for the implementation, monitoring and evaluation of guidelines. This should be recognised as an important investment for clinical governance and for improving the quality of patient care. Effective and widespread use of appropriate clinical guidelines will help nurses to raise the standards of care and to be able to demonstrate this through completing the clinical audit loop with continuous and ongoing monitoring and evaluation. Nurses need to gather this evidence to demonstrate that the clinical guidelines do work, that the guidelines can influence nursing practice and behaviour and to demonstrate cost and clinical effectiveness. There should be close links between clinical audit, clinical guideline development and the monitoring of changes in health outcomes through the nursing care improvement model. Clinical guidelines can enhance nursing practice and demonstrate the importance of evidence-based nursing care and the professional application of clinical governance.

CHAPTER 2

WHY CLINICAL GUIDELINES? A MEDICAL PERSPECTIVE

DJ Tuffnell

SYNOPSIS

The growth in clinical guidelines has gathered pace in the United Kingdom with the advent of clinical governance and the arrival of the National Institute for Clinical Excellence (NICE). There are substantial benefits to the introduction of clinical guidelines but they are dependent upon the guidelines themselves being developed, presented and implemented in a robust and appropriate way. The benefits accrue from the consistency of care offered across groups of patients and by groups of professionals. This leads to the delivery of clinically effective care which, in an appropriately written guideline, will also be cost-effective. Clear guidance will reduce errors and provide a clear standard for care to be subsequently or even prospectively audited. This framework then creates an environment for education, either in the gathering of knowledge for the development of the guideline or in the implementation phase, for staff and patients alike.

As with all things there are problems with guidelines. However, most of the problems stem from poor guideline development or implementation rather than because there is anything intrinsically poor about guidelines themselves. The concerns stem from the principles of 'clinical freedom' and the infringement of it by guidelines. Well-written guidelines will include a framework which allows departure from the guideline as long as clear and reasonable explanations are present. These reasons should be recorded contemporaneously in the case record. This also answers the concerns over the possibility that guidelines may be used as a medico-legal imperative. Out of date or ineffective guidelines also create concern. This is easily avoided by good development and built-in review periods.

What should the key attributes of a clinical guideline be? The principle attribute which leads to a guideline being used – which is the primary aim – is ease of use. A guideline written in an easily understood way with built-in points of referral for senior help is likely to be successful. Plainly, the guideline must be easily available and based in the most relevant evidence. The wider the initial consultation, the wider ownership is created, and this encourages use of the guideline.

There is always a debate about the differing importance of national or local guidelines. National guidelines are usually produced by acknowledged experts with a large evidence base and exhaustive referencing. They are seen as powerful documents that, quite rightly, can influence practice in a positive way. The concern arises when there is the development of national guidelines with grade C evidence. This is evidence based on expert opinion rather than from randomised trials. The difficulty is that this may not be relevant in smaller or non-teaching units. Also, national guidelines will have less ownership at a local level and may not be as widely disseminated, particularly to junior staff. Inevitably they cannot include important pragmatic information, such as local contacts. Local guidelines often have a less rigorous evidence base, in part because of resource constraints. However, they are a powerful tool to influence local practice. This is particularly due to the ability to develop wide ownership and to obtain the opinion and consent of the local clinicians before introducing the guideline. Local guidelines also can cover a wider range of issues than national guidelines and can be amended more easily in the light of changing evidence or practice.

When developing a guideline the first step is to determine the scope or subject of the guideline. A new member of staff, an incident within the unit, the publication of new evidence, or a new national guideline may trigger this. Once the subject is defined the drawing together of a group to collect evidence to draw into a working document is needed. The wider the net is cast with this group, the more likely implementation is to be successful. The opinions of dissenters need to be considered and mechanisms developed to take account of their concerns. This may incorporate an audit of the guideline into its introduction to demonstrate compliance and effectiveness.

Once the guideline is produced the difficult bit starts. The guideline must be made widely and easily available. In order to grab the attention of busy clinicians it must be presented in a way which makes it worthy of reading. Whilst some guidelines are useful as reference documents and so do not necessarily need to be read before they are used, others for emergency situations need understanding before the situation arises if they are to improve care.

Once guidelines are introduced it is amazing how quickly time can pass, so it is important that review dates are determined in advance. Once a review takes place a copy of the old dated guideline needs to be stored for medico-legal reasons.

INTRODUCTION

The Institute of Medicine has defined guidelines as 'systematically developed statements to assist practitioner and patient decisions about appropriate health care for specific clinical circumstances'.[1] The development of guidelines has blossomed into an industry within medicine with the advent of clinical governance, the requirements of risk management and now the arrival of the National Institute for Clinical Excellence (NICE)[2] (NICE are developing guidelines that cover a wide number of clinical conditions, such as multiple sclerosis, hypertension and depression). NICE are encouraging all possible stakeholders to contact them to ensure the guidelines they produce take into account as many views as practicable.

This demonstrates that clinical guidelines can relate to the management from a purely medical perspective, such as which drug to use or which operation to perform. They can also relate to the process of care for patients, such as when referral should take place and the time frames within which that is reasonable.

The other element of the process for which guidelines are increasingly being developed surrounds the expertise of the doctors who will be involved in the management of particular conditions.

This last area often determines the development of tertiary referral or regional centres, which look after less common conditions or problems.

Commonly this sort of guideline is developed in relation to cancer services. It is often justified by the requirement that for expertise to be maintained it is necessary to have exposure to enough cases per year to maintain skill levels.

BENEFITS OF GUIDELINES

With this proliferation of guidelines it must be perceived that there is an importance and a benefit to the development of common ways of approaching a particular medical problem. These benefits accrue not simply from the existence of a guideline but from how it is presented and implemented, adapted and improved. However, before considering those elements we need to examine how the ideal guideline may improve clinical care.

CONSISTENCY OF CARE

The primary aim of a good clinical guideline is to ensure that all the right things and none of the wrong things are done when a patient presents with a

---

1   Field, MJ and Lohr, KN (eds), *Guidelines for Clinical Practice. From Development to Use*, 1992, Institute of Medicine, Washington DC: National Academy Press.

2   National Institute for Clinical Excellence (NICE): website www.nice.org.uk.

particular clinical problem. This is regardless of which health care professional sees them and regardless of the part of the country or time of day they are being seen. This is also referred to as uniformity of care. It is not aimed at somehow limiting excellence, but is aspiring to ensure excellence for all. A well-written guideline will include all the necessary elements of the process of care to ensure that this occurs. It must be appreciated that consistency will not occur simply because the guideline exists, but is dependent on the appropriate training and education of staff, availability of the resources required and also feedback from audit.

CLINICAL AND COST-EFFECTIVENESS

The development of a guideline requires consideration of the evidence available about the most effective way to manage a condition. This must take account not just of which treatment is most clinically effective, but also which is most cost-effective. One reasonable criticism of clinical guidelines is a failure to consider costs alongside improvements in clinical outcome.

ERROR REDUCTION

A major source of concern in clinical care is error. This requires a systematic approach to its reduction. A guideline can assist by ensuring that no important elements are omitted in either the investigation or treatment of patients. This is recognised by the requirement of the Clinical Negligence Scheme for Trusts (CNST) in their risk management standards for guidelines for the conditions that carry highest risk.[3] At the present time these guidelines all refer to obstetric conditions, but the range of required guidelines will undoubtedly increase with time. Compliance with a well-recognised guideline will help to rebut allegations of negligence

PROVIDING A STANDARD FOR AUDIT

As stated earlier, the success of a guideline is not based simply in its construction and existence but also how it is implemented. Audit will indicate whether a guideline is viable in practice.

---

3   Clinical Negligence Scheme for Trusts (CNST), *Clinical Risk Management Standards*, National Health Service Litigation Authority (NHSLA), June 2000, London.

Audit must continue once a guideline is up and running. The symbiosis of audit and clinical guidelines is an important element in the delivery of high quality care.

EDUCATION

The group that considers the evidence and constructs the guideline will improve its own knowledge, but the greatest educational benefits of a guideline will be gained by those who use the guideline in their own clinical practice. A well-constructed guideline is self-explanatory, in theory at least. However, the guidelines that are followed most often, and are therefore most effective, have an educational programme running alongside them. This can work in a cascade fashion rather than all users needing central training.

Clinical guidelines can also be used to educate patients. The development of a guideline provides a background against which it should be straightforward to produce clear information for patients. This information can be verbal, but is more useful if it is also provided in written form.

DISADVANTAGES OF GUIDELINES

As with all treatments, guidelines have disadvantages as well as benefits. A number of these are concerns rather than actual difficulties. The concerns are caused by the way in which the guidelines are developed and implemented, rather than because there is an intrinsic deficiency in the theory of guideline usage. It is important to consider the concerns raised by clinicians to explain how they can be reduced or eliminated.

INTERFERENCE WITH CLINICAL FREEDOM

Those who are uncomfortable with clinical guidelines often raise the accusation of 'cookbook medicine'. The suggestion that medicine can be reduced to a list of instructions ignores the fact that each patient is an individual with different requirements. The 'art' of medicine is needed to take account of this individual variation and provide individually based treatment. This argument ignores the benefits that come from the introduction of guidelines, many examples of which will be described in this book. It also ignores the fact that a guideline should include enough flexibility to take account of the factors that may alter the treatment or investigation required in a specific clinical circumstance. A guideline is just that – a guideline. It should not be followed slavishly but should provide a framework for clinicians to work in. Clinicians with different levels of experience should all be able to use the same guideline. Less experienced clinicians should only deviate from a guideline if they have discussed the case with a more senior clinician. This means that for trainees many guidelines could be construed as policies. Guidelines should build in referral points so that it is clear when help should be sought. However, senior clinicians will not be constrained in the same way as trainees. This should not mean that they deviate from the guideline at an early stage in the management of the condition. However, the extra experience they have should allow them to realise when the guideline is less useful and when to deviate from the guideline. The responsible clinician will document the justifiable reasons for departing from the guideline.

All clinicians have to pass examinations before they are considered competent to practice. A guideline should be the perfect answer to the examination question, which asks how a particular condition or treatment should be managed. This allows the majority of patients to be managed in a safe and effective way. If you cannot write or comply with a guideline, you probably should not be practicing.

INEFFECTIVE GUIDELINES

One reasonable concern about guidelines is the perpetuation of unsafe or ineffective practice. This arises when guidelines are poorly constructed without taking into account all available evidence. Those responsible for national guidelines usually ensure that a great deal of effort is used to avoid this, but the same may not be true of local guidelines. However, this problem is less likely to occur when guidelines are published. It is more likely that guidelines will become obsolete because of new evidence or because they are not reviewed. There is also the danger that an old guideline will remain in circulation and be used even though it has been updated. This can be avoided with electronic publication. The responsibility for a guideline does not end once it is introduced. A mechanism must be in place for regular review and updating.

RATIONING

Many doctors and patients are worried that the introduction of a clinical guideline will lead to rationing, particularly of expensive treatments. This concern can be avoided if it can be demonstrated that when the evidence is considered, both clinical effectiveness and cost-effectiveness are used to determine the appropriate guidance. This will still cause discomfort for some clinicians who believe that clinical effectiveness should be the only parameter used when determining the choice of care for patients.

KEY ATTRIBUTES OF GUIDELINES

Ease of use

Guidelines with complicated descriptions or with large expositions of the theory of clinical care are unlikely to be useful in everyday practice. Those who put guidelines together often forget that they will often need to be used when there are time constraints. Therefore an easy to read guideline, or even an easy algorithm, is more likely to be translated accurately into appropriate action than one which includes too many explanations of why the action is appropriate. A successful guideline is more likely to include what to do rather than why to do it.

A guideline which eases the decision about the appropriate course of action is preferable to one which provides numbers of alternatives which the claimant has to choose between. The process of guideline development should aim to eliminate difficult decisions rather than create them. This can be achieved by building in clear referral points for less experienced clinicians rather than expecting them to reach a point where they are unsure and uncertain. Whilst they may realise at this point that help is needed, clear advice in a guideline is helpful and desirable.

Ease of availability

It is self evident that a guideline cannot be used if it cannot be found. A number of techniques can be used to make a guideline available. The guideline should be widely disseminated and often short versions, or *aide memoires*, will be produced in poster or laminated card form. The difficulty with this approach is that most clinicians manage dozens of conditions and so cannot have paper versions easily available of all the relevant guidelines. Even if they did, the volume of paper would be so large as to make the finding of an individual guideline, particularly in an urgent situation, dangerously impractical. An increasingly used alternative is electronic publication using an intranet-based system.

Wide ownership

Most aspects of the delivery of health care rely on strong team-working. Teams work best if the individual members feel that their opinions are valued and represented in the work of the team. Nowhere is this truer than in the development and use of guidelines. 'Ownership' can only come from all members of the team being involved in the guideline at as many stages as possible, from deciding the remit of the guideline, to its use and review. It has to be recognised that there are very few areas of clinical care which have such a strong evidence base that it is clear exactly which form of care is best. However, the value of consistent care justifies teams making a decision about the way care will be delivered by them. The more members feel they were involved in the decision about what the guideline will contain, the more likely they are to comply with it once it is introduced. Wide ownership should also include the ability to influence any changes to the guideline once it has been introduced. A feedback mechanism is of value in spreading the feeling of ownership as long as changes do occur in response to reasonable suggestions.

Evidence based

The increasing dissemination of clinical evidence means that clinicians have access to up-to-date high quality information about the best way to manage patients. If this information is not translated into the guideline, then the guideline will quickly fall into disrepute. It is essential that those responsible for a guideline examine the primary sources of evidence before determining the guideline's content. As stated above, few clinical conditions have an absolutely clear management based on the highest level of evidence – the randomised controlled trial. This means that some interpretation and evaluation of potentially conflicting sources of evidence is required before a guideline can be established. The more the people who are going to use the guideline are involved in the determination of how that equivocal evidence is interpreted, the more likely the guideline is to be followed.

The referencing of a guideline is often seen as a vital part of demonstrating the evidence base which justifies the guideline. Many institutions, such as the CNST and the United Kingdom Central Council (UKCC) suggest that all guidelines require referencing. This can create a conflict with the aim of ensuring that the guidelines are easy to use. Also, many areas of clinical care are not governed by absolutely unequivocal evidence. It is entirely possible to use the same paper to justify two entirely different courses of action. An example of this is pre-labour rupture of membranes of women at term in pregnancy. The TERM PROM trial[4] demonstrated that it made no difference to operative delivery rates whether labour was induced or awaited. This evidence can therefore be used to justify both courses of action – and some in between. For consistency of care purposes a unit may choose to adopt

---

4   Hannah, ME *et al*, 'Induction of labour compared with expectant management for pre-labour rupture of the membranes at term' (1996) 334 NEngl J Med 1005–10.

induction as the management of first choice, justifying its choice with the same paper as the unit next door used to justify its choice of expectant management. When there is less ownership of the document at a local level, such as with a national guideline, then a clear demonstration of the sources of evidence is needed. This imperative is less when ownership is wider within organisations.

Clinically relevant

Some guidelines concentrate on the organisational aspects of patient management.

Whilst this can be helpful, it is more useful if a guideline concentrates on the clinical aspects of care and incorporates the organisational elements as a secondary feature.

NATIONAL v REGIONAL v LOCAL GUIDELINES

The production of guidelines is seen as the responsibility of many bodies. The Royal Colleges all produce guidelines and NICE will increasingly produce a number of guidelines at a national level. These are potentially very influential documents. Also, specialist bodies at regional level produce guidelines with the intention of improving services and standards of care in smaller areas.

However, the majority of clinical guidelines are produced at a local level by clinicians hoping to influence the delivery of care in their own units with the knowledge of local circumstances. Which of these guidelines are most likely to be effective?

National guidelines

National guidelines are produced by groups of experts drawn together because of their knowledge of the particular condition or treatment. These guidelines usually incorporate the most up-to-date evidence and are exhaustively referenced. Therefore they are respected for the evidence base. However, the need to incorporate all the evidence means that the documents are usually lengthy and are not practical for day-to-day use. Also, those who draw up the guidelines always seem unable to stop themselves from expressing opinions for which there is no clear evidence from trials or observational studies. They then describe this as grade C evidence – expert opinion. This opinion is often dominated by those from large institutions with high staff levels and resources. This may not be relevant or appropriate for smaller hospitals or different areas of the country. It may be better if national guidelines avoided the use of this type of opinion, but instead identified the area as one for local decision-making. Whilst, normally, good guideline construction avoids options wherever possible, it may be better if national guidelines adopted more often the approach of outlining the available clinical options. This is particularly true of those parts of guidelines which are supported only by grade C evidence. Here a range of acceptable opinion would be more useful than a dogmatic statement, given the gravitas which national guidelines are given.

National guidelines may include parameters which help units or individuals to judge whether it is appropriate for them to be managing a particular condition or performing a specific technique. The rationale for this is that a minimum level of continuing experience is necessary to maintain expertise. These parameters may be most appropriate for considering the level of experience for satisfactory training rather than for continuing practice. However some conditions require multidisciplinary working at a level which necessitates careful organisation. Clinicians must audit their own outcomes to ensure they are satisfactory.

National guidelines struggle to develop widespread ownership. Even though on many occasions senior staff can be asked for their opinion of the guideline before it is introduced, junior staff or staff from other disciplines may not be. As the majority of the benefits accrued from the introduction of guidelines stem from the advantage of consistent care delivered by large numbers of staff, this is a significant disadvantage of national guidelines.

The dissemination of national guidelines is also problematic. Although these guidelines are often sent to all consultants, hospitals or general practitioners, they are not universally available. They are often copyrighted, which makes it difficult to disseminate them in a cheap way as a charge is often made for further copies. It is also difficult to incorporate them into guideline booklets in ward areas, as they are either the wrong size or already bound. If an electronic system is used locally it can be difficult to copy them into the same format as local guidelines.

National guidelines are aimed at many units. This means that local organisational issues are not included in the guideline. Key information for local use, such as local telephone numbers, cannot be included, which reduces the practical value of the guideline.

Despite these concerns, national guidelines will remain the most influential in directing public policy and as a reference source for local guidelines. They are also the most likely to be considered if there is a criticism of the way in which care has been provided in a particular case.

Regional guidelines

A regional guideline could be described as one which is used in a number of hospitals or across a group of general practices. It does not have to be used across the whole of a health region, such as the West Midlands, to achieve the aims of a regional guideline. The principal aim of a regional guideline is to develop a commonality of practice across a number of linked units or practices. This may be because the area has overlapping populations, or because of rotation of staff. This type of guideline can have a number of the advantages of both national and local guidelines.

Regional guidelines should have a solid evidence base. They should take into account randomised controlled trials as well as observational data. Whereas a national guideline will have expert opinion or grade C evidence which may not take into account local factors, the regional guideline should take such local factors into account. The ability to take local factors into account allows regional guidelines to be more precise about the decisions that should be made. It is much more likely that all the clinicians that will use the guideline will have the opportunity to decide upon the detail, or at the very least, the lead clinicians in each area will be able to. Regional guidelines also benefit from the fact that the local experts are known to the clinicians using the guidelines. This would hopefully allow them to be more credible and open to local discussion. This more local ownership can be enhanced by attaching educational and feedback sessions to the introduction and development of the guidelines. Ownership of regional guidelines will of course still be lower than ownership of local guidelines.

Regional guidelines are generally developed in areas of clinical practice which have given rise in the relevant region to specific clinical worries. These guidelines will often be more practically based than national guidelines as they can include some local information, such as contact points, which cannot be included in a national guideline.

Local guidelines

Local guidelines are powerful tools for influencing practice at a local level. They will reflect practice in a single hospital, department or general practice. They will not have the same depth as national guidelines. This is a strength as well as a weakness. The strength of this lies in the fact that the content is determined by local clinicians and reflects the way in which they expect care to be delivered in their own department. This commitment to the way in which care should be delivered means that compliance with the guideline should be high. This presumes that the guideline has been constructed with the consent and involvement of a wide range of clinicians. It is important that the process which establishes the guideline involves all disciplines and all levels of staff that are going to be affected by the guideline. This process develops the ownership of the guideline, which is a fundamental strength of local guidelines.

A weakness of guideline production at a local level is often the clarity of the evidence used. There is an expectation from regulatory bodies that all guidelines will be referenced. The difficulty with that approach is that the guideline can then become overloaded with the detail required to support the references, and so lose the practical value of brevity and precision. It does not make the guideline more valid simply to attach the references. A local guideline should not be developed without consideration of the randomised controlled trials or observational studies relevant to the area of clinical practice. However, a guideline based in sensible, safe clinical practice, developed by senior clinicians, is of great value. This emphasises the point that a good guideline is simply the model answer to an examination question asking about the management of a problem. This is most true at local level.

A local guideline can and should include information about the referral routes for admission, investigations and treatment. This means telephone numbers, the appropriate forms or bottles for tests, names and contact points of relevant clinicians, and the points at which senior help should be sought. Pragmatism is integral to the usefulness of the guideline. The collection of all this relevant information in one point will lead to clinicians being more likely to consult the guideline. The inclusion of referral points within a local guideline ensures that there are clear mechanisms in place to avoid deviation from the guideline by those not experienced enough to be certain that the guideline's advice is appropriate. All members of the multidisciplinary team need to be considered when compiling the guideline. For instance, a guideline should direct and encourage a nurse who is not happy with the course of action proposed by a junior doctor to seek help elsewhere. At a local level, the level of expertise expected from each level of staff can be made much clearer.

Local guidelines can deal with a much wider range of problems than national or regional guidelines. They can generally be developed quicker and can be implemented within a short period of time if needed. Whilst all guidelines should have built-in review times, local guidelines can be changed much more easily than national or regional guidelines if there is a change in evidence. If a clinical trial, such as the Term Breech trial,[5] shows an important new message, local guidelines can change within days. The Term Breech trial showed that planned vaginal breech delivery at term is associated with a statistically significant increase in the risk of foetal death or serious morbidity. Once the trial was published, local guidelines in our own unit were changed in days. The national guidelines on management of breech presentation from

---

5   Hannah, ME *et al*, 'A multicentre randomised controlled trial of planned caesarean section versus planned vaginal birth for breech presentation at term' (2000) 356 The Lancet 1375–83.

the Royal College of Obstetrics and Gynaecology were unchanged several months later. The fast development of local guidelines assumes that local clinicians are aware of the publication of important trials. This unfortunately is by no means always certain.

Development stages and validation

When developing any guideline there are a number of important steps, whether the guideline is local or national. The first step is to determine the subject for the guideline. It is unusual now for no guidelines to be in place in a clinical area, so the subject for a new guideline will be determined by an event. This may be the employment of a new member of staff with a specific interest in the new subject, or an adverse event occurring which identifies weaknesses in the current way in which the problem is managed, or national or regional pressure to improve a particular aspect of clinical care.

The event initiates a review of practice, which leads to new guidelines. Also, the publication of a national guideline may lead to local clinicians reviewing their own local guideline.

After deciding that a guideline is needed, someone will need to take responsibility for its development. Whilst an individual will need to take a lead, the development of a guideline in isolation is the best way to ensure it never gets used. The ownership of the process of development is integral to the guideline being used effectively once it is introduced. Therefore, a group of clinicians from all disciplines involved needs to be established. This should include all levels of staff. Junior staff often have an important part to play in ensuring that the guideline includes the practical elements that will make it more usable. They can also ensure that it makes sense to all levels of staff. When only senior staff are involved, decisions can be made which wrongly assume knowledge.

This group then needs to explore the evidence available to them about the subject. This is the area of guideline development which seems to vary most. Some groups hunt exhaustively for all the evidence before writing the guideline. Other groups write the guideline and then search the evidence to ensure the guideline is correct. National guidelines favour the former approach; one of the weaknesses of local guidelines is that often the latter approach is used. The preferred methodology is to gather evidence first but some subjects and aspects of all areas of clinical care do not have a complete grade A evidence base. The detailed analysis of evidence forms part of a later chapter. The main danger at a local level of detailed evidence gathering is that the process becomes unduly lengthy. This can lead to the guideline never being produced.

Once the evidence has been considered, the subject area of the guideline should be refined. This is most likely to place constraints upon what will and will not be included. The larger and more detailed a guideline becomes, the less likely it is to be used. Hence the decision has to be made as to whether the guideline is to be aimed at providing a large and detailed evidence base with explanations (as would be suitable for a national guideline) or to provide detailed but short and precise instructions (as is optimal for local guidelines).

A first draft of the guideline should then be produced, covering the areas determined at the last stage. This draft should be reviewed by the core guideline group before having as wide a dissemination as possible. The staff in all clinical areas should have a chance to make comments before the guideline is introduced. The setting of a deadline for comments and suggestions is vital. One problem at this stage is that there are often diametrically opposed views expressed; obviously the greater the number of clinicians consulted, the more likely this is to be true. It is better for it to be debated at this stage rather than when the guideline is in place. If those responsible for the guideline take the opportunity at this stage to talk to dissenters and discuss the evidence for the proposed guideline there is a better chance that a common view can be found. In this situation the importance of consistency of care needs to be stressed. It also invaluable to build into the introduction of a guideline provision for an audit of compliance and outcome. This allows the dissenters to be reassured that they will have the opportunity to review the guideline with local 'evidence'.

Ultimately a final decision does need to be made as to the final version of a guideline. As one of the main strengths of a guideline is the consistency of care that stems from its introduction it is axiomatic that different versions within the same unit of the same guideline are destructive. Different consultants within hospital practice may have differing views on how to manage a particular condition. However, it would be very unusual for them to be the only professionals dealing with a patient. Even if that is the case, patients come into contact with other patients with the same condition. This is a common source of concern for patients. The value of consistent information, a clear plan and a particular path being followed in all cases is likely to outweigh hugely any possible benefits from the difference between two treatments. Ideally a form of cabinet policy should exist. This is where a discussion occurs about the options available but once one is agreed all involved adhere to the common line. The development of this type of policy can be aided if several guidelines are developed alongside each other and there is seen to be 'give and take' on all sides.

This process in itself creates a form of validation for guidelines – certainly in the local context. At a more regional or national level the process of validation needs to be wider. Once a guideline is developed by the core group it needs to go to representative bodies, such as the Royal Colleges, before it can be accepted. It is this part of the process which makes national guidelines more credible than local ones.

The publication and dissemination of guidelines is vital to their successful implementation. It is surprising how commonly the start date for guidelines passes before the guidelines are available in the clinical area. The wider the guideline is distributed the more likely it is to be used. However, clinicians are faced on a day-to-day basis with a barrage of paperwork. In order for a guideline to stand out from the other paperwork it needs a feature which makes it worthy of reading. It can be argued that the guideline does not necessarily have to be read prior to needing to use it. This is true when there is time to read a guideline within the clinical time to treat the patient. It is less likely to be possible when it is an emergency treatment such as thrombolysis for myocardial infarction.

It has to be accepted that on some occasions guidelines are only used when the patient is already in need of treatment. This is particularly so if locums are treating a patient in a setting they are not used to. In these situations it is important to ensure that the guidelines are available in the clinical area. It is also important that the guideline can be easily found within the guideline booklet or folder. This may be facilitated by electronic publication. The availability of guidelines within an electronic format does not preclude the use of the guideline on paper. Indeed, one advantage of guidelines published in this way is that a copy can easily be run-off and used at the bedside or stored in the notes.

The review period for clinical guidelines is an integral part of their development. National guidelines usually have a two or three year review period. Local guidelines can be reviewed at more frequent time periods. It is crucial that there is provision for the review of guidelines in the light of new evidence. It is important that guidelines are responsive to other changes in local practice. This means that a change in one area may create a conflict with another guideline. It is important for these reasons to be able to modify guidelines fairly quickly. However, a formal review should take place at a pre-determined time interval. It should be very rarely necessary to withdraw a guideline. If a guideline was important and relevant when it was introduced it should be updated rather than withdrawn.

Increasingly if a claim of negligence is made, a request will come for the guideline in place at that time. It is therefore important for copies of all guidelines to be kept. Guidelines must be dated and the dates when modifications occurred should be appended. This aspect is aided by electronic storage as otherwise mountains of paper can be created. The reasons for deviation from guidelines should be documented.

SUMMARY

The principal aim of the introduction of a guideline, from a medical perspective, is to ensure that the optimal way to manage a patient or series of patients is clearly documented. The production of a successful clinical guideline will be a rigorous process. A successful guideline will deliver consistent evidence-based, cost-effective care. It will provide a standard against which the quality of care can be audited and will provide a focus for education and continuing professional development. Within this framework errors are less likely to occur and consequently risks to the patient and the organisation are reduced.

Guidelines often attract legitimate criticism because of failures in the process of development and implementation of the guideline, rather than because there is intrinsically a flaw in the concept of working to guidelines. Clinical guidelines are accused of interfering with clinical freedom but do so only if they are not developed in a multidisciplinary way with clear parameters as to when the guidelines apply. The guidelines should include referral points and should be applied so that it is clear that they are guidelines and nothing more. Experienced clinicians are at liberty to deviate from guidelines but should document the reasons for their actions. This is simply good clinical practice. Guidelines are also accused of supporting rationing of health care. Again, if the guideline is constructed properly the care described should be cost-effective, evidence-based care. This does mean that the most expensive treatments will not be included unless they are demonstrated to be more effective.

A well-written guideline will be easy to use and practical. It should be relevant to clinical care as delivered to the patient and based in the best evidence available in the light of local circumstances. It should be widely discussed before its introduction in order to develop wide ownership. The dissemination of the guideline should be easily apparent and the guideline must be available in the clinical areas that it is aimed at. Once introduced, it should be reviewed regularly and altered as new evidence becomes available or if problems become apparent with the guideline.

There are strengths and weaknesses of national and local guidelines. National guidelines tend to include a more thorough review of the evidence but still include a great deal of 'expert opinion' (grade C evidence). This type of evidence is better confined to more local guidelines where local circumstances can be taken into account. National guidelines tend to be longer and be more theoretical than practical. However they are more influential as they are validated by prestigious bodies. Local guidelines will tend to be more intimately owned by those who use them. They can include more of the day-to-day practical details of patient care. They can be audited more easily by those who introduce them and changes introduced more easily. The best guidelines will use the highest level evidence from national guidelines and include the wide ownership and practical details of the best local guidelines.

CHAPTER 3

DESIGNING CLINICAL GUIDELINES: STEPS AND PROCEDURES

DJ Tuffnell and J Wright

SYNOPSIS

The design of a clinical guideline is fundamental to its success. The more planning that goes into the way in which the guideline is put together the more credible it will be, the more ownership it will have and the more likely it is to be followed. This runs from identifying the general subject area and then refining it, through drawing together a group to work on the guideline. Then all the evidence needs to be considered before deciding the evidence relevant to the subject area and, importantly, to local circumstances. This all needs translating into a working document before being circulated for opinions from outside the group responsible for the guideline. In the end a process has to exist to resolve conflicts of opinion. Ultimately a final document has to be produced.

The identification of subject areas for clinical guidelines will be driven by the various priorities that exist within the healthcare system. Guidelines which cover the 10 most common conditions, procedures or reasons for referral may cover over 90% of patient episodes in a hospital setting. It could quickly be seen that to give maximum coverage this would be an easy way to identify initial priorities. External bodies may also determine guideline priorities. The four confidential enquiries into peri-operative death, maternal death, stillbirths and deaths in infancy and suicide are also sources that determine guideline priorities. The Clinical Negligence Scheme for Trusts mandates that for risk management purposes maternity units should have guidelines for certain key conditions.

To establish a guideline a group needs to be drawn together. It is helpful to think about those areas that will be affected by the introduction of a guideline. From a medical staff viewpoint you need to consider medical staff at each part of the referral process. For nursing and midwifery staff, think about relevant specialist nurses as well as those directly involved. It may well be that some professions allied to medicine are involved, such as physiotherapy. Managers are often forgotten with clinical guidelines but will be important when resource changes are needed and the impact on other services needs to be thought out. A number of questions need to be asked when considering patient involvement. Can patients with the condition be asked their opinions? Can they be involved in the group? Can patients with past experience of acute conditions help? Can you rely on individual patients, or do you need a focus group?

The roles within the group need to be determined. Often a natural leader will become apparent but there are other important responsibilities. Not least of these is to establish timescales to work to and how to ensure all members contribute appropriately. It is also vital to develop a mechanism to get a wide range of views. The wider the ownership of a guideline is established in its development the more likely it is ultimately to be used.

A successful guideline will be evidence-based. Gathering the evidence can be a protracted process unless carefully undertaken. It may well be that other guidelines exist, either nationally or locally, and these can be adapted or used as the framework for your own guideline. When considering external evidence it can be graded in two different ways. First, it can be classified by the experimental studies from which it is derived. These could, for example, be either randomised controlled trials or observational studies. Secondly, it can be categorised by the recommendations for clinical practice drawn from the experimental studies.

There are three key steps to developing guidelines that are based on the best available evidence.

The first is to form an answerable question. This should be as clear as practicable to help the other steps. Then you need to track down the best evidence. Finally you critically appraise the evidence you have obtained.

There are a number of useful sources of evidence. There are various databases to search and which one you chose will depend on how much time you have and how in-depth you want to go. The main library databases include *Medline*, which is North American; *Embase*, which is European; and *CIANHL*, which has a nursing/therapy emphasis. A number of journals are now acting as filters to try and pick out all the high quality, rigorous clinical research evidence from the mountains of curriculum vitae-enhancing rubbish. The Cochrane Collaboration publishes its Database of Systematic Reviews on all clinical areas on the Cochrane Library, a quarterly CD-ROM that aims to provide the best single source of reliable evidence about the effects of health care.

In appraising the evidence you have to consider whether the results are valid and, indeed, what the results indicate, then you have to decide if the results apply to your patient in your situation.

Once all the evidence has been appraised and considered it needs to be turned into a practical document. This should be produced in a way that is understandable and readable. Finally, an agreed version needs to be circulated, published or placed on to the electronic system. It is helpful if meetings disseminate the guideline or announcements and that a start date is clear. At this point the authors will sit back and feel that their work is done – unfortunately this is not the case. The birth of a guideline is just the beginning of the process.

INTRODUCTION

The design of a clinical guideline is fundamental to its success. In order to ensure the guideline is well designed a number of steps will need to be followed. It is possible that a guideline thrown together on the back of an envelope by a single person and then distributed as a memo will work, but it is unlikely. The more planning that goes into the way in which the guideline is put together the more credible it will be, the more ownership it will have and the more likely it is to be followed. It is clear that not all guidelines require in-depth and detailed analysis before they are used. However, the more complex the condition, the more valuable a guideline is likely to be. The more complex the condition, the greater the importance of the guideline being based in evidence and being accepted by all the disciplines that will be involved in the use of the guideline.

This chapter will discuss the steps involved in developing a guideline. This is not the end for the guideline but merely the beginning. However, the implementation and revision of the guideline will be considered in Chapter 4, 'Implementing Clinical Guidelines'.

IDENTIFYING AND REFINING THE SUBJECT AREA

This has been described as the first step in developing a guideline. The first aim of guideline development is to determine the priorities, in terms of areas of clinical practice, which may be facilitated and improved by the development of a guideline. Guidelines can relate to the management of conditions, such as asthma, or procedures, commonly operations, or to processes, such as referral criteria. There may well be overlap between these areas and it is important to establish the parameters for the guideline.

The identification of subject areas for clinical guidelines will be driven by the various priorities that exist within the healthcare system. Guidelines which cover the 10 most common conditions, procedures or reasons for referral may cover over 90% of patient episodes in a hospital setting. In primary care a large part of clinical practice would be covered by creating guidelines which deal with the conditions which lead to the most referrals in a number of clinical specialities. However, a guideline can still be very useful in areas outside common practice. First, since common things are common, many practitioners will have established patterns of (hopefully good!) behaviour. This means that the added value from a guideline may not be significant. The problem with rare conditions is that, because they are rare, individual practitioners may not be sure about the best way to manage the condition or referral. In this situation, a guideline can provide practitioners with the confidence to initiate the right treatment and use the referral points built into the guideline if difficulties arise.

External bodies may also determine guideline priorities. The four confidential enquiries (The Confidential Enquiry into Stillbirths and Deaths in Infancy (CESDI), the National Confidential Enquiry into Peri-operative Death (NCEPOD), the Confidential Enquiry into Maternal Death (CEMD) and the Confidential Inquiry into Suicide in Hospital (CISH)) each produce recommendations that may require clinicians to establish guidelines in particular areas. They often include an outline guideline. This is the case with the CEMD, which has produced a guideline for the management of pregnant women who refuse blood transfusion. More recently, the Clinical Negligence Scheme for Trusts has produced a list of guideline requirements for obstetrics. These are required to be available in all maternity units wishing to pass the assessment for the CNST risk management standards at level 1.

The area for the guideline needs some initial refining before establishing the core group to tackle the project. If the guideline, for instance, were to cover diabetes, then an all-encompassing guideline would need physicians, primary care doctors, vascular and ophthalmic surgeons, nurses, dieticians, chiropodists, etc. However, if the guideline were to consider the management of diabetes in pregnancy then the group could be more limited. It is important to consider the relevant professionals at an early stage, as excluding relevant people may miss important issues. It is valuable to involve patients or patients' representatives wherever possible. However, it can often be difficult to identify appropriate representatives for patients, particularly in acute rather than chronic settings.

Figure 3.1:   Stakeholders for initiating and developing clinical guidelines

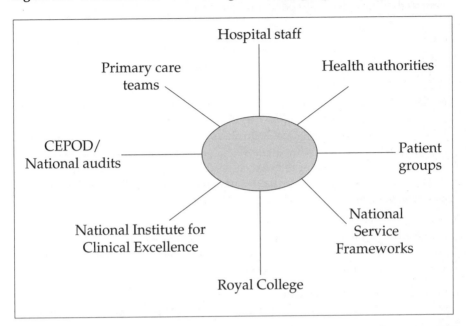

Hospital staff

Primary care teams

Health authorities

CEPOD/ National audits

Patient groups

National Institute for Clinical Excellence

National Service Frameworks

Royal College

ESTABLISHING STAKEHOLDERS

In drawing together a group to examine an area suitable for a guideline it is helpful to think about those areas that will be affected by the introduction of a guideline. The one certain way of ensuring that a guideline will not be used is to impose it upon a group without their knowledge or involvement.

In determining the stakeholders it is important to establish a mechanism which allows consultation and involvement, but is also efficient in time management. Whilst it may be helpful to have advice from the renal physicians when drawing up the guideline for diabetes management, they will not need to be at each meeting nor to check each element of the guideline. However, their input may be essential when considering the evidence for using certain interventions, such as ACE inhibitor use in diabetes. The initial task in establishing stakeholders revolves around identifying those that are key for each particular element of the guideline.

It has to be acknowledged that it is not always possible to involve all stakeholders from the outset. This can be because the stakeholders do not recognise themselves as such. Initially, a clinician may not feel the guideline is of significance to him. However, as the guideline develops, and sometimes as it is implemented, a clinician may want to have input into the guideline. It is important that the process allows for such involvement, though not in a way which compromises the clinicians who have been involved through the whole process. Simply being involved last should not allow clinicians to require changes that have been agreed in a wider forum.

Box 1

Stakeholders

Medical staff – Consider medical staff at each part of the referral process. Does it involve primary, secondary and tertiary care? Have you representatives of all the primary care groups/trusts? Does it involve surgeons and physicians? What about radiology, pathology and other diagnostic services? Will it involve other specialists than the primary receiver of referrals eg renal physicians or vascular surgeons in diabetes? Have you involved medical staff at all levels, including training grades? Have you thought about anaesthetists and HDU/ITU?

Nursing and midwifery staff – Are there relevant specialist nurses? Will the guideline impact on nurse training – are the nurse tutors involved? Will nurses be involved from a number of clinical areas – have you got representation from them all? Have you got nurses directly affected or only senior nurses?

Professions allied to medicine – Will your guideline affect physiotherapists, occupational therapists or other PAMS? Will your guideline change or affect drug or pharmacy use?

Managers – often forgotten with clinical guidelines. Will the guideline affect the costs or demands for a service? Are the right contracts, referral mechanisms in place? Will the guideline require budgetary changes or new capital costs? Is the project management support in place? Will it be possible to follow up the guideline in line with clinical governance? Will it change the need for administrative and clerical staff? Will it change the way referrals are dealt with? Will it need to change configuration of theatre time?

Patients – last but not least. Can patients with the condition be asked their opinions? Can they be involved in the group? Can patients with past experience of acute conditions help? Can you rely on individual patients or do you need a focus group?

ROLES WITHIN THE GROUP

Often the stimulus for the development of a guideline will come from an individual who views the proposed area as important. They will become the natural leader of the group. This may well be appropriate, but it is important that the person leading the group is credible with the other members and, perhaps more importantly, credible with the professionals who will be expected to follow the guideline. Therefore, the initiator of the process may not be the best person to be seen externally as the lead. This does not mean that the initiator will not end up driving the process by keeping up momentum, but may have to accept that someone else leads the group.

The initial discussions within the group will be about the scope of the guideline and who will develop which areas within the guideline. If the guideline is about a limited topic, then one person may develop the whole guideline. More typically, with a guideline relevant to a number of professional groups, different areas of the guideline will initially be developed separately. The nominated leader of the group will have the responsibility of determining who will be gathering the evidence and developing each area. The most important task at this time is to develop timeframes within which the members of the group are expected to work.

It may be that the initial timeframe is about when the evidence should be gathered. It can be appropriate to suggest that a first draft of the topic should be available, along with the evidence to justify the guideline as written. Ideally the draft of the guideline should be circulated prior to the next meeting. This gives all the participants the opportunity to review the draft and even the provided evidence. Then at a subsequent meeting it should be possible to get close to a guideline for circulation outside the group. If a number of areas within the guideline have been developed separately then it is important to ensure that they are compatible with each other. There is nothing more confusing for staff than finding guidelines for the same condition written by different professional groups that contradict each other. In fact, this is the major reason for ensuring that all stakeholders are involved in the process of developing guidelines.

At this point the person leading the group has to find a way to resolve differences. One of the principal advantages of guidelines is that they provide a common way to manage a condition or procedure for all similar cases. Inevitably there will be some disagreements about elements of the guideline. The strength and success of the guideline is largely determined at the point of disagreement. If it is not possible to get a consensus from the people who are most closely identified with the guideline then it is unlikely that people outside the development group will see the guideline as credible. A successful leader will develop a system of compromise within the group. It is possible to build options into a guideline and still maintain most of its advantages, but having fewer options will make the guideline less complicated and easier to follow. An alternative to having options within the guideline is to have referral points. The difference is that the first-line staff can take options whereas referral points require contact with senior staff. Obviously having referral points too early in the course of management destroys the value of a guideline in allowing consistent care to be delivered by those with initial contact with the patient.

GATHERING THE EVIDENCE

The previous section discussed who might gather the evidence for discussion by the group but what evidence may be useful. There are a number of sources of evidence to be considered.

OTHER GUIDELINES

It is always worth remembering that it is not necessary to reinvent the wheel. Clinical guidelines are developed in many areas. Source of guidelines will include the various Royal Colleges in the United Kingdom. Guidelines are increasingly being produced by the National Institute for Clinical Excellence (NICE). Various guidelines are also produced by pharmaceutical companies and other groups related to clinical practice. It is likely that other hospitals or practices or districts may have already developed a guideline in the area that you are considering. It can often be helpful to check with 'neighbours' to establish if they have already done the work you are starting on. Also, at many national or specialty meetings clinicians may discuss guidelines they have used. Commonly it will be possible to get copies of these guidelines to allow you to have a starting point from which to develop your own guideline with local relevance.

It is also important to check that you do not have guidelines already in place. Whilst it may seem obvious that you would know about your own guidelines this is not always the case. Often new members of a clinical team feel that they can make their mark by producing a new guideline. If the old guideline has been in place for a while, often gathering dust on a shelf, it may not be obvious. However, to ignore the old guideline may well create problems. It may also be helpful to understand how much change is needed and this can help in determining the best way to implement the guideline once it has been established. It is always possible that it may not need changing, just 'readvertising'. It is also important to remember that other disciplines may have guidelines which overlap with your proposed guideline. The evidence from those guidelines will be very important in the development of the new guideline. This links to the necessity to involve all the stakeholders in the process.

VALIDITY OF EXTERNAL EVIDENCE

External evidence is graded in two different ways. First, it can be classified by the experimental studies from which it is derived (Box 2). Secondly, there can be recommendations for clinical practice drawn from the experimental studies, which are often categorised differently (Box 3).

Box 2

Classification of evidence levels

Ia Evidence obtained from meta-analysis of randomised controlled trials.

Ib Evidence obtained from at least one randomised controlled trial.

IIa Evidence obtained from at least one well-designed controlled study without randomisation.

IIb Evidence obtained from at least one other type of well designed quasi-experimental study.

III Evidence obtained from well-designed non-experimental descriptive studies, such as comparative studies, correlation studies and case studies.

IV Evidence obtained from expert committee reports or opinions and/or clinical experience of respected authorities.

Box 3

Grades of recommendations

A Requires at least one randomised controlled trial as part of a body of literature of overall good quality and consistency addressing the specific recommendation. (Evidence levels Ia or Ib)

B Requires the availability of well controlled clinical studies but on randomised clinical trials on the topic of recommendations. (Evidence level IIA, IIb, III)

C Requires evidence obtained from expert committee reports or opinions and/or clinical experiences of respected authorities. Indicates an absence of directly applicable clinical studies of good quality. (Evidence level IV)

Good practice point

Recommended best practice based on the clinical experience of the guideline development group.

DEVELOPING EVIDENCE-BASED GUIDELINES

There are three key steps to developing guidelines that are based on the best available evidence:

- Form an answerable question. This requires clinical decisions to be broken down into specific components that can then be addressed. So rather than 'Should patients in atrial fibrillation be anticoagulated?' in the development of stroke prevention guidelines, the question should be 'Will the benefits of warfarin in reducing the risk of stroke outweigh the harm from bleeding in the secondary prevention of stroke?' The latter defines the patient group, the treatment, the desired outcome and the potential harm.

- Track down the best evidence. This is discussed in the next section. For the question asked above we can find a systematic review of all the randomised controlled trials demonstrating that elderly people with atrial fibrillation and a risk factor for stroke have a 68% reduced risk of stroke on warfarin relative to placebo (4.4% absolute risk reduction).

- Critically appraise the evidence. What are the results? Are the results of the systematic review valid? Are they applicable to local patients? This is discussed below.

SEARCHING FOR EVIDENCE

There are various databases to search and which one you chose will depend on how much time you have and how in-depth you want to go.

DATABASES

The main library databases include *Medline,* which is North American, Embase, which is European, and CIANHL, which has a nursing/therapy emphasis. When performing searches it is important to consider the scope of the search that you wish to undertake. Often excluding non-English and animal studies will not jeopardise the quality of your review of evidence. With some topics, reviews may have been published already and it may be time-saving to search for reviews initially and only look for separate studies if reviews are not available.

Medline is the most popular medical database. It is possible to access some *Medline* services online free of charge. One such service is PubMed at www.ncbi.nlm.nih.gov/PubMed/. It contains millions of references categorised by time (for example, 1987–92), clinical area and study design.

Relevant studies can be searched by combining the clinical topic (using free text words or MESH (medical subject) headings) and the appropriate trial design to find the best evidence. Different questions require different trial designs. For example:

- Studies of treatments should be limited to randomised controlled trials.
- Studies of diagnostic tests should be limited to cross-sectional studies.
- Studies of prognosis should be limited to inception cohorts.

If no studies are found then the search can be broadened. If too many are found then they can be limited by making the search terms more specific. Reference lists of papers identified can be checked and experts in the field written to for additional relevant studies.

The problem with using databases such as *Medline* is that you may miss many relevant trials that are mis-classified (for example, about a third of randomised controlled trials will be missed), or be swamped by irrelevant papers. To be confident about your search terms and search strategy you also need to be well-trained and a regular user. Medical librarians can provide essential expertise; it may be better to start your research elsewhere.

JOURNALS

A number of journals are now acting as filters to try and pick out all the high quality, rigorous clinical research evidence from the mountains of curriculum vitae-enhancing rubbish. Journals such as ACP Journal Club and Evidence Based Medicine screen all the major clinical journals for studies that fulfil clear criteria for validity and reliability of methods and results. Fewer than 1% of papers meet these criteria, but this research cream can provide an excellent source of evidence about therapies, diagnostic tests, prognosis, causation, quality improvement, professional development, economic appraisals and systematic reviews.

These summaries have been collated since 1991 to form Best Evidence. This is available on CD-ROM and in health libraries.

Another international collaboration is Clinical Evidence. This is produced by the BMJ Publishing Group and the American College of Physicians. It aims to provide an up-to-date (published every six months) compendium of the best available evidence on the effects of common clinical interventions.

THE COCHRANE LIBRARY

The most comprehensive source of good evidence is the Cochrane Library. The Cochrane Collaboration publishes its Database of Systematic Reviews on all clinical areas on the Cochrane Library, a quarterly CD-ROM that aims to provide the best single source of reliable evidence about the effects of health care. It may be that a systematic review has already taken place and this will provide a review of the evidence together with the criteria that have been used for developing the review. This details all the trials and studies that have been considered and what criteria were used for inclusion and exclusion. If a review has not been published it is possible that the relevant Cochrane review group may know whether anybody is developing a review. If a review has not been written or is underway then the Cochrane controlled trials register will give access to over 200,000 trials and provide references for them. Further details can be found at www.cochrane.co.uk. Also in the library is the York Database of Reviews of Effectiveness (DARE) and a register of controlled clinical trials (to try and prevent future publication bias). An alternative source of reviews of evidence-based healthcare is Bandolier which is available online at www.jr2.ox.ac.uk:80/Bandolier.

The reviews in the Cochrane Library attempt to define the important clinical questions, undertake thorough searches for all available trials and systematically review these trials to end up with clear answers for clinicians. They are published with synopses, abstracts and full reviews, so that busy clinicians can obtain quick answers when they need them, or more in-depth discussions when appropriate. Although the Library has many gaps (either lack of reviews or lack of primary research trials) and excludes all non-randomised controlled research, it is becoming more and more useful with time, not necessarily as a clinical reference document, but as a definitive source of medical knowledge.

APPRAISING THE EVIDENCE

After searching for the evidence, the next step is to sift through all the papers and exclude irrelevant or poor methodological articles. Selected studies should be categorised according to study design and the hierarchy of evidence mentioned above. The next step is to read the selected studies and decide on the strength and the quality of the research findings. This is often called critical appraisal. We tend to be over-simplistic in reporting research findings, categorising them into black or white (the drug worked or it didn't). However, research results are rarely so neat and tidy. There are many grey areas around how much the treatment worked and with what harm or side effects. We must weigh up the costs and benefits to make our own decision about whether or not the treatment is suitable to our particular patient (and increasingly individual patients will want to do so themselves).

There is nothing clever about appraising a paper, though many people are not used to doing it and lack the confidence to believe their own conclusions.

Just as taking a clinical history or performing a clinical examination seems complex and difficult to the novice, so can critical appraisal of a paper. The key, as with history taking or clinical examination, is to start with a clear structure. In reading a paper there are three key questions to ask:

- *Are the results valid?*
- *What are the results?*
- *Are the results applicable to my patient?*

If the study is of poor quality, with potential biases, then there is no point knowing what the results are, as they will not be valid. If the results are valid, then you need to decide how appropriate they are, based on the patient's values and preferences.

The more detailed questions to ask about a paper depend on what the paper is about. For example, if it is an evaluation of a therapy then you need a randomised controlled trial with double blinding of patients and researchers, on an appropriate population of consecutive patients in order to provide the base evidence. The following questions should be addressed:

Box 4: Critical Appraisal Questions for a Treatment Study

	Yes	Can't tell	No
Are the results valid?			
1 Was the assignment of patients to treatments randomised?			
2 Were all patients who entered the trial properly accounted for and attributed at its conclusion?			
3 Was follow-up complete?			
4 Were patients analysed in the groups to which they were randomised?			
5 Were patients, health workers, and study personnel blinded to treatment?			
6 Were the groups similar at the start of the trial?			
7 Aside from the experimental intervention, were the groups treated equally?			
What are the results?			
1 How large was the treatment effect? (What outcomes are measured?)			
2 How precise was the treatment effect? (What are the confidence intervals?)			
Will the results help me care for my patients?			
1 Can the results be applied to my patient care?			
2 Were all clinically important outcomes considered?			
3 Are the likely benefits worth the potential harms and costs?			
4 Are patients' values and preferences addressed?			

Evidence can be synthesised using qualitative methods (meta-analysis). However, this depends on having suitable randomised controlled trial results to undertake meta-analysis, and having the technical skill to do so. Qualitative methods of data synthesis are more commonly employed. The results of papers are summarised and some form of weighting applied based on methodological rigour, generalisability and validity.

There are many areas where research evidence is lacking. Where recommendations are made by consensus in the guideline group, this should be explicitly acknowledged.

PULLING IT ALL TOGETHER

Once all the evidence has been appraised and considered it needs to be turned into a practical document. This should be produced in a way that is understandable and readable. All too often guidelines are produced which contain the most up-to-date information yet they are buried under a huge mountain of theory and discussion. In general, the most successful guideline will include all the main evidence in a shortened form, with a clear distillation of the practical elements. The main users of a guideline will not wish to read a lengthy document, but will want to know what they should or should not do.

Therefore the next step after putting the evidence together is one of brutal editing, include the practical and particularly the local elements, and agree a final draft version. It is at this stage that wide consultation is needed to ensure that future implementation is successful. This is discussed in the next chapter. It is at this time that the guideline can be seen to be open to debate, perhaps even when it is not! However, the opportunity to comment is always welcomed by users.

Finally an agreed version needs to be circulated, published or placed on to the electronic system. It is helpful if the guideline is disseminated by meetings or announcements. The start date should be clear. At this point the authors will sit back and feel that their work is done – unfortunately producing a guideline is a bit like a pregnancy. The birth of a guideline can seem a long and difficult process but being a successful parent takes just as much work and effort and toil.

SUMMARY

The process of developing a clinical guideline should follow a sequence of logical steps. This starts from the point of determining those that may be interested in the topic being considered. They then need to meet to try to refine down the question or topic that the guideline will cover. At all stages it is important to keep under consideration who might need to be involved, as widespread ownership of a guideline increases the chances of successful implementation. Once the topic is clear a search for evidence to develop the guideline is needed. Commonly now, local guidelines can be based on national guidelines where the major work in the relevant area has been done. If that is not the case, then a search needs to be done for the evidence. It may be that a review is available, either from the Cochrane Library or elsewhere. If not then a search of the journals and/or databases is required.

The purpose of collecting all this evidence is to ensure that the practice encouraged by the guideline is up-to-date and the most appropriate available. It is clear that the successful implementation of a guideline depends upon the guideline being clear and easy to follow. A long detailed guideline is unlikely to be easily followed in a busy clinical situation. At all stages the production of the guideline document or pathway must be developed with an eye to implementation. To continue the analogy with childbirth – a perfectly formed child will not flourish without attention. However, a less than perfect child with a lot of care and attention may perform very well.

Further reading

Jackson, R and Feder, G, 'Guidelines for clinical guidelines' (1998) 317 BMJ 427–28.

Shekelle, PG, Woolf, SH, Eccles, M and Grimshaw, J, 'Developing guidelines' (1999) 318 BMJ 593–96.

CHAPTER 4

IMPLEMENTING CLINICAL GUIDELINES

J Wright and DJ Tuffnell

SYNOPSIS

When implementing a guideline it should be clear that this is not a process which begins once the guideline is published. The elements that go into producing the guideline in the first place are key to its implementation. This includes ensuring that all the stakeholders are involved in the process and that ownership is developed widely. The guideline should be based in evidence appropriate for the setting in which it will be used.

There are a number of barriers to implementing guidelines and these should be considered early in the process to encourage the change that will be needed. There can be concerns about lack of time and funds for the new guideline and there may be organisational or professional issues that impact on the guideline. Whilst these inhibit successful implementation, they need to be tackled at the development stage. It is possible to include incentives for guideline use, such as extra resources or training leading to improving practice.

The design and presentation of a guideline will be key to successful implementation. There is no single method but a number of alternatives are available. These include the use of algorithms or flow charts and computer packages to make them easy to follow. The guidelines also need to be accessible and this can also be achieved by different methods, depending on the guideline. These include posters, folders in clinical areas, handbooks, desktop packs, computer packages and even mouse mats. The proliferation of guidelines can lead to either saturation or loss of the guideline in a large volume of material. It is essential to develop some system for accumulating all the guidelines in an organised way in each clinical area. Traditionally this has been done using either a folder or booklet, but it can sometimes be impossible to find the right guideline. This has led to the wider use of electronic publication, often using an intranet facility.

Software packages are available and it is wise to consider the facilities that would be helpful. The software must be user-friendly as most users will not be highly skilled in computer terms. Therefore, publication should not rely on HTML but allow commonly used word processing skills. Publication should be separate from the users for security reasons. This is to ensure that the users do not change the guidelines. The software could also include some of the elements of good guideline practice such as a classification, clear authorship and review periods. Within the guideline links to other guidelines should be possible. As guideline numbers increase, an efficient mechanism to search for the appropriate guideline should be available. This may be simply on the basis of searching for a stem such as hypert** for hypertension. Electronic publication also ensures the right guideline is available and not an out-of-date one. It can also archive the guidelines and avoid storage difficulties. Feedback to the author through the package is also possible.

Dissemination of the guideline through educational meetings is important to raise awareness. It can be helpful to get local opinion leaders involved in the educational process. If mechanisms can be developed to include prompts in clinical areas this improves compliance. The use of audit aids implementation. Feedback about performance increases awareness and training. Targeting patients, particularly with chronic conditions, about what to expect can encourage them to prompt professionals. Each guideline will need different implementation strategies for each area it is used. Although audit is used to aid implementation in the first place, it is important to use it also to demonstrate a change in practice. Care pathways can be used to incorporate guidelines into the healthcare process. This also builds in explicit standards and aids multidisciplinary communication by improving documentation.

Ultimately guideline implementation is about managing change and this requires leadership. This initially may come from an individual but ultimately relies on the development within the clinical team of confidence in the way in which things are done. This ensures that new or locum members of the team are guided in the right direction.

INTRODUCTION

So now you have a clinical guideline, based on the most up-to-date evidence and with the weight of local expertise behind it – what now? Sadly, guidelines are not self-implementing and most clinicians recognise that they usually end up either in the bin, or being added to the guideline mountain in the corner of the clinic room. All that effort of reviewing the evidence, obtaining consensus from all the different stakeholders and putting the information into a presentable form, and what happens next? They get posted out to all relevant professionals, printed in the relevant specialist journal and backed up by a few lectures from the authors.

This chapter will deal with how to change the clinical practice of your colleagues. There is pretty good evidence about what works in changing professional practice and implementing guidelines. What does not work is posting guidelines out, publishing them in journals and giving a few didactic lectures. So why are these methods the mainstay of professional development? Partly this may be due to habit, partly it may be due to lack of awareness about how ineffective these methods are.

Although there are no magic bullets for implementing change, some things clearly work (see Box 1 below). Implementation should try to be multi-faceted to target different reasons for resistance to change and different learning needs. Different professionals have different ways of learning – some need only to read the guidelines to change. Others will need more intensive education, training and reminders.

The problem lies in translating knowledge into practice without additional resources. It would be great to copy the drug companies and send out academic detailers to every doctor, give out mugs with 'Prescribe Aspirin' on them, or set up snappy computer-aided prompts. However, this costs money. In practice, we rely heavily on the use of existing resources.

Box 1: Interventions to promote behavioural change among health professionals

---

Consistently effective interventions
- Educational outreach visits
- Reminders
- Multifaceted interventions
- Interactive educational meetings

Interventions of variable effectiveness
- Audit and feedback
- The use of local opinion leaders
- Local consensus processes
- Patient mediated interventions

Interventions that have little or no effect
- Educational materials
- Didactic educational meetings

(Adapted from Bero *et al*, BMJ, 1998.)

GET TO THE RIGHT STARTING POINT

As the man in the joke replies when he is asked directions, 'I wouldn't start from here', the same is true for implementation of guidelines. If you reach the stage of your final, beautifully designed guideline without having considered implementation, then you are in the wrong place. Implementation should be integral to the whole process of guideline development. Before the first viewpoint is uttered, or evidence citation referenced, it is essential to plan for getting the guidance into everyday practice.

Barriers and incentives: spending a bit of time at the start of a new topic to understand potential barriers and incentives to change as well as local politics is essential if success is to be achieved.

Potential barriers may include the following:

- *Lack of time*. There is never enough time, but improving patient care must be a priority, and good guidelines may save time in the end by reducing inappropriate referrals or complications.
- *Lack of funding*. Insufficient local services, for example, low numbers of staff or diagnostic services, may hinder change. Involvement of managers may be important.
- *Organisational*. Lack of support from the hospital, or different priorities.
- *Professional*. Conflict between different demands from different disciplines or between professional and patient needs.
- *Individual*. Lack of knowledge or skills in local staff.

Try to link guidelines with incentives such as resource allocation, feedback of performance or training. Subsequent motivation for change may be greater.

Discuss the topic with key clinicians and other staff in the district. Ask them to identify the barriers and incentives, and find out how they would set about the task of developing guidelines or improving practice. Find out what current practice is and why it differs from best practice. Assess whether local consensus is achievable and whether subsequent change is likely.

CHOOSE THE RIGHT GROUP

As discussed in the previous chapter, guideline development has moved on from being a solitary affair with a kitchen table. Involving the right people in development is important for two reasons. First, the care of a patient depends on different health professionals. Each different professional group will have its own important contributions to make to a guideline and useful messages to get across. Secondly, if the guideline is to be effective then several different professional groups must be signed up to it. If one group has been left out then its members are unlikely to feel particularly motivated to adhere to the guidelines developed. The right membership will promote the right credibility and it is important to start by thinking who the guideline is aimed at.

Box 2:   Choosing a guideline development group

Leadership: does the group have a chair who has the skills of communication and facilitation to develop consensus guidelines?

Expertise: are the staff with the specialist knowledge on hand?

Medical staff: are the different specialties represented? If the guideline is aimed at junior doctors, are they represented?

Nursing and therapy staff: few topics are the sole preserve of doctors and most other health professionals will have knowledge and know-how about particular topics.

Primary care: again, few topics are the sole preserve of hospital care and local general practitioners and practice nurses should be invited if the guidelines will impact on them.

Managers: many guidelines have implications of costs or changes in demand for particular services.

Administrative or project management support: clinical governance departments should ensure that they have staff with the skills to support the process.

Patients: this may be difficult, and not always appropriate, but guidelines are all about improving patient care, and their voice should be heard.

Crossing the interface between primary and secondary care is often neglected when it comes to guidelines. There is a tendency to have one rule for hospital care and one for the rest. While many of the patients seen in hospital will be different from those seen in primary care (in severity of illness, for instance), the evidence base for treatment or investigation will mostly be the same. So, for example, access to upper gastrointestinal endoscopy for a patient in hospital should not be governed by different guidance just because the endoscopsist is close at hand.

Few patients are aware of the (artificial) distinction between primary and secondary care. Each contact is just another stop on their health journey. Clinical guidelines need to acknowledge this movement across 'borders'.

The other frequently forgotten group to involve in guideline development is the managers. This is short sighted: a clinician will get little sympathy if he turns up six months after the guidelines have been agreed saying that he needs a new drug, or more staff or another echo machine. Managers have control of staff and resources, and they are better on-side than off-field.

One last, but very important group is the patients themselves. In many cases this may not be appropriate, for example, in acute emergency guidelines or diagnostics. But more and more patients want to know the basis of clinical decision-making, particularly in chronic diseases such as diabetes, epilepsy or angina. Where possible a patient should be included in the group. It may be appropriate to involve non-medical carers, for example, in the case of stroke patients. Ask around and select someone who will be assertive enough to contribute in a potentially intimidating professional environment.

Guideline discussions are often very technical and the environment can be intimidating. Alternative methods to obtain patient involvement should be considered, such as running separate focus groups to allow the consensus group to be informed by what patients and their carers think are the important points to include in guidelines.

OBTAIN CONSENSUS

Guidelines and supporting evidence should be circulated to the group. In a perfect world you could identify suitably valid guidelines, approve them with a large group, rubber stamp and stick them on the shelf on the ward or in the clinic. Simple endorsement may sometimes be all that is needed, but clinical practice can be hard to change and the process of change is important. Your consensus group needs to meet and discuss the guidelines. This ensures that all the stakeholders are signed up to the recommendations and provides an excellent opportunity to spend some time reflecting on what current practice is and what it should be.

It is always interesting to review guidelines and their recommendations in a group. It reveals different practices between different clinicians – different drugs or doses used, different use of investigations, different surgical techniques. It allows debate about what is best practice, backed up by explicit evidence. It provides a forum for different voices that may have previously been ignored. It also identifies what the potential barriers to adopting local guidelines may be, for example, lack of diagnostic equipment such as echocardiography to diagnose heart failure, restricted access because of waiting times that limit the diagnosis of epilepsy, or disagreement with the evidence such as grommet insertions for glue ear.

Using the circulated guidelines and evidence as a foundation, adaptations can be made to take local circumstances into account. The group should take into account the specific health needs of the local population and the availability of current services. Changes agreed by the group can be made and circulated outside the meeting or discussed at a subsequent meeting. Circulate early drafts to people outside the group – the wider the net is cast in seeking people's opinion, the earlier disagreements can be resolved and ownership encouraged.

Figure 4.1

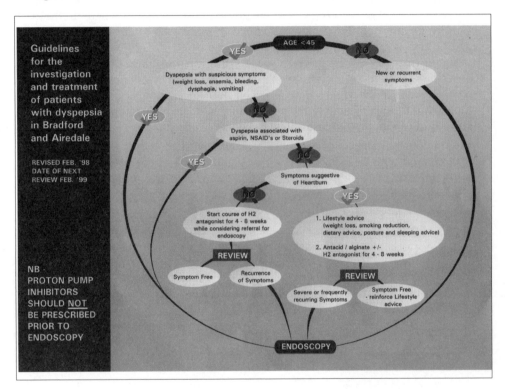

PRESENTATION AND ACCESS

With consensus achieved, the next step is to package the guidelines so that they will be accessible and readable. Many national guidelines, and some local guidelines, tend to end up as bulky tomes with slabs of text and reams of references. Guidelines should be quick reference documents for busy clinicians making frequent and pressurised clinical decisions, so design and presentation are important. Having invested so much effort to develop the guidelines, it is worth spending a bit of time to make sure they are used.

There is no single method for presentation of guidelines. Some may be best conveyed as algorithms or flow charts (Figure 4.1), with the diagnosis as the starting point (for example, endometrial carcinoma). Patients, however, tend not to be aware of the need to present with a diagnosis, and the symptom may be the most suitable starting point (for example, post-menopausal bleeding).

Cheap and easy-to-use computer design packages are now widely available, and it is worth thinking about transferring dull lists of recommendations into more eye-catching formats (Figure 4.2).

Finally, try to ensure that the guidelines are accessible. Where are they going to be used most? Which staff are going to use them and where do those staff go for information? A few years ago there was an interesting little trial published which randomised two junior doctor's residences. In the intervention residence posters were stuck on the back of toilet doors describing patient resuscitation methods. The other residence acted as the control. After a few weeks they assessed both groups of junior doctors and found that those allocated to the posters in the toilets had significantly greater knowledge about how to resuscitate patients.

The logical extreme of guideline posters could be wards and residences wallpapered with them. This is obviously going too far, but there is no reason why important topics should not be promoted this way. Methods of dissemination to consider include:

- ward folders;
- ward or clinic posters;
- junior doctor handbooks;
- desktop packs for clinics;
- computers and even mouse-mats to improve access to the guidelines (Figure 4.2).

Figure 4.2

Computer access, either on stand-alone computers or on networks such as intranets, will become increasingly important as a source of guidelines. This allows widespread access of guidelines throughout a hospital and between primary and secondary care. It also allows guidelines to be updated quickly and efficiently, without the danger of out-of-date guidelines lying around on wards and being used.

ELECTRONIC PUBLICATION

With the move towards the electronic patient record and the slow but steady advancement of information technology within health care in the UK, the publishing of guidelines in an electronic format should be considered. Many hospitals now have an intranet or access to the Internet. Many national guidelines are available through Internet sites of the organisation which has published them. Some guidelines are, unfortunately, only available in summary form and the whole guideline needs to be purchased in booklet format. However, local guidelines can be easily published using an intranet and some software applications are available to facilitate this. What should be the properties of a software application?

SOFTWARE PROPERTIES

The software should, in the first place, be user friendly. Most clinicians will not have the computer skills to use any software that is not intuitive. Therefore it must function in publishing terms in a similar way to word processing software. It should not use HTML, even though this is the publishing language for most Internet sites or intranets. Ease of use creates the problem that unauthorised users may feel able to alter the guidelines if they disagree with them. This means that the publishing of the guidelines must be disconnected from the site on which they are published. This leads to the requirement of the software having security levels established, determining who can access which guidelines through the software, and who can edit which guidelines. It may mean that each department will only have one authorised publisher. The way in which the guideline is published should allow the author to be established separately from the publisher.

Within the layers of security it is possible to allow some guidelines, particularly those in development phases, to be available to selected individuals. This allows the development of the guidelines to proceed in a newsgroup type format rather than requiring regular meetings. This may be a clear advantage, particularly if the authors have difficulty in meeting.

The software should also be able to include, in the formatting, some of the essentials of good guideline practice. A classification of the guideline may add to the clarity provided by the title. It is also possible to put in place a clear reminder as to when the guideline should be reviewed. It should be possible to set different review periods for different guidelines. The software should also provide an area for references or further reading. It is the authors' preference that these should be hidden in order to facilitate the use of the guideline.

Within the guideline it should be possible to develop links. This should allow an index to be placed at the beginning of a long guideline, particularly if there are multiple sections. It should also be possible to allow linkage to other guidelines which are on similar topics, or relate to the same condition. This will allow clinicians to filter through the available guidelines to ensure that they can find the appropriate one.

When large numbers of guidelines are available in electronic format, a new problem can develop. It can be difficult to find the appropriate guideline. This can also be a problem with multiple paper guidelines. However, with electronic guidelines it should be possible to search for key words or even parts of words. For example, one could search for guidelines related to hypertension or to hypert**, if the software is configured appropriately. The software should then be able to produce a list of guidelines that match. This allows the user the opportunity to search more effectively.

The format of the published guidelines can also be made uniform by the publishing constraints of the software. There are advantages and disadvantages to this. Whilst uniformity may be constraining it can also ensure that key features are included with each guideline. It is important that the publishing allows the guidelines to be read easily on the computer screen, and also printed in an easily read format. Whilst computer terminals are becoming more widespread they still tend to be one per ward or clinical area. They are still not present at the bedside. This means that a printed version is still useful and important. It can also be helpful to include in the clinical record a copy of any guideline used. This can act as an *aide memoire* and also can allow a clear pattern of care to be identified should any subsequent allegations be made about the quality of care.

This medico-legal aspect of the guidelines also demonstrates a major advantage of electronically published guidelines. It should be easy to archive and date stamp the guidelines. This avoids the common problem of trying to determine which guideline was in place at the time of the incident that led to allegations. Importantly, the process of archiving also removes out-of-date guidelines, thus ensuring that a clinician will not inadvertently use a guideline that has become out-of-date.

One other difficulty of paper guidelines is that it is often difficult for staff to know if minor changes have been made to guidelines. The electronic format allows for a 'notice board' to come up when the guideline software is opened, showing either new or recently amended guidelines. This advertising of new or amended guidelines can be important in maintaining the awareness (and hopefully therefore the effectiveness) of guidelines.

Electronic publication can also incorporate a feedback mechanism for guidelines. This can be an extremely helpful way to encourage ownership of the guidelines. If clinicians not directly involved in the process of development have the opportunity to comment if they have problems, it will allow them to feel involved in the process of the evolution of the guideline. It also allows small but important changes to be made to a guideline, without the need to withdraw many copies of the guideline. In our own unit the comment sections of the electronic guidelines are used by all professionals to discuss areas that they have concerns about. They also highlight areas of problems even if they do not have a solution! The comments facility has also been used to develop themed discussions about areas of practice that are changing or developing.

We also use the guidelines software to publish details of clinical trials, the presentations from departmental meetings in powerpoint format and the newsletters from clinical governance meetings. Our 'clinical incident reporting system' often leads to lessons to be learnt. We use the guideline system to publish these lessons in a reverse chronological way. This allows clinicians to read about the most recent events first but also allows old lessons to be retained. This can be important when new staff start as they can learn the old lessons as well as the new. An example of the guidelines software is demonstrated in Figure 4.3.

Figure 4.3

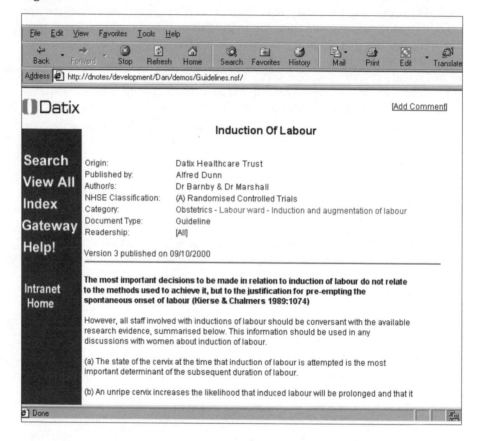

Box 3:   Advantages of electronic publication

Ease of availability

Consistency of format

Guaranteed up-to-date and not out-of-date

Ease of alteration

Reminders when updating requires

Ease of feedback comment

Can be used to develop newsgroup format about guideline

Guaranteed archiving

Ease of searching

Ease of adding references

Ease of notifying staff about new guidelines

Can be used to publish and archive newsletters, presentations, research details

Can be used to publish lessons learnt from clinical incidents

Allows copy to be placed easily in clinical record

DISSEMINATION AND IMPLEMENTATION

When you come to getting your guideline, or any other clinical change, into routine practice there are a number of different methods that can be used. All require resources. Some require more resources than others. The more effort that is put into the implementation phase, the more you will see change and subsequent improvements in patient care. The following interventions should be considered.

RAISE AWARENESS

Try and involve as many people as possible in commenting on the draft guidelines so that there is early ownership. Publicise the guidelines though local newsletters in the hospital or in primary care. Simple postal dissemination does not seem to be effective in promoting change, but it may promote recognition and awareness that can then be built upon. This is facilitated by the electronic process discussed above. Email may also be used if available.

Identify local 'opinion leaders'. These are local health professionals who are considered to be influential in educating other staff about the guideline area. They are likely to be listened to and their clinical opinion respected and adopted. They should be used to lead or support the educational and training events as part of the guideline implementation process. These opinion leaders usually have the enthusiasm to promote their messages, but will have limited time. Thought should be given to how to use this time most efficiently.

It is not always easy to identify clear opinion leaders in a particular field, but local knowledge and enquiry as part of the preliminary guideline work (see above) will usually identify suitable candidates.

Educational meetings. Use existing educational events such as postgraduate lectures or clinical governance meetings (for hospital departments or primary care groups) to promote the guidelines to hospital staff and general practitioners.

Didactic lectures are of dubious effectiveness, but are still the mainstay of medical education. Interactive and participatory sessions are more likely to promote change and subsequent guideline adoption. Involve your audience, listen to what they want to learn and provide concrete examples for them to learn from.

Educational outreach visits by relevant medical and nursing specialists – taking the message out to the clinicians. These visits take place in the practice setting (for example, general practitioners' surgeries, or individual departments) and so tend to be more interactive and less formal. This is a strategy commonly used by the pharmaceutical industry and one that appears to be effective, yet one that the health service has been slow to adopt. The main reason for this inertia has been the lack of time and resources to send someone out to train other staff. However, it may be the only way to influence doctors who would not otherwise attend existing educational events. Such a targeted strategy may be valuable in changing the practice of those who deviate from guideline recommendations the most. A 10 minute discussion may prevent many time-consuming, inappropriate referrals.

Prompts and reminders. These can be valuable aids in getting timely access to the right guideline. Posters for wards and stickers or markers in medical records can be simple methods of reminding staff (for example, to prompt staff to check that all post myocardial infarction patients are discharged on aspirin and beta blockers). Guideline mouse-mats, desktop calendars and computer versions which can be accessed via local intranet are more sophisticated methods (Figures 4.2 and 4.3). Guidelines can also be incorporated into relevant referral forms to encourage compliance with referral requests, for example, with radiology requests. Recommendations can also be incorporated into reports (such as laboratory investigations) or referral letters, to reinforce desired practice. Computerised decision support will become an increasingly powerful method of reminder as it allows prompts to be made at the same time as clinical decision-making.

Audit and feedback. This allows individual wards and departments to see how their own clinical practice matches up with recommended standards and subsequently to monitor change. This information on performance can be important in demonstrating weaknesses in practice that justify the need for local guidelines. This can be used in the educational and training events to link key messages with evidence about current practice. It can also provide the basis for evaluating guideline uptake (an aspect which is important if you are to be objective about the effectiveness of your efforts) and sustainability of changes in clinical practice.

Patient involvement. Patients themselves can be influential in encouraging health professionals to make the right decisions. Well-informed patients will know what treatments they should be taking and what standards of care should be provided. This is particularly true of patients with chronic diseases and younger, more empowered, patients. It is worth considering strategies that target patients themselves, such as posters in waiting areas, messages in the local press or discussions with local patient organisations.

Different mechanisms will work for different individuals, so try to tailor local approaches using the above menu of methods. Try to be systematic in the approach to implementation. Adopting a stepwise approach may allow the best use of limited resources available. For example, record attendance at educational and audit feedback events to monitor coverage. Where possible, health professionals who do not attend should be offered a group or individual outreach visit by the audit/guideline facilitator or other relevant staff (for example, consultant or specialist nurse). When this is not possible, and as a last resort, guidelines should be sent by post to the remaining health professionals.

The final stage of implementation should be to evaluate the process of change and learn any lessons from it. Has there been the desired change? If so, what worked? If not, what were the barriers and how can they be overcome? Changing practice is an ongoing process that must be reflective and adaptable if it is to succeed. Evaluation can be through audit of guideline standards or more qualitative techniques of interviews with guideline users and developers.

CARE PATHWAYS

One way of encouraging adherence to guidelines or clinical standards is to build these recommendations and standards into the patient records. Typical medical records are unstructured and poorly completed. Different professionals tend to use different parts of the records and frequently ignore what their colleagues are writing. This encourages haphazard documentation and much duplication.

Care pathways, or integrated care pathways, are health plans that describe the process of care from admission through to discharge for a particular condition (for example, myocardial infarction or stroke) or particular surgical operations. They have a number of potential advantages:

- They can incorporate guidelines into records so that they act as prompts and reminders to health professionals.
- They highlight explicit standards to be met in the patient's pathway of care – standards that can be audited simply from the records to inform staff.
- They are multidisciplinary and so can improve communication between different professionals as well as cut down on unnecessary duplication of information recorded.
- They can reduce variation in clinical practice.
- They can improve documentation in health records.

The process of developing care pathways is just as important (and as time-consuming) as developing guidelines. Spend some time identifying potential barriers to pathway adoption and avoid areas where there will be too much resistance. Choose a suitable clinical topic and convene a multidisciplinary team to develop the pathway. Standards and clinical prompts are then incorporated into a patient pathway and after piloting, reviewing and modifying the pathway, it can then be put into practice with an appropriate training programme for ward staff. Audit of records can then identify the degree of staff compliance and describe the common variations in care.

There is considerable experience in developing care pathways in different clinical areas in the National Health Service. Rather than start from scratch, try to identify suitable pathways that have been developed elsewhere. These can then be modified to the local context.

Care pathways share some of the problems of guidelines. Like guideline development, the development of care pathways requires time, leadership and energy. They can become too inflexible and fail to take adequate account of the uncertainty of clinical practice. They may also stifle clinical decision-making by making it too automatic. Recording variations and deviations from the care pathway is important if these potential barriers are to be overcome and better pathways developed.

The development of electronic patient records will allow integrated care pathways to become electronic. This will allow much greater flexibility and the tailoring of prompts and standards to individual patients. It will also cut down on the excessive consumption of paper that generic care pathways tend to require. This is discussed in the next chapter.

MANAGING CHANGE AND LEADERSHIP

These two processes are inextricably linked. When introducing a new guideline, the role of clinical leaders is vital to the success or failure of clinical guidelines. This underlines the importance of the points made earlier about involving the appropriate people in the process of guideline development. If a respected clinical leader is not involved, or is uncomfortable with the guideline as developed, it is unlikely that it will be implemented successfully as it will be undermined from the outset. For this reason, the person who leads a guideline development group may not be the person who wishes to drive the process, but their role as a figurehead requires them to be seen as the lead.

However, once the guideline is in the public domain it should not be dependent on the support of a single clinician. This is self evident, as clinical care rarely depends on single individuals. If a guideline depends on a single person it will falter when that person is away or busy with other matters. This undermines one of the primary aims of a guideline, which is to provide consistent care at all times. Therefore one of the roles of the group developing the guideline is to bring along the leaders of each clinical team and/or shift to ensure leadership is available at all times.

One situation that can often lead to difficulties in ensuring compliance with guidelines is when new staff or locum staff are employed. This is because they may well have been used to working in a different way to the way described within the unit guidelines. It is at this point that leadership from other members of the clinical team is required. This can be difficult. For instance, for a ward sister to explain to an experienced locum doctor that the way they are intending to manage a clinical situation falls outside the way which is accepted in the unit can lead to confrontation. It is at this point that the support and leadership of other senior clinicians is required to reinforce the behaviour of the ward sister. This is important for two reasons. First, it reinforces the appropriateness of the guideline and the importance of following it. Secondly, it increases perceptions of ownership of the guideline by the staff working in the clinical area and strengthens their role within the development of practice within the unit.

The role of clinical leaders stretches beyond ensuring that others comply with the guidelines. It is vital for the guideline and the development of consistent practice within the unit that senior clinicians follow the guidelines. If it becomes perceived that the guidelines are only in place for junior staff, then they will rapidly lose the credibility of the staff they are aimed at influencing. The senior staff must be seen to document reasons for practice outside the guidelines. It is also important to spend time discussing with new and junior staff why the guidelines are interpreted in particular ways in the unit. This education process should be part of the underlying philosophy of leadership within a successful unit.

SUMMARY

All this work to develop and implement one guideline may appear to be daunting. However, the outcome is not simply about a piece of paper with a flow chart on it. The outcome should be the better care of patients, a goal we all share and strive towards. This may involve time and effort, but along the way you will provide wonderful opportunities to:

- develop teamwork and communication;
- reflect on current practices;
- provide interactive and educational discussions about the evidence-base behind clinical practice;
- inspire different professionals towards a common goal;
- set standards to measure future performance.

Be prepared for requests from the group for more!

Time and resources are required to support this process. These requirements should be identified and provided for clearly in departmental and organisational development plans. The process requires:

- leadership;
- enthusiasm and energy;
- careful planning and efficient use of time;
- good communication with staff involved in the development and staff who will be using the guideline.

Implementation of guidelines starts at the stage of planning the guideline. This process is continued through development by ensuring that all interested parties are involved. This is essential to ensure that the barrier of opposition is removed and that potential opponents are brought into the process. Once the guideline is written and ready for sharing with the world this must be done in a way that ensures that all the relevant people have access. This can be achieved in a number of ways. The format that the guideline is published in is important. Electronic publishing is useful where available but can be substituted or supplemented by other formats, such as laminated guidelines, mouse-mats or *aides memoires*.

Publication of the guideline is only a small part of the implementation process. Implementation relies on clinicians having ownership and feeling that the guideline represents the way that they wish to practice. It also relies on them having a sense that they can influence the development of the guideline over time. The involvement of senior clinicians in demonstrating their confidence in the guidelines by following them is also integral to successful implementation. Ultimately the use of guidelines has to be audited and this should demonstrate that outcomes have improved. At this point it becomes clear that a guideline has been successfully implemented.

Appendix – Some guideline implementation examples

An example of a local guideline for best practice of patients with dyspepsia and *H pylori* in primary care is shown in Box 4.

Box 4: **Evidence into practice: management of patients with peptic ulcers and dyspepsia**

Background: Eradication of Helicobacter pylori is effective in healing the majority of peptic ulcers and preventing relapses. In many patients with ulcer disease this eradication may eliminate the need for long term maintenance with acid-suppressing therapy. These drugs comprise one of the most expensive cost categories in the NHS drug budget and there is therefore great potential to improve patients' health at a reduced cost to the health service. This topic was chosen to promote the implementation of effective management of patients with dyspepsia and peptic ulcer disease.

Implementation methods: A multifaceted approach which included the development of evidence-based clinical guidelines, audit and feedback, outreach visits, educational workshops, patient reminders and the development of patient information linked to the guidelines.

Impact: 229 (86%) of general practitioners attended group or personal education and feedback sessions. 44 (44%) of practices took part in the audit. 1,306 patients with a diagnosis of peptic ulcers were identified from audit of records. Follow-up after nine months was completed for 66% of patients. 10% of patients with ulcers had been prescribed eradication therapy for *H pylori* at baseline compared to 50% at follow-up. Patients who had been prescribed eradication therapy were more likely to be off treatment with acid-suppressing drugs compared to those who had not (71% v 19.1%). Costs of the project were £140 per patient known to have been treated with eradication therapy.

An example of using a regional network to implement severe pre-eclampsia guidelines is shown in Box 5.

Box 5: Implementing Regional Guidelines in pre-eclampsia

Background

Regional Guidelines for the management of severe pre-eclampsia were developed in 1997 in the Yorkshire region and incorporated a complete multidisciplinary clinical management plan. The recommendations within the 1990–93 Confidential Enquiry into Maternal Mortality stated that:

> All units should have a lead consultant, clear guidelines for the management of severe pregnancy induced hypertension, including eclampsia, and ready access to a Regional advisory service led by a consultant with special expertise.

Implementation

The initial guidelines were well received but the accompanying audit had a poor response. Awareness had to be raised throughout the region. Funding for a regional audit midwife was obtained. The midwife developed contact midwives in each unit and developed an education and feedback process. This involved meetings at a regional level to feedback results as well as meetings in each unit. Within each unit the regional and individual units results were given. This benchmarked practice and detailed areas of improvement. At each annual meeting changes to the guideline were made after discussion about the impact of the guideline. The network midwives met regularly to feedback any problems to the coordinating group.

Impact

In three years 649 women were managed using the guidelines. Compliance with the guidelines improved, particularly in the areas of involvement of senior staff, performance of blood tests, management of hypertension, thromboprophylaxis and use of magnesium sulphate. There was no improvement in fluid management or routine observations. Outcomes were improved with a reduction in intensive care admission (from 11.3% in 1998 to 5.7% in 2000). There were also less complications, particularly pulmonary oedema.

The development of the link midwives has led to an increase in confidence when managing these complex cases. They have, in turn, facilitated the development and audit of the guidelines improving the outcome for the women.

Further reading

University of Leeds, *Effective Health Care. Implementing Clinical Guidelines*, 1994.

NHS Centre for Reviews and Dissemination, *Effective Health Care Bulletin. Getting Evidence into Practice*, 1999, University of York.

Wensing, M, van der Weijden, T and Grol, R, 'Implementing guidelines and innovations in general practice: which interventions are effective?' (1998) Br J Gen Pract 48:991-7.

Bero, LA, Grilli, R, Grimshaw, JM, Harvey, E, Oxman, AD and Thomson, MA, 'Closing the gap between research and practice: an overview of systematic reviews of interventions to promote the implementation of research findings' (1998) 317 BMJ 465–68.

Dunning, M, Abi-Aad, G, Gilbert, D, Gillam, S and Livett, H, *Turning Evidence into Everyday Practice*, 1998, London: Kings Fund.

Cambell, H, Hotchkiss, R, Bradshaw, N and Porteous, M, 'Integrated care pathways' (1998) 316 BMJ 133–37.

CHAPTER 5

THE ROLE OF THE CLINICAL INSTITUTIONS AND CENTRAL GOVERNMENT IN GUIDELINE CREATION AND DEVELOPMENT

AJ O'Rourke

SYNOPSIS

Attempts to codify physicians' practice are almost as old as the profession, but only in the last century has this produced objective clinical guidelines. More recently, the writing and dissemination of guidelines has been driven by the evidence-based movement's demand that clinical care must be based on the appraisal and application of research work and a desire to deal with poor quality care by promoting 'best practice' through levelling up. More controversial applications of guidelines include cost effectiveness and rationing. In many countries, all too public defects in the quality and regulation of health care have given governments a remit to establish programmes for quality assurance, clinical audit, detecting substandard performance and professional re-accreditation.

In America, guideline development was lead by the Agency for Health Care Policy and Research (AHCPR), but having crossed swords with one professional group and suffered a reduction in its funding, this body now concentrates on disseminating rather than commissioning guidelines. Many European countries also have mechanisms for issuing clinical guidelines. In the UK, the government has established National Service Frameworks for specific conditions; a National Institute for Clinical Effectiveness (NICE); a system to ensure that clinical standards are maintained and improved (clinical governance); and a Commission for Health Improvement (CHI).

NICE will work with a Partners' Council and a wide range of professional and statutory bodies involved in healthcare to evaluate drugs and other interventions, produce guidelines for their use and design audit methodologies to monitor their application. Recently NICE's workload increased to over 30 appraisals and about 15 guidelines a year, with a focus on work to support the National Cancer Plan. Areas for future work include infertility. Although NICE has delivered much solid work, it has drawn fire over the openness of its decision making, the evidence base for some of its recommendations, and the potential impact on the health service of implementing these, in terms of workload and cost. Although NICE recommendations are not legally binding, it is not clear how closely CHI will expect to see them followed when it begins its review of clinical standards.

Many professional bodies have also established research, effectiveness and audit units, and some have developed their own clinical guidelines. From April 2001, NICE proposes to support six Collaborating Centres, involving the Colleges and professional associations in partnerships. NICE also commissions appraisals from academic units and is developing diabetes guidelines in collaboration involving the Royal College of General Practitioners.

Possible future developments include: pathways of care (guidelines which have been customised for local use, to produce a document that functions as the medical record, and has built-in quality monitoring components); incorporating guidelines into decision support software; and dealing with manpower problems by allowing guideline-controlled delegation of some clinical tasks. A strong theme in the New NHS is patient empowerment and greater involvement in clinical decision-making. Patients and the public would not only play a role in choosing topics for guidelines, but should contribute actively to the process of devising them, which may shift the emphasis to 'softer' outcomes like equity and speed of access to healthcare. Demands that healthcare encompass alternative and complementary therapies, many of which have a weak evidence base, may mean making guidelines flexible enough to respect traditions other than the western reductionist world view.

THE ROLE OF THE CLINICAL INSTITUTIONS AND CENTRAL GOVERNMENT IN GUIDELINE CREATION AND DEVELOPMENT

The Physicians draw their support from the public funds and administer their treatment in accordance with a written law which was composed in ancient times by many famous physicians. If they follow the rules of this law as they read them in the sacred books and yet are unable to save the patient, they are absolved from any charge and go unpunished; but if they go contrary to the law's prescriptions in any respect, they must submit to a trial with death as the penalty, the law-giver holding that but few physicians would ever show themselves wiser than the mode of treatment which had been closely followed for a long period and had been originally prescribed by the ablest practitioner (Diodorus Sicculus, Greek historian of the 2nd century BC, commenting on Egyptian military medicine):

> We have left undone those things which we ought to have done; and we have done those things which we ought not to have done; and there is no health in us. (*Book of Common Prayer.*)

INTRODUCTION

Codes, regulations and recommendations as to how doctors should practice are almost as old as the profession, but for most of history, they have been little more than *ex cathedra* pronouncements from influential individuals, or at best a summary of the experience of the good and the great.[1] Early examples of national guidelines included the American Academy of Paediatrics (treatment of infectious diseases, 1938) and the American College of Obstetricians and Gynaecologists (practice standards, 1959). Only recently have we moved on from such consensus to systematic guidelines as concise summaries of 'best evidence' for a specific clinical condition that can support clinical decisions. Healthcare organisations across the world, whether publicly or privately funded, have to grapple with common problems such as:

- Delays of up to 10 years between publication of good research and its clinical application.

- Costs rising faster than inflation, and the need for probity in the use of public funds.

- Variation in clinical practice: clinicians manage the same problem in many ways. Not all variation is bad: it may represent lack of evidence about the best methods, or sensible adaptation to local factors, but some represents sub-standard care.

- The continued use of treatments for which there is little evidence of effectiveness beyond tradition and anecdote: some of these may be at best a waste of resources, at worst detrimental to the patient: 'The history of medicine is richly endowed with therapies that were widely used and then shown to be ineffective or frankly toxic.'[2]

- Failure to employ techniques validated by robust studies.

A generic approach to the financial issues has been to divide healthcare into purchasing organisations (who hold budgets and negotiate contracts) and providers (who deliver clinical services). Guidelines can be used for cost effective healthcare by making explicit what will and what will not be funded. Few would disagree with guidelines as tools for overcoming the barriers to disseminating research and helping doctors choose appropriate care. However, when guidelines determine which treatments can be used and which cannot, or decide which interventions will be funded, they become more controversial. Some clinicians have the uneasy feeling that ultimately

---

1   Spiegel, AD, and Springer, CR, 'Babylonian medicine, managed care and Codex Hammurabi circa 1700 BC' (1997) 22(1) J of Community Health 69–89.

2   Passamani, E, 'Clinical trials, are they ethical?' (1991) 324 New England J of Medicine 1589–92.

guidelines may be mechanisms of healthcare rationing. Guidelines also tend to be drafted for discrete clinical problems whereas patients often present with multiple pathologies, with possible conflict between the guidelines for each.

Another question is: to what degree should scientifically rigorous national guidelines be 'customised' for local use? This is a trade-off between the benefits of motivating clinicians to establish ownership by fitting them to local resources, and the risk of reducing them to a consensus endorsement of current practice.

MAKING MEDICINE MORE RATIONAL

The phrase 'evidence-based medicine' (EBM) has almost become a mantra in recent years, along with the broader terms of 'evidence-based practice' (EBP) and 'evidence-based health care'. It is misleading since medicine has always acted on some sort of evidence, even if that 'evidence' was little more than a concoction of inaccurate cribs of ancient texts and anecdotal observations. EBM is about explicit decision-making, based on objective appraisals of scientific research. It may have been better to start with 'research-based' but EBM has stuck. One definition of EBM is:

> ... the conscientious, explicit, and judicious use of current best evidence in making decisions about the care of individual patients. The practice of evidence based medicine means integrating individual clinical expertise with the best available external clinical evidence from systematic research.[3]

Again, this addresses the old question 'is medicine an art or a science?' by answering 'both!' There is the art of establishing rapport with a patient, taking a history and performing physical examination, combined with the science of diagnosis and choosing the most appropriate course of action. Similarly, the skills of clinical acumen apply to using guidelines. Some fear that they are 'cookbook medicine': for A, do B. Old-fashioned clinical freedom (in its grossest form the right 'to treat the patient in whatever way I choose') has passed, but guidelines are tools not rules: they help clinicians decide what they may do, not tell them what they must do.[4]

As with much of bio-medical science, EBM depends on supporting technologies, notably:

1 Electronic databases, with indexing systems allowing rapid, systematic searches.

---

3   Sackett DL, Rosenberg, WMC, Gray, JAM, Haynes RB and Richardson WS, 'Evidence based medicine: what it is and what it isn't' (1996) 312 BMJ 71–72.

4   James, PA, Cowan, TM, Graham, RP and Majeroni, BA, 'Family physicians' attitudes about and use of clinical practice guidelines' (1997) 45(4) J of Family Practice 341–47.

2   Techniques of systematic review and meta-analysis to summarise the results of many smaller studies.

3   Statistical techniques and critical appraisal to convert clinical data into valid conclusions.

A leading principle of EBP is making systematic use of the bio-medical research; a key stage in designing any guideline is the literature review. The traditional review article was often little more than a subjective collection of 'everything we know about malaria' or all viewpoints on a topic, giving each equal weight. The modern systematic review addresses a focused clinical question ('What is the best treatment for malaria contracted in Kenya?'), with explicit inclusion and exclusion criteria for selecting primary research. Each article will also be appraised for its methodological robustness. A meta-analysis goes one stage further by using statistical analysis to combine the raw data from the individual studies. This process is not a 'one off.' As more research is published, a review only remains valid if updated: a good guideline will include an explicit review date.

Scientific evidence is now ranked in a hierarchy something like Figure 5.1: the higher up a methodology is ranked, the more robust and closer to objective truth it is assumed to be.

Figure 5.1: A hierarchy of bio-medical evidence

Rank	Methodology	Description
1	Systematic reviews	Review using explicit methods to locate and assess quality in primary studies
	Meta-analysis	Statistical integration of several independent clinical trials classed as combinable usually to the level of re-analysing and combining the original data (also called: pooling, quantitative synthesis)
	Both are sometimes called overviews	
2	Randomised controlled trials (RCTs)	Individuals are randomly allocated to control and intervention groups, identical for all significant variables apart from the intervention, and followed up for specific end points
3	Cohort studies	Groups are selected on the basis of their exposure to a particular agent and followed up for specific outcomes
4	Case-control studies	Cases with the condition are matched to controls without it; retrospective analysis looks for differences between the two groups
5	Cross-sectional surveys	Survey or interview of a sample of the population of interest at one point in time
6	Case reports	A report based on a single patient or subject; sometimes collected together into a short series
7	Expert opinion	A consensus of experience from the good and the great
8	Anecdotal	Casual and often second-hand clinical observations

This ranking has an evolutionary order, moving from simple observations up through increasingly sophisticated methodologies. The physical sciences are relatively consistent: repeated measurements of the acceleration due to gravity give a fairly constant value. But biological systems are multivariate and less predictable: if you studied diet and growth in different groups even from the same species, you would get very mixed results. Social phenomena are even more complex. Many bio-medical discoveries had to wait for statistical techniques capable of dealing with populations. For instance:

- Observation proves that sewing up torn veins stops bleeding to death.
- 1950s cohort studies established the link between smoking and lung cancer.
- Nowadays, detecting small but important differences in survival with different drugs for cancer needs large multi-centre RCTs.

There are three more points about this hierarchy:

1 Techniques ranked lower are not obsolete: any ethics committee would quite rightly reject a proposed RCT studying risk factors by exposing half the subjects to some noxious agent! Here, you need a cohort (a group exposed to the agent by chance or choice) to compare how they fare with an unexposed group. One study methodology is not always best: for each question there will be an appropriate method.

2 This hierarchy is not fixed in tablets of stone: there is debate over the relative positions of systematic reviews and large RCTs. Traditionally, the RCT has been regarded as the most objective method of removing bias and producing comparable groups. But the technique is often slow, expensive and produces results that are difficult to apply to 'real situations'. In the future, computer capacity may make observational studies with multiple variables possible.

3 Some statisticians object to the emphasis given to significance defined by probability tests and suggest other ways of evaluating studies, such as Bayesian methods. In the future, we may need to revise the tools we use to decide whether a study changes our existing knowledge.[5]

HEALTH QUALITY PROGRAMMES

In the last 20 years, many countries have recognised the importance of explicit programmes of quality assurance and quality improvement in healthcare, rather than depending on professional integrity. The emphasis has moved

5 Sterne, JAC and Smith, GD, 'Sifting the evidence – what's wrong with significance tests?' (2001) 322 BMJ 226–30.

from dealing with under-performance by self-regulation towards anticipating and preventing it by insisting that clinicians actively examine the quality of the care they deliver. So, in the 1990s, the UK introduced compulsory clinical audit where staff would have to identify standards of care, examine current practice against these and produce action plans to address deficits. Guidelines, once endorsed, can form the basis of audits:

> Medicine is now well into the era of explicit professional and clinical standards. Clinical guidelines flow from the drive to secure clinical decision making which is based on the best research evidence available and which is therefore as demonstrably effective as possible.[6]

Most healthcare professionals would agree with this broad sentiment, while debating how 'well into' we are.

In America, guideline development was led by the Agency for Health Care Policy and Research (AHCPR). Congress established AHCPR in December 1989 with the aim of 'systematically studying the relationships between health care and its outcomes'. AHCPR used two mechanisms to evaluate outcomes: Patient Outcomes Research Teams (PORTs) and less extensive reviews or effectiveness and outcomes. Each PORT had four components: a review of the research; analysis of data to explain variations in practice; recommendations concerning the effectiveness of clinical practices; and dissemination of the information.[7] AHCPR used a multidisciplinary panel, including the public and voluntary bodies, to define the content and target audience for each guideline. Where robust studies were lacking, the panel fell back on consensus. The end product consisted of three documents: a summary for clinicians; a summary for the public; a review of the supporting evidence.[8] But, in 1995, after producing 18 guidelines, AHCPR fell foul of the surgeons when it concluded that most surgery for back-pain was unnecessary. The backlash resulted in a substantial cut in the organisation's funding, and it now concentrates on disseminating guidelines developed elsewhere and getting research into practice rather than commissioning its own guidelines. Along with the American Medical Association and the American Association of Health, AHCPR is now developing an on-line national database of clinical guidelines.

In the Netherlands, the Dutch College of General Practitioners has produced guidelines since 1987; Finland has issued more than 700 guidelines

---

6   Irvine, D, foreword in Hutchinson, A and Baker, R, *Making Use of Guidelines in Clinical Practice*, 1999, Abingdon: Radcliffe Medical Press.

7   Marwick, C, 'Federal agency focuses on outcomes research' (1993) 270 J of the American Medical Association 164–65.

8   Miaskowski, C, Jacox, A, Ferrell, BR, Hester, NO and Paice, JA, 'Clinical Guideline Development: a historical perspective and nursing implications' (1994) 21 Oncology Nursing Forum 1067–69.

since 1989; Sweden has a Council on Technology Assessment in Health Care; France, the Agence Nationale de l'Accréditation et d'Évaluation en Santé; in Germany, Italy, Spain, Australia and New Zealand, the health services also use guidelines.

In the UK, the Labour Government elected in May 1997 set out its plans for modernising healthcare in *The New NHS: Modern, Dependable*,[9] which explicitly acknowledged the importance of national standards and guidelines by establishing:

- Evidence-based National Service Frameworks for specific conditions.

- A National Institute for Clinical Excellence (NICE) established 1 April 1999 'to promote clinical and cost-effectiveness by producing clinical guidelines and audits, for dissemination throughout the NHS'. NICE has the status of a special Health Authority, that is, it has national rather than regional responsibilities in promoting healthcare.

- A system to ensure that clinical standards are maintained and improved (clinical governance).

- A Commission for Health Improvement (CHI) to 'support and oversee the quality of clinical governance and clinical services', and to monitor the quality of clinical care.

THE NATIONAL INSTITUTE FOR CLINICAL EXCELLENCE (NICE)

To date, many professional bodies have produced guidelines at local, regional and national level. But it was not clear how valid, up to date and generally applicable many of these were; some gave ambivalent or even conflicting advice. Developing a national database of guidelines with an explicit description of the evidence base for each seems to be a good idea. This is the sort of resource that the National electronic Library for Health (NeLH) could provide. Ideally, each entry would include a critical appraisal on the validity of the guideline (allowing clinicians to decide if it is applicable locally) and a date for revision.

The rationale behind NICE is to reduce duplication and increase confidence in the production and dissemination of clinical guidance by producing 30 to 50 annual evidence-based appraisals of medical drugs, interventions and devices, the actual topics being determined by the Department of Health and the National Assembly for Wales. Initially, it was

---

9   Department of Health, *The New NHS: Modern, Dependable*, 1997, London: HMSO. www.official-documents.co.uk/document/doh/newnhs/forward.htm.

planned to concentrate on clinical issues, with the future options of also addressing preventative and public health issues.

NICE will not work in isolation: it has a Partners' Council, comprising some 40 members representing patients and carers, health management, the healthcare industry, professional bodies and the Unions. Members are appointed by the Secretary of State for Health and the National Assembly for Wales. NICE will also forge links with a wide range of 'stakeholders': public health, the NHS Research and Development and Health Technology Assessment programmes, regional Development and Evaluation Committees, the York NHS Centre for Reviews and Dissemination, the Medicines Control Agency, the Medical Devices Agency, health authorities, primary care organisations, NHS regional offices, academic bodies and the Royal Colleges.

Structurally, NICE has a board appointed by the Health Secretary on individual merit, rather than as representatives of specific bodies, and a secretariat. Initially, Department of Health staff provide technical and administrative roles in co-ordinating the NICE programme. The Board, appointed by the Health Secretary and the Welsh Assembly, has a chair, six non-executive members (a mix of lay, clinical, NHS management and health economics backgrounds) and four executive members (Chief Executive, communications director, planning and resource director, clinical director). The Chief Executive is accountable to the Board for progress on the agreed programme and the use of resources. The Department of Health and the Welsh Assembly currently select technologies for appraisal by NICE, which is accountable to them. The current Chair is Professor Sir Michael Rawlins, a professor of pharmacology and previous chair of the Committee on Safety of Medicines. NICE also has two important sub-committees: the Appraisal Committee and the Guidelines Advisory Committee who advise on both its guidance and guidelines.

NICE has three main outputs: appraisals of healthcare technologies; clinical guidelines for specific conditions; methodologies for clinical audits. These recommendations apply to England and Wales and will be based on evidence of both clinical and cost effectiveness and the advice of its sub-committees. With devolved government, Scotland has its own Clinical Resource and Audit Group, Clinical Standards Board, Health Technology Board and the Scottish Intercollegiate Guidelines Network (SIGN). Presumably, the Northern Ireland Assembly will duly sort out arrangements in that province. NICE plans to work closely with the Scottish bodies and the Irish ones when they mature.

NICE health technology appraisals will operate at six main stages:

1   *Topic identification*: the original plan envisaged examining clinical practice where there was doubt about the most effective clinical intervention or evidence of wide variation; or 'horizon scanning' to anticipate new technologies and drugs under development, leading to discussion with the

sponsoring companies. At present, topics are determined by the Department of Health and the Welsh Assembly, but this mechanism is under review.

2   *Evidence collection*: at this stage gaps may appear, which can be addressed by the NHS R and D Programme. Evidence for appraisal should include clinical outcomes, health improvements in terms of length and quality of life, net costs to the NHS, and social services, impact on NHS resources including manpower. In addition to literature reviews, patient groups, manufacturers and professionals may submit evidence.

3   *Appraisal of the evidence*, leading to guidance drafting.

4   *Dissemination of the guidance along with methodologies for supporting audits*: here NICE incorporates the functions of the former National Centre for Clinical Audit. In the future it may also oversee the four National Confidential Enquires: maternal death; still births; suicide and homicide by the mentally ill; peri-operative deaths.

5   *Implementation*: NICE is not prescriptive, so this is likely to occur through clinical governance.

6   *Updating recommendations* as new evidence arrives.

So far, all but one technology assessments have concerned products that already have licences. About one year before anticipated launch, the Department of Health will formally request a NICE appraisal, and gives the sponsoring company, patient groups and healthcare professionals six to eight months to submit evidence for review by the NICE secretariat, which will add a commentary including likely impact on the NHS: the sponsors may see and comment on this. A multi-professional appraisal group, under NICE, reviews the evidence against the guidance scope and the appraisal committee produces draft recommendations, which the sponsors, the Department of Health and the Welsh Assembly are consulted on, as are patient and professional groups. The appraisal committee issues its final recommendations, and circulates them to the stakeholders who may appeal at this stage. These conclusions may require review as new evidence comes to light, and NICE guidance includes such a date.

The NICE remit covers medical devices and diagnostic interventions as well as drugs. Requiring these to demonstrate that they are effective, rather than merely safe, is a new departure. The Health Technology Assessment Programme, one of the NHS research and development initiatives, will prepare assessment reports and the National Co-ordinating Centre for Health Technology Assessment integrates this work with NICE. Once the NICE guidelines are complete, the report appears on the NICE Website and the HTA publishes them as monographs. Up to December 2000, this process had produced guidance on:

- Removal of wisdom teeth.
- Hip prostheses.
- Taxanes for ovarian cancer and breast cancer.
- Coronary artery stents in the treatment of ischaemic heart disease.
- Liquid-based cytology for cervical cancer screening.

In July 2000, the *NHS Plan: A Plan for Investment, A Plan for Reform*[10] reinforced the role of NICE, increasing its workload to about 50 appraisals and about 20 guidelines a year. A large part of the first year's work will be directed to assessing a number of drugs used to treat malignant disease, as part of the National Cancer Plan, leading up to guidance on their clinical and cost effectiveness in mid-2001:

> The funding we are making available will mean the NHS is able to implement the National Institute of Clinical Excellence's recommendations, tackling the postcode prescribing lottery for cancer drugs. Some 30,000 people can be confident as a result that they will receive newly licensed drugs where this is clinically appropriate.[11]

Up to 2005, NICE will also develop or update guidance on urological, haematological, head and neck, breast, bowel and lung cancer and palliative care.

In December 2000, the Health Secretary turned his attention to infertility treatment, and suggested that he would refer this topic to NICE with the object of devising a National Standard for England and Wales. As health authorities have adopted a wide range of approaches to providing this service, it is a particular example of 'postcode rationing': women of the same age and with the same obstetric history but living in different parts of the country have different access to treatment. The Health Secretary has determined that with its new resources the NHS can afford a uniform level of service based on nationally binding guidelines.[12] This, however, introduces a subjective element and this means making value judgements. Once a health authority has decided it will provide fertility treatment to women over 35 with primary infertility (that is, no previous confirmed pregnancy), it is a relatively objective process to review the literature for the most effective way of ensuring a live birth. However, deciding if access to fertility treatment should depend on age, stability of domestic partnerships, having already

10 Department of Health, *The NHS Plan: A Plan for Investment, A Plan for Reform*, 2000, London: HMSO.
    www.doh.gov.uk/nhsplan/default.htm
11 *Ibid*, p 115.
12 Kmietowicz, Z, 'NICE to tackle infertility treatment' (2000) 321 BMJ 1432.

borne a child, is a subjective process, not an appraisal of clinical trials. NICE acknowledges these issues, and will establish a Citizens' Council to advise it.

Although NICE has produced much solid, reliable appraisal work, more publicity has gone to a few controversial projects, and it is worth considering these because they lead some health care professionals to lack confidence in NICE. The very first NICE recommendation was that zanamivir (Relenza) should not be prescribed for the treatment of 'flu by the NHS. The company that manufactures the drug did not accept this with equanimity, and even suggested such decisions would lead to the pharmaceutical industry re-locating outside Britain. Another concern of some professionals is that NICE will waste resources re-inventing wheels where there are already well used and respected guidelines, such as for asthma.[13] However, some of these works may not be sufficiently evidence-based for NICE to endorse them, although of course it will take note of any existing systematic reviews or guidelines.

Another NICE appraisal declined to endorse the use of beta-interferon for the treatment of relapses of Multiple Sclerosis, drawing criticism from patient groups (for failing to give the evidence they produced due weight) and the Association of the British Pharmaceutical Industry for the slowness of its decision-making process. Another problem, which emerged at the time, was the 'transparency' (or otherwise) of the NICE appraisal and decision-making processes. Many assumed that in the era of 'open government', all the evidence would be available for public scrutiny, and that if a sponsor was unwilling to submit its 'evidence' for the usual channels of peer review and publication, then NICE should not have to accept it. However, Sir Michael has explained that NICE labours under restrictions:

> Some of the material provided by individual companies may be given to us 'In Confidence'. Whilst we make every effort to get their approval for us to disclose important data (and many companies have done so even when our final advice has not been to their satisfaction) it may not invariably be the case in the future. We have contemplated refusing to accept data which is not, or cannot be put, in the public domain. To do so, however, may deny us the opportunity to undertake a full evaluation of the available evidence; and thus may result in us giving advice that is not in the best interests of patients ... We have made no secret of the fact that we would have wished both our provisional and final appraisal advice, on the use of particular technologies, to be published on our web-site. We have been persuaded from doing so, so far, at the request of relevant manufacturing industries because of the potential impact on share prices. Whilst many on the mailbase will find this difficult to

---

13 British Thoracic Society, British Paediatric Association, Royal College of Physicians, King's Fund Centre, National Asthma Campaign, Royal College of General Practitioners, General Practitioners in Asthma Group, British Association of Accident and Emergency Medicine, British Paediatric Respiratory Group, 'Guidelines on the management of asthma' (1993) 48 Thorax 48, S1–24.

accept, there is a real issue for us because of the requirements of the Financial Services Act.[14]

In the future, it seems that 'confidential' information from the commercial sector will not directly influence guideline drafting, but it will be used for the assessments of individual products and technology.

Rather oddly, at the same time, the manufacturers of zanamivir commented that they enjoyed 'a very good working relationship with NICE'.[15] In November 2000 NICE revised its decision, making the drug available under certain criteria, having received evidence from the manufacturers showing that it reduced the duration of symptoms and possibly the risk of complications requiring antibiotics. It also emerged that a pharmaceutical physician employed by the manufacturers sits on the NICE appraisal committee, which caused some suspicion. Sir Michael Rawlins explained that the physician was appointed for his expertise, not to represent the company, and that he is not present when the company's products are discussed. Both the 'evidence-base' for the change in recommendation, and the usefulness of the guidance have been questioned, and many in primary care expressed concern for the impact on prescribing budgets and GP workload. The argument resulted in the public exchange of vitriol between NICE and the professions, with on the one hand Richard Smith, editor of the British Medical Journal, writing:

> One failing of NICE is that it's living a double lie. The first lie – which is as Orwellian as its name – is to deny that it's about rationing health care, which might be defined as 'denying effective interventions'. Denying ineffective interventions is not rationing; rather it's what the Americans call a 'no brainer'. The population is smart enough both to know that NICE is rationing health care and that rationing of health care is inevitable. The second, and related, lie is to give the impression that if the evidence supports a treatment then it's made available and if it doesn't it isn't. In other words, the whole messy problem of deciding which interventions to make available can be decided with some data and a computer.[16]

And Sir Michael Rawlins replying:

> First, Dr Smith has a continuing obsession (clearly shared by a few others) about notions of rationing. The use of the term has now become futile. It means such different things to different people that it would be better if it were avoided altogether. If he now wishes to define rationing as 'denying effective

---

14 Rawlins, M, 'NICE and Beta-interferon', 2000, E-mail to the evidence-based health discussion list, 22 June.
www.mailbase.ac.uk/lists/evidence-based-health/2000-06/0096.html

15 Kmietowicz, Z, 'NICE's appraisal procedures attacked' (2000) 321 BMJ 980.

16 Smith, R, 'The failings of NICE' (2000) 321 BMJ 1363–64.

treatments' he is, of course, quite at liberty to do so; but his readers should be aware that the way NICE approaches appraisals is more sophisticated.[17]

The crux of this dispute is whether NICE is an agency of rationing (Smith's view) or 'prioritisation' with a role of insuring that the NHS gets value for money (Rawlins). NICE also accepts short term increases in prescribing costs as worth long term saving in caring for degenerative diseases.[18] But this reasoning sounds rather close to one concept the NHS was founded on in 1948: initially the service would be expensive as it cleared a huge backlog of untreated illness. Then, as the health of the nation improved, costs would fall. In fact, they steadily rose. In practice, working out the impact of implementing NICE guidance is very complex: provisional estimates for the first year suggested that the 15 drug appraisals saved £47m; but the implementing the recommendations for cancer, heart disease, defibrillators and hearing aids cost £130m.[19]

Ultimately, NICE does not determine the total size of the health budget, but its guidance will influence how the cake is divided up. Primary care in England is now organised into Primary Care Groups (PCGs) which will evolve by 2004 into Primary Care Trusts (PCTs). Similar bodies called Local Health Groups cover Wales. Each PCT will receive a unitary budget from its health authority, which will not have ring-fenced pots of money for particular areas of care: the PCT is expected to set its own priorities and allocations. Control down to individual practices may be achieved by indicative budgets (for example, for prescribing). PCTs must demonstrate probity for the public money they are entrusted with. Innovations like zanamivir have to be paid for by juggling existing budgets. In Devon, 20 practices decided, on cost grounds, not to prescribe zanamivir.[20] In view of the fragmentary nature of the health budget, some healthcare economists doubt that NICE can end postcode prescribing. Indeed, although NICE hoped its guidance on taxanes for advanced breast cancer would end geographical variation in provision of such treatment, six months later it was far from clear if all health authorities had adopted this policy.[21]

Even though NICE recommendations do not carry legal weight, CHI will use them in its clinical governance monitoring to ensure that every health

---

17 Rawlins, M, 'The Failings of NICE', 2000, electronic response to Richard Smith's editorial, 8 December.
    www.bmj.com/cgi/eletters/321/7273/1363#EL13

18 Rawlins, M, 'In pursuit of quality: the National Institute for Clinical Excellence' (1999) 353 The Lancet 1079–82.

19 Timmins, N, 'Medicines arbiter has "added £100m to treatment bill"' (2000) The Financial Times, 30 November, p 2.

20 Browne, A, 'GPs warned as they snub advice on anti-flu drug' (2000) The Observer, 10 December, p 12.

21 Ferriman, A, 'Milburn to monitor implementation of NICE guidance' (2000) 321 BMJ 1431.

authority and NHS trust in England and Wales is taking 'full and proper account' of each appraisal.[22] The Department of Health also seems to adopt the Chilean national motto of *by reason or force*:

> We will expect the guidance produced by NICE to be implemented consistently across the NHS. How well this happens in practice, to ensure that unacceptable variations in care for patients are not allowed to persist, will determine whether and how NICE's and the Commission for Health Improvement's powers will be strengthened in the future.[23]

There are two other influences NICE recommendations bring to bear:

1   Re-accreditation. A number of high profile cases have exposed clinical under-performance. Originally CHI would examine clinical standards including adherence to NICE recommendations. The government now has a mandate to reform, or even move away from, traditional self-regulation for doctors, nurses and other professions, who will periodically have to produce documented evidence of their continuing education and performance to retain their qualifications. It is not clear how CHI, the Performance Assessment Framework and the reformed General Medical Council will fit together in this role. However, it would seem prudent for clinicians to prepare themselves to defend variance in their practice from NICE recommendations. It has yet to be tested whether CHI will accept shortfalls in resources or funding, or failure to negotiate for a large enough slice of a devolved PCT unitary budget, as justification for departing from NICE guidance.

2   The existence of such 'national' standards will lend ammunition to individuals or patient support groups campaigning for access to any interventions they endorse.

ROLE OF INSTITUTIONS

In recent years, many professional bodies have established research, effectiveness and audit units, and some have developed clinical guidelines (see Figure 5.2). Most, if not all, of this guideline development has been funded separately from project grants. Initially, each of the 23 Royal Colleges and professional associations received a grant from NICE to fund its effective clinical practice activities. The Institute inherited this system of funding from arrangements to support clinical audit.

---

22   Department of Health, *A First Class Service: Quality in the New NHS*, 1998, London: Department of Health.
www.doh.gov.uk/newnhs/quality.htm

23   *Ibid*, p 22.

In June 2000, NICE decided to re-deploy these resources to support six Collaborating Centres, established in April 2001. Each represents a clinical topic area: acute care; chronic care; nursing and supportive care; mental health; primary care; and women's and children's health. The Colleges and associations will band together to form these using a 'board'-type model. It seems likely that the larger bodies, such as the Royal Colleges of Surgeons and Physicians, will be housing and staffing these Centres; smaller Colleges will no longer receive central funding for this work but will be nominal partners in the new Centres. Each Centre will bring together a wide range of professional, patient, academic and managerial skills for developing national NHS guidelines and audits. Skills and experience in these areas are in short supply, and the resources needed to develop a national, robust, evidence-based guideline are considerable. Each centre is likely to be led by a professional partnership with academic support. So, for instance, the primary care Centre will include the Royal College of General Practitioners, with academic input from the School of Health and Related Research (ScHARR) at Sheffield University and also Leicester University for clinical audit. NICE will commission these Centres to each write guidelines, initially two for each Centre each year, but possibly more in subsequent years. The topics of these guidelines will be determined by the Department of Health and the Welsh Assembly.

The original plan for NICE included commissioning research as required from academic bodies, where there were gaps in the evidence. An example of this is the five-year contract to perform 12 annual appraisals (effectively systematic reviews of a clinical intervention including economic aspects) recently concluded between the Department of Health and ScHARR.

Another example of partnership is the development of diabetes guidelines by the Royal College of General Practitioners (RCGP), in collaboration with other bodies such as the Royal College of Physicians and the Royal College of Nursing. The RCGP had already decided to review this condition before NICE was formulated, and repetition of this work would clearly be a waste of scarce professional resources: even though limited to type II diabetes in adults, the volume of literature is huge – something like a 27-inch pile of abstracts! The completed guidelines from the College will undergo two rounds of consultation and revision with NICE stakeholders, before going to the NICE secretariat and guidelines committee for endorsement. These processes will take about six months. Once endorsed, it is not yet clear whether NICE or the College will have final ownership of the guidelines, including responsibility for the content and periodic updating.

Figure 5.2: Examples of guideline activity by the Royal Colleges

College	Activity
Royal College of Pathologists	Has a unit for professional standards, with speciality groups producing guidelines on audit and best practice; representative link with NICE to contribute to relevant audits; no immediate plans to be a collaborating centre in itself, but the College will be a partner with the Physicians' and Surgeons' Colleges in their collaborating centres.
Royal College of Surgeons	Established a Surgical Epidemiology and Audit Unit in 1990. Now functions as a Clinical Effectiveness Unit (CEU) with an academic partnership with the Health Services Research Unit at the London School of Hygiene and Tropical Medicine. The CEU is assisted and advised by the Clinical Effectiveness Committee, which has the task of developing strategies for implementing the government's quality assurance agenda for the NHS. The CEU receives Effective Clinical Practice funding from the National Institute for Clinical Excellence (NICE) and is looking forward to clear collaboration on projects relating to NICE's appraisal, audit and guidelines programmes.
Royal College of Nursing	Developing nurse-led guidelines in topics like leg ulcers and pain relief in children as part of its clinical effectiveness work. As well as working on its own guidelines, the RCN works with other bodies, to provide a nursing perspective in developing guidelines, participating on steering groups and piloting them.
Royal College of Paediatrics	Has a Quality of Practice Committee (QPC) committed to publicising evidence-based guidelines to College members. The QPC is initially identifying existing guidelines developed by other groups. These will be appraised and those meeting the College standards will be disseminated. In addition the QPC also wishes to become involved in the development of evidence-based clinical practice guidelines. In 1999, the College identified 10 priority areas for guideline development, later honed down to three (epilepsy; meningococcal infection; urinary tract infection). For the last one, the College hopes to endorse guidelines developed

	by the American Academy of Paediatrics. The College continues to invite suggestions for guideline development from its members, and intelligence about relevant evidence-based guidelines under construction at other organisations.
Royal College of Obstetricians and Gynaecologists	Has a Guidelines and Audit Committee, which has produced 22 'green-top' guidelines, each described as 'an educational aid' rather than 'a standard of care', and recognising that variation of practice to allow for patient needs and resources may be appropriate. The College Clinical Effectiveness Support Unit is a multi-disciplinary team drawing on clinical, midwifery, statistical and epidemiological skills for its work in clinical audit, clinical outcomes indicators and the development, so far, of seven National Evidence-based guidelines. Several more are under development, but funded by NICE, who will ultimately own these. NICE is assessing an existing guideline, on the use of Anti-D immunisation to prevent Rhesus incompatibility in new-born, and the infertility guidelines will be updated and adopted by NICE.
Royal College of Physicians of London	Has a Research Unit, which undertakes clinical effectiveness work rather than original clinical studies; Website lists some 35 guidelines, plus various audit proformae and supporting papers, produced since 1992.
Royal College of Anaesthetists	Has also produced extensive guidelines for the provision of anaesthetic and critical care services.
Royal College of General Practitioners	Webpage has one guideline on back pain. The College is developing a national evidence-based clinical guidelines on depression and one on type II diabetes, which will be endorsed by NICE (see above).

Some Colleges give their members much professional discretion in their use of any guidance. The Anaesthetists introduce their published collection thus:

This document should be considered as guidance only. It is not intended to replace the clinical judgement of the individual anaesthetist; the freedom to determine the treatment of individual patients should not be constrained by a rigid application of the guidance contained with in.[24]

Another body producing guidelines following systematic literature reviews is the North of England Evidence-based Guidelines Development Project, funded by the research and development directorate of the Northern and Yorkshire Regional Health Authority. The group aims to produce guidance which will be customised for use depending on the strength of recommendation and local preferences and resources. So far this group has tackled pain control in degenerative arthritis, dementia, aspirin use in vascular disease, angina and some of the drugs used for heart failure.

FUTURE PERSPECTIVES

Related to guidelines are pathways of care, well developed in America, but relatively new to the UK. These are guidelines which have been customised for local use, to produce a printed document that functions as the medical record. The patient has access to this and can watch their own progress, becoming active in their own healthcare. Deviation from the pathway ('variance') is not automatically wrong, but must be acknowledged and justified.[25] Pathways have two specific strengths: built-in measures of quality such as audit loops and risk management strategies; and they are usually drafted by a multidisciplinary team. Increasingly, healthcare involves many professional groups (doctors, nurses, pharmacists), and this approach recognises the skills and responsibilities of each. The traditional guideline was often designed for one profession only, with rather loose involvement of other disciplines ('If symptoms do not resolve, consider physiotherapy referral'). A potential weakness in pathways is the generation by consensus: effectively the process trades scientific rigor for acceptability.

The new NHS stresses greater provision for the public and patients in terms of services, access to information and involvement in decision-making. A particular problem is communicating information about risk and adverse events in ways that are realistic but not alarmist to the public. A potential tool harnessing guidelines to this end is a discussion of the risks and benefits of different approaches to managing a given condition, such as 'decision analysis trees'. Here, the 'forks' represent clinical choices, and the 'branches' take account of the probability of various outcomes, including side effects, and patient preference.[26]

24 Royal College of Anaesthetists, *Guidelines for the Provision of Anaesthetic Services*, 1999, London: Royal College of Anaesthetists.

25 Johnson, S (ed), *Pathways of Care*, 1997, Oxford: Blackwell Science. Hutchinson, A and Baker, R, *Making Use of Guidelines in Clinical Practice*, 1999, Abingdon: Radcliffe Medical Press.

26 Baker, R and Feder, G, 'Clinical Guidelines: where next?' (1997) 9 Int J for Quality in Health Care 399–404.

To be valid, a guideline must deliver positive health outcomes. But in addition to clinical trials, showing which interventions work best in a rarefied research atmosphere, more qualitative data may be needed as to how these studies translate into the 'real world'. In EBP, this is described as the utility or generalisability of the study. Involving patients and carers produces a whole new angle as to what makes for 'quality' in healthcare. The American AHCPR did include one lay member on its guideline panels and the British Royal College of Nursing has patient involvement in guidelines steering groups. Other methods include focus groups and in-depth interviews. With adequate training and support, patient representatives can play active roles in the production of guidelines: for instance, the National Childbirth Trust has trained members to undertake literature searches.[27] Patient input must be active, not just asking opinions, and cover the whole guideline process, starting with the selection of topics, rather than merely being brought in to endorse or fine-tune the draft. Also, the guideline group needs a neutral chair to ensure fair opportunity to contribute. One beneficial spin-off might be shifting the emphasis in guideline development away from secondary care, towards the neglected areas of primary care and community services.

In involving patients, those drawing up guidelines may have to consider softer issues like equity and speed of access and user friendliness, as well as traditional 'hard' outcomes like cure and survival rates. The public also shows increasing interest in alternative and complementary therapies,[28] many of which have a weak evidence base, and some of which do not even acknowledge western reductionist scientific theories. We also live in a multi-cultural society: some of these traditions have strong beliefs about health that do not accept the empirical logic that most 'evidence-based' guidelines are derived by. Designing guidelines for these situations will require novel methods.

Incorporating guidelines into desk-top decision support software looks a promising method of enhancing their uptake, but will need better understanding about clinicians' choice of therapeutic and diagnostic interventions.[29]

The Department of Health has also recognised the risks that medical interventions themselves can pose to patients, and is developing a new theme of making the NHS safer for patients undergoing treatment by documenting medical errors and adverse events and instigating a pro-active policy to

---

27 Duff, LA, Kelson, M, Marriott, S, McIntosh, A, Brown, S, Cape, J, Marcus, N and Traynor, M, 'Clinical guidelines: involving patients and users of services' (1996) 1 J of Clinical Effectiveness 104–12.

28 Owen, DK, Lewith, G and Stephens, CR, 'Can doctors respond to patients' increasing interest in complementary and alternative medicine?' (2001) 322 BMJ 154–57.

29 Johnson, ME, Langton, KB, Haynes, RB and Mathieu, A, 'Effects of computer based clinical decision support systems on clinician performance and patient outcomes: a critical appraisal of research' (1994) 120 Annals of Internal Medicine 135–42.

prevent recurrence. To do this, from July 2001, there will be a new independent body, the National Patient Safety Agency, which will collect and analyse such data, provide feedback on improving safety and promote research in this area. Clear guidance on local reporting mechanisms will be needed to support the process, specifically around topics like clinical negligence, medical devices, adverse drug reactions, Mental Health Act incidents, reporting of injuries, certain diseases and hazardous events. In some cases mechanisms for reporting already exist (for example, the yellow card system for drug problems to the Medicines Control Agency), and these will be integrated into new reporting systems rather than replaced or duplicated by new plans. Where specific problems around devices or drugs become apparent, direct action involving the manufacturers is envisaged. There are specific targets for intrathecal (spinal) injections given in error (to be in place by the end of 2001), suicides by psychiatric patients (March 2002), obstetric practice (the end of 2005) and for drug errors (also by the end of 2005).[30]

In some disciplines the NHS is already suffering a recruitment problem, such as nurses in the acute sector and GP principals in inner cities. It is also apparent that professionals often waste time on routine tasks. One solution is to specially train less highly qualified staff to manage chronic stable conditions within a defined protocol, which would specify when they should involve a doctor. Such protocols may also allow limited prescribing according to strict rules and nurse practitioners in both primary and secondary care already deliver much effective care using them.

SUMMARY

- EBP tackles the problems of slow and uneven application of research to clinical practice by insisting that interventions should be justified by objective appraisal of the scientific literature.

- Guidelines are a way of summarising this evidence: a guideline is only as good as the evidence it is based on, and as more research is published, it may need updating.

- Professional bodies have produced clinical guidelines for specific conditions, which have generally been well received by practitioners, although often customised before application to take account of local resources and existing practice.

---

30 Department of Health, *Building a Safer NHS for Patients: Implementing an Organisation with a Memory*, 2001, London: Department of Health.
www.doh.gov.uk/buildsafenhs

- As part of the New NHS, the government has established the National Institute for Clinical Excellence (NICE) and the Commission for Health Improvement (CHI).
- NICE will appraise clinical evidence, produce guidelines and promote audit.
- CHI will investigate quality in healthcare in general, and the uptake of NICE recommendations in particular.
- NICE has produced much good work, but some of its decisions have proved controversial and there is concern that it is obliged to use unpublished data.
- There is concern about the financial impact of NICE recommendations, especially on primary care prescribing budgets, and whether NICE can 'opt out' of the rationing debate.
- Although NICE recommendations are not legally binding, the government is keen to end 'postcode' rationing in health care.
- NICE plans to work more closely with professional and academic bodies through partnerships and Collaborating Centres.
- Future developments will include pathways of care; the delegation of some clinical tasks from doctors to nurses, and possibly other staff, using specific protocols; and increased involvement of the public in guideline development. The Department of Health is also planning a programme to make the NHS safer for patients undergoing treatment.

Websites

NICE: http://www.nice.org.uk

SIGN: http://www.show.scot.nhs.uk/sign/index.html

The Health Technology Assessment Programme: http://www.ncchta.org

CHAPTER 6

THE DEVELOPING ROLE OF CLINICAL GUIDELINES

JH Tingle

SYNOPSIS

This chapter discusses clinical guidelines within the context of the government's developing health care quality agenda and within the tort of negligence. Clinical guidelines are a major tool in the government's health quality reforms and feature in a number of areas. Organisations such as NICE develop and actively encourage the use of clinical guidelines. This increased frequency of use of clinical guidelines cannot be looked at in isolation from the law. As clinical negligence litigation is increasing, clinical guidelines will be seen more as part of the environment of care. Lawyers and judges will scrutinise them. A key issue discussed is how lawyers and judges will use clinical guidelines.

On the basis of case law, it could be argued that there is a legal duty on health carers to research and to keep up to date with developments in their field of professional expertise, which would include knowledge of the main existing and new clinical guidelines. The judiciary also seem to be adopting a much more pro-active approach to assessing expert clinical evidence, and clinical guidelines can be seen to feature in this new approach. As clinical guidelines contain best, evidence-based care principles, they should work to reduce the level of adverse incidents occurring and in turn clinical negligence litigation should be reduced.

INTRODUCTION

Clinical guidelines occupy an important position in the NHS care environment with government and many healthcarers seeing them as effective health care quality improvement tools. Clinical guidelines are being increasingly used. That increased use has highlighted a number of important practical legal issues which this chapter and others in this book will explore. Could it be said, for example, that a healthcarer could be found to be negligent for missing a guideline which would otherwise have helped a patient? How do guidelines relate to the assessment of the standard of care in negligence? Some cases have gone to court on guidelines and it is possible to make some general observations on how the courts treat guidelines, pointing to possible future trends. This chapter takes an English tort law perspective of issues, focusing largely on the standard of care in clinical negligence actions.

CLINICAL GUIDELINES AND HEALTH QUALITY

The Labour Government signalled early on in its life its aim of reducing regional inequalities of care and increasing quality in the NHS. This was, and is, to be done through national standards and guidelines for treatments and services:

> 3.5 Nationally there will be:
>
> new evidence-based National Service Frameworks to help ensure consistent access to services and quality of care right across the country ... a new National Institute for Clinical Excellence to give a strong lead on clinical and cost-effectiveness, drawing up new guidelines and ensuring they reach all parts of the health service.[1]

The National Institute of Clinical Excellence (NICE) has issued a number of national clinical guidelines and has an ongoing work programme. Guidance has been issued on a variety of topics, including pressure ulcer risk management and prevention and prophylaxis for patients who have experienced myocardial infarction.[2] The NICE clinical guidelines initiative also exists alongside other government initiatives, such as Clinical Governance,[3] The NHS Plan,[4] and the National Patient Safety Agency.[5] These initiatives all focus on increasing quality throughout the NHS and involve strategies which can utilise clinical guidelines. The net effect of all these government initiatives is to enhance the profile of clinical guidelines at nearly every level of the NHS.

CLINICAL GUIDELINES IN A MORE LITIGIOUS HEALTHCARE ENVIRONMENT

The environment in which healthcarers practice has also become more litigation-orientated in recent years, with more patients complaining and

---

1 Department of Health, *The New NHS: Modern, Dependable*, December 1997, Cm 3087, London: HMSO.
2 NICE, 'Clinical Guidelines', www.nice.org.uk/cat.asp?c=16422.
3 Department of Health, *Clinical Governance: Quality in the New NHS*, 1999, London: NHS Executive.
4 Department of Health, *The NHS Plan*, July 2000, Cm 4818-1, London: HMSO.
5 Department of Health, *Building a Safer NHS for Patients*, April 2001, London, www.doh.gov.uk/buildsafenhs.

suing then ever before. Clinical guidelines could well now feature more in cases and complaints. The National Audit Office (NAO)[6] state that the rate of new clinical negligence claims per 1,000 finished consultant episodes rose by 72% between 1990 and 1998. The estimated net present value of outstanding claims at 31 March 2000 was £2.5 billion for England (up from £1.3 billion at 31 March 1997). In addition, there is an estimated liability of a further £1.3 billion for negligent treatment but where claims have not yet been made by patients.

This factor must be taken in conjunction with other issues, such as the high-profile medical scandals of recent years, the Shipman and Bristol paediatric surgery to name but two. Healthcarers are now under increasing pressure to implement evidence-based, reflective treatment practices to ensure quality-based healthcare practices. These practices will often require the development and application of clinical guidelines.

NEW PRESSURES

The NHS is also being moved by the government and the NHS Executive firmly towards developing a culture where failures, mistakes, errors and near misses are reported and lessons learnt. A new compulsory adverse clinical incident system is being developed to be applied right across the NHS.[7] Clinical guidelines can consolidate good, safe and evidence-based practice and can be viewed as an essential pre-requisite of an effective clinical risk management process underpinning patient safety.

GUIDELINES AND CLINICAL NEGLIGENCE

When the increased level of litigation in the NHS is considered, the discussion of how clinical guidelines can influence the litigation process assumes an increased significance. Ronni Solomon, in Chapter 9, discusses the US research findings on guideline impact. Whether this research is transferable to the UK, however, remains an open question, given that both countries have markedly different healthcare systems and litigation cultures. The US research value lies in the perspectives it provides on the issue of the potential legal impact of guidelines.

---

6 National Audit Office, *Handling Clinical Negligence Claims in England*, May 2001, report by the Comptroller and Auditor General, HC 403, Session 2000–01:3, London: HMSO.

7 Chief Medical Officer (Chair), *An Organisation with a Memory*, 2000, report of an expert group on learning from adverse events in the NHS, London: HMSO.

From an English tort law perspective, a central issue is the possible impact of a clinical guideline on the standard of care. As Stern argues:

> One possible effect of clinical guidelines is that they will come to be understood as setting the parameters for legally safe medical care. Thus, the perceived threat of liability in negligence being imposed because of non-compliance may prove to be the most effective tool to ensure that clinical guidelines are effective in modifying clinical practice.[8]

Could a clinical guideline be viewed as determinatively laying down the standard of care in a case? If a healthcarer was, for example, unaware of the guideline, or refused to follow one for no good reason, does that show a breach of duty?

BOLAM

In *Bolam v Friern Hospital Management Committee*,[9] the *locus classicus* of the test for the standard of care required of a doctor or any other professional person was stated. The test is the direction to the jury given by McNair J at p 587:

> I myself would prefer to put it this way, that he is not guilty of negligence if he has acted in accordance with a practice accepted as proper by a responsible body of medical men skilled in that particular art ... putting it the other way round, a man is not negligent, if he is acting in accordance with such a practice, merely because there is a body of opinion who would take a contrary view.

It seems unlikely that a clinical guideline would be viewed by any court as determinatively laying down the standard of care to be adopted in a particular case. This would not happen, as other factors would also be relevant. Under the *Bolam* principle, even minority medical opinion can be regarded as reasonable and proper, subject to a judicial determination of *Bolam* reasonableness. The judge remains the final arbiter of what is reasonable practice. It is clear, as a matter of practical common sense, that medicine and healthcare will not always fit neatly into a conceptual strait-jacket. There will rarely be only one proper way of doing something, though this can sometimes happen. There are often a number of reasonable and proper ways of treating patients, and a clinical guideline may offer only one approach. Healthcarers would not be viewed as negligent simply because they took another proper approach to treatment rather than the one stated in the guideline. Guidelines are not straight railway lines, which always have to be followed. In some circumstances, it could be negligent to follow or apply a guideline, where, for example, the patient's condition contra-indicated its application. Clinical

---

8   Stern, K, 'Clinical guidelines and negligence liability in clinical effectiveness', from Deighan, M and Hitch, S (eds), *Guidelines to Cost Effective Practice*, 1995, Essex: Earlybrave.

9   *Bolam v Friern Hospital Management Committee* [1957] 1 WLR 583.

guidelines do not suspend the clinical autonomy of healthcarers. That such an approach applies is clear from tort jurisprudence.

The precise circumstances of each case require detailed consideration. Tort cases are very fact-specific and what may be clinically appropriate in one case may not be in another. Doctors and other healthcarers can often only agree to differ in a complex area such as healthcare. A balance has to be achieved between the clinical autonomy of the healthcarer, the exact clinical situation facing the healthcarer, and the particular clinical guideline in question.

The GMC[10] emphasises the importance of being aware of guidelines in its advice to doctors and managers on maintaining good medical practice. The GMC recognises that most doctors will practice in medical and clinical teams:

> To help maintain quality, clinical teams will normally use:
> - an active and supportive approach to the professional development of each member;
> - the standards set by professional organisations;
> - recommended clinical guidelines …

The term used is 'normally use' not 'must use'; to say 'must use' would have been totally inappropriate for the reasons given above.

NEW *BOLAM*

The *Bolitho v City and Hackney HA*[11] case clarifies the *Bolam* principle and provides support for the practice of evidence-based healthcare and, therefore implicitly, the use of clinical guidelines. In this case, the House of Lords was asked to determine, in the context of medical negligence, the correct approach to causation and the correct approach to expert evidence. As Brazier and Miola state:

> Two questions were central to the appeal before the Law Lords. (1) Did the *Bolam* test have any application at all in deciding issues of causation? (2) Does the *Bolam* test require a judge to accept without question truthful evidence from eminent experts? The House of Lords answered the first question in the affirmative … As to the second issue before their Lordships … Lord Browne-Wilkinson (with whom his brethren agreed) forcibly rejected any such proposition. The court is not bound to find for a defendant simply because he leads evidence from a body of experts who genuinely believe that the defendant's practice conformed to sound medical practice.[12]

---

10 General Medical Council, *Maintaining Good Medical Practice*, July 1998, London: GMC.

11 *Bolitho v City and Hackney HA* [1998] Lloyd's Rep Med 26.

12 Brazier, M and Miola, J, 'Bye-bye *Bolam*: a medical litigation revolution?' (2000) 8 MLR 1, pp 85–114.

Lord Browne-Wilkinson stated that the courts will not just blindly accept what medical experts say is proper or reasonable practice. The judge must be satisfied that the experts have directed their minds to the benefits and risks of treatment and that opinion has a logical basis:

> The use of these adjectives responsible, reasonable and respectable all show that the court has to be satisfied that the exponents of the body of opinion relied upon can demonstrate that such opinion has a logical basis. In particular in cases involving, as they so often do, the weighing of risks against benefits, the judge before accepting a body of opinion as being responsible, reasonable or respectable, will need to be satisfied that, in forming their views, the experts have directed their minds to the question of comparative risks and benefits and have reached a defensible conclusion on the matter.[13]

Lord Browne-Wilkinson went on to say:

> I emphasise that in my view it will very seldom be right for a judge to reach the conclusion that views genuinely held by a competent medical expert are unreasonable ... It is only where a judge can be satisfied that the body of expert opinion cannot be logically supported at all that such opinion will not provide the bench mark by reference to which the defendant's conduct falls to be assessed.[14]

This speech provides the current conceptual focus for judges dealing with clinical negligence cases, as Foster argues after *Bolitho*:

> Experts will have to appear not only respectable but reasonable. The defendant will be judged not only by the cut of the expert's suit. Experts will have to be prepared to say not only that they do something a particular way, but why. Justifications to the effect: 'I was taught to do it that way and lots of others do it that way, too' will not work any more ... Reports will have to be more carefully reasoned and referenced. The question of referencing raises another spectre. Evidence-based medicine might begin to play a part in medical litigation. If the published evidence makes a wholly one-sided case against a particular medical practice, it will be difficult for any expert to say that its adoption by the defendant was reasonable, even though he or she is in august medical company in doing so.[15]

Clinical guidelines are an essential feature of evidence-based medicine and will no doubt be influential on judges. Carefully formulated clinical guidelines will be good evidence of the reasonableness of a practice. This will be so even if there are contradictory guidelines in other institutions.

---

13 *Bolitho v City and Hackney HA* [1998] Lloyd's Rep Med 26, p 33.

14 *Ibid*, p 34.

15 Foster, C, '*Bolam*: consolidation and clarification' (1998) Health Care Risk Report, vol 4, issue 5, pp 5–7.

CLINICAL GUIDELINE CASES

There are a number of reported cases on clinical guidelines which show how the courts can use and be influenced by guidelines.

Early v Newham Health Authority[16]

The claimant, Sarah Early, then aged 13, went to the operating theatre to have an appendectomy. The anaesthetist gave her an intravenous injection of thiopentone, 100 micrograms of phentonyl and 100 milligrams of suxamethonium. He was unable to intubate successfully and the effect of the thiopentone wore off before the effect of the suxamethonium wore off. The claimant came to in a state of panic and distress as her body was still partly paralysed. The defendants were sued on the basis that: (1) the anaesthetist was negligent; and (2) the procedure which he adopted when he discovered he was unable successfully to intubate the claimant was faulty.

Both claims failed. It was not established that the anaesthetist or the procedure he adopted was negligent.

Deputy Judge Patrick Bennett QC's comments on the procedure adopted for failed intubation are interesting as they show how a judge can deal with the issue of clinical guidelines. The procedure used for intubation, which in fact failed, was a clinical guideline, though at the time of the event it was orally stated. By the time of the trial, the (failed) intubation procedure was reduced to writing. The judge stated:

> It is, of course, common for attacks to be made against the medical profession but having heard Dr McAteer describing how, in relation to this procedure, it was put before the division of anaesthesia in the hospital, all the consultants at Newham got together, there are about ten of them there, seven or eight of whom are consultants, who then decided that this was the proper procedure to follow and minutes of the discussion were kept. I find it somewhat unfortunate that Professor Robinson should suggest that those consultants and the drill that they adopted was nevertheless such that no reasonably competent medical authority could have adopted it. I am quite satisfied from what I have heard ... that I am dealing with a competent medical authority who applied its mind to this problem and came up with a reasonable solution.

The *Early* case was decided at least three years before *Bolitho* and the judge did not therefore have the benefit of Lord Browne-Wilkinson's views on handling expert evidence. However, he clearly demonstrated an informed view of the expert evidence and made a reasoned decision, influenced by the fact that a meeting of consultants had taken place where the guidelines were discussed,

---

16   *Early v Newham Health Authority* [1994] 5 Med LR 214.

and also that there were minutes of that meeting available. He was satisfied that the guidelines were *Bolam* reasonable. A more contemporary case on clinical guidelines, post-*Bolitho*, follows.

Penney, Palmer and Cannon v East Kent Health Authority[17]

This case concerned cervical smear tests and negligence allegations concerning the test findings. Some slides had been labelled negatively when they should not have been and there was then no medical follow-up for the claimants, who subsequently went on to develop invasive adenocarcinoma of the cervix and had to undergo surgery, which included hysterectomy.

The Court of Appeal dismissed the Health Authority's appeal. There were abnormalities there to be seen on the slides and no reasonably competent cytoscreener could with confidence have concluded that the appearances on the slides were not pre-cancerous. The standards of the Cervical Screening Programme (CSP) had not been complied with. The trial judge had relied on a test of screener satisfaction known as 'the absolute confidence test' which, according to the judge, all the experts in the case seemed to endorse. The trial judge used this test in deciding the correct standard of care to be adopted and whether it had been met. This test is incorporated into the clinical guidelines of the CSP.

This case clearly shows the judge, HHJ Peppitt QC, at first instance being influenced by a national clinical guideline and by Lord Browne-Wilkinson's approach to expert evidence in *Bolitho*. The judge tested the evidence of experts and stated:

> ... I do not consider that the evidence of Drs Hudson and Boon stands up to logical analysis as that phrase was used by Lord Browne-Wilkinson in *Bolitho* ... This is not to disparage the evidence of either. It is rather that in my judgment their opinions cannot stand 'the absolute confidence test' which Dr Hudson herself propounded with the agreement of the other experts.

The Court of Appeal would not interfere with the judge's findings and approach. He had adopted the correct approach with a clear and logical judgment.

PERSONAL UPDATING

It is always possible that a claimant's expert could raise in evidence the existence of a guideline and argue that had it should have been applied. Not to apply the guideline was, it could well be argued, negligent practice. As

---

17   *Penney, Palmer and Cannon v East Kent Health Authority* [2000] Lloyd's Rep Med 41.

mentioned earlier, under the *Bolam* principle, a healthcarer is able to choose any number of ways to treat a patient; a clinical guideline indicates just one treatment method. As long as these other ways are *Bolam* defensible, the defendant will escape. What happens, however, when it emerges that the defendant clinician was ignorant of the guideline in question through poor professional updating? Charles Foster, in Chapter 7, discusses the use that can be made of guidelines at trial and points out that, procedurally, an expert must produce them.

The question of ignorance of guidelines and of research can be seen in the following two cases.

Crawford v Board of Governors of Charing Cross Hospital[18]

The claimant developed brachial palsy as a result of his arm being kept in an extended position on the operating table. Six months before the operation took place an article had appeared in The Lancet pointing out this danger. The anaesthetist in question had not read this article and the first instance judge, Gerrard J, held the defendant hospital liable for negligence. The Court of Appeal allowed the defendant's appeal. There was no negligence. Lord Denning stated:

> ... it would, I think, be putting too high a burden on a medical man to say that he has to read every article appearing in the current medical press; and it would be quite wrong to suggest that a medical man is negligent because he does not at once put into operation the suggestions which some contributor or other might make in a medical journal. The time may come in a particular case when a new recommendation may be so well proved and so well known, and so well accepted that it should be adopted, but that was not so in this case (quoted from Mason and McCall Smith).[19]

Mason and McCall Smith comment on this case:

> Failure to read a single article, it was said, may be excusable, while disregard of a series of warnings in the medical press could well be evidence of negligence. In view of the rapid progress currently being made in many areas of medicine, and in view of the amount of information confronting the average doctor, it is unreasonable to expect a doctor to be aware of every development in his field. At the same time, he must be reasonably up to date and must know of major developments ... The practice of medicine has, however, become increasingly based on principles of scientific elucidation and report and the pressure on doctors to keep abreast of current developments is now considerable. It is no longer possible for a doctor to coast along on the basis of

---

18 *Crawford v Board of Governors of Charing Cross Hospital* (1953) *The Times*, 8 December.

19 Mason, JK and McCall Smith, RA, *Law and Medical Ethics*, 5th edn, 1999, London: Butterworths.

long experience, such an attitude has been firmly discredited not only in medicine but in many other professions and callings.[20]

Crawford was a case of the late 1950s, before the information technology age, an age which we are now in. Today's healthcarers have access to, and are exposed to, a wide range of information. The Internet and intranets are powerful information resources which are increasingly being used by both patients and healthcarers. The *Crawford* approach now needs to be considered in the context of the above information revolution. Whilst it is now easier to obtain information, there is also much more of it. A balancing exercise has to take place. Healthcarers cannot just bury their heads in the sand and say that they have no time to up-date their professional knowledge. They must demonstrate a reasonable, personal, professional updating regime. Guidance on this is contained in the judgment of Mitchell J in *Gascoine v Ian Sheridan and Co and Latham*.

Gascoine v Ian Sheridan and Co and Latham[20a]

This case concerned a number of issues, one of which was the responsibility of a hospital consultant to keep informed about changes and developments in his speciality. Mitchell J said that the consultant in question was a very busy man:

> ... who clearly had a responsibility to keep himself generally informed on mainstream changes in diagnosis treatment and practice through the mainstream literature such as the leading textbooks and The Journal of Obstetrics and Gynaecology. Equally clearly it would be unreasonable to suppose that [he] had the opportunity to acquaint himself with the content of the more obscure journals.

This case is authority for the proposition that all professionals should be able to demonstrate a personal, systematic and professional up-dating regime.

If a healthcarer pleaded ignorance of a clinical guideline, key issues would be how widely disseminated it was and the evidence and authority behind it. NICE guidelines in particular will be very persuasive and it will be hard to justify ignorance of them, as they are so well researched and disseminated.

PRACTICAL LEGAL ISSUES AND CLINICAL GUIDELINES

Clinical guidelines can be developed nationally or locally. Hospital wards or a particular health authority may develop them. If a clinical guideline becomes evidence in a case it will be examined very carefully and its development

---

20 *Ibid.*

20a *Gascoine v Ian Sheridan and Co and Latham* [1994] Med LR 437.

process examined. This was done in the *Early* case. The Department of Health have issued some guidance on the development steps to take and possible relevant legal issues.

It is argued[21] that a number of aspects of clinical guidelines development would diminish the risk of legal actions:

(1) the objectives for the clinical guidelines need to be clear, and clearly stated. This will affect their subsequent legal standing;

(2) the intended use and applicability of clinical guidelines should be spelt out clearly in the introduction;

(3) the guidelines must make clear for whom they are intended. The recommendations will usually be intended for a particular group of practitioners;

(4) clinical guidelines that no longer reflect best practice might conceivably become actionable, and developers need to incorporate specific statements about their validity and review procedure;

(5) they should be constructed in such a way that allows deviation and does not suffocate initiative that might bring about further improvements;

(6) the development of clinical guidelines must involve all the relevant professions and managers.

While action could be taken against a clinician for not keeping up to date, a College is probably not actionable, as it would be difficult to show that it owes a duty or obligation directly to the patient.

The above are common-sense steps, which all clinical guideline developers should adopt.

It makes sense, for example, for clinical guidelines to have a review date, otherwise how do you know that best current practice is being incorporated? However, many clinical guidelines are undated. The research of Hibble, Kanta, and Pencheon *et al* on p 855 found:

... that 38 per cent of all the guidelines collected were undated.[22]

WILL CLINICAL GUIDELINES HELP CHANGE THE CURRENT NHS LITIGATION CULTURE?

Clinical guidelines do have the potential to reduce litigation. If clinical guidelines incorporate best practice, then surely the incidence of adverse events occurring must be reduced if they are used?

---

21 Mann, T, *Clinical Guidelines: Using Clinical Guidelines to Improve Patient Care in the NHS,* May 1996, London: NHS Executive.

22 Hibble, A, Kanka, D, Pencheon, D and Pooles, F, 'Guidelines in general practice: the new Tower of Babel' (1998) 317 BMJ 26, pp 862–63.

Clinical guidelines are also an essential feature of a number of the government's initiatives designed to end regional variations of care and to drive quality through the NHS. With this amount of government-sponsored activity there should be some discernible changes and improvements over time in health care quality as the reforms bed in.

More research needs to be done in the UK on the effect of guidelines on litigation practices. We have the Hyams 1995[23] study, discussed by Ronni Solomon in Chapter 9, but there seems to be no equivalent UK study.

If clinical guidelines can help improve the quality of health care and assist in reducing clinical negligence actions by being a tool for lawyers to weed out bad cases earlier, then clinical guidelines will be doing a good and useful job.

---

23 Hyams, AL, Brandenburg, JA, Lipsitz, SR, Shapiro, DW and Brennan, TA, 'Practice guidelines and malpractice litigation: a two way street' (1995) 122(6) Annals of Internal Medicine, pp 450–55.

CHAPTER 7

CIVIL PROCEDURE, TRIAL ISSUES AND CLINICAL GUIDELINES

C Foster

SYNOPSIS

Clinical guidelines are multiplying. Their proliferation, and the related growth of evidence-based medicine, means that many areas of medicine and surgery, which attract the attention of civil litigators, are or will be governed by clinical guidelines. Increasingly it will be possible to plead just one particular of negligence: 'Failing to follow guideline X.' In such circumstances the guideline will, of course, be discloseable. If compliance with a guideline is said to exculpate, the reasonableness of the guideline will be scrutinised. Here, documents evidencing the reasonableness of the guideline-drafting process may become discloseable. If there are no guidelines, and it is said that there should have been, again, documents evidencing the decision-making process may be discloseable. Public interest immunity and ordinary confidentiality considerations may be good reasons for refusing to disclose.

Guidelines are no substitute for expert evidence about acceptable practice. Compliance with well recognised guidelines is likely to exculpate. Deviation from well-recognised guidelines may be *Bolam*-defensible. There are complex and interesting causation problems where there has been a failure to follow a guideline.

INTRODUCTION

This chapter deals with the way that clinical guidelines can be used in civil proceedings for clinical negligence.

It starts by outlining the criteria used by the English courts in deciding whether or not clinical guidelines and documents related to their creation can be disclosed. It does not pretend to set out exhaustively the law of disclosure. It then moves on to consider how disclosed guidelines and documents can be used in litigation. That necessarily entails looking at some of the rules of evidence as well as some rules of procedure. The chapter concludes by discussing the likely effect of clinical guidelines on the outcome of clinical negligence trials. This concluding section needs to be read in conjunction with Chapter 6.

DISCLOSURE: THE BASIC RULES

The Civil Procedure Rules 1998 (CPR) swept away a great deal of old law on the obligation of disclosure. The Woolf Reports which led to the CPR acknowledged that disclosure of documents was important in litigation, but noted that the disclosure process was often extremely onerous and resulted in the disclosure of lots of documents which were never used. It was often, in the terms beloved of the new Rules, 'disproportionate': the time, money and effort expended on disclosure bore little relationship to the effect of that disclosure on the just resolution of the dispute.

One of the reasons for this disproportion, said the Reports, was that the criteria used to determine whether a document should be disclosed were far too wide. Under the old law a party in civil proceedings had to disclose not only admissible documents, or documents which might tend to prove or disprove a matter in issue, but any document which, it was reasonable to suppose, contained information which may enable the party applying for disclosure either to advance his own case or damage that of his adversary, or 'fairly lead him to a train of inquiry which may have either of those two consequences'.[1]

'Disclosure' means stating that a document exists or has existed: CPR Pt 31.2. A 'document' is anything in which information of any description is recorded: CPR Pt 31.4.

The default position is that 'standard disclosure' will be given: CPR Pt 31.5. The parties may agree to vary, or the court may order variance from, this standard obligation.

By CPR Pt 31.6:

Standard disclosure requires a party to disclose only:

(1) the documents on which he relies; and

(2) the documents which

    (1) adversely affect his own case;

    (2) adversely affect another party's case; or

    (3) support another party's case; and

(3) the documents which he is required to disclose by a relevant practice direction.

---

1   *Compagnie Financière du Pacifique v Peruvian Guano Co* (1882) 11 QBD 55, *per* Brett LJ, pp 62–63.

There is a Pre-Action Protocol for the Resolution of Clinical Disputes which deals, *inter alia*, with obtaining health records.[2] The relevant part of the Protocol seems only to contemplate at the pre-action stage the disclosure of the patient's own clinical records, but the Protocol more generally advocates openness[3] and if the preliminary letter written on behalf of the patient clearly raises an issue to which clinical guidelines are relevant, any court looking later at the conduct of the case will take a very dim view of non-disclosure of the relevant parts of the guidelines.[4]

DISCLOSURE OF CLINICAL GUIDELINES AND RELATED DOCUMENTATION UNDER THE BASIC RULE OF DISCLOSURE

There will be many instances where clinical guidelines are discloseable under the criteria in CPR Pt 31.6. Those instances are easy to identify.

Where the alleged tort involves departure from clinical guidelines, the guidelines will clearly be relevant. Where it involves conduct which falls within the guidelines, the existence of the guidelines will tend to exculpate (see below) and accordingly the guidelines will of course be disclosed. Sometimes (and increasingly), allegations will relate to a failure to lay down or implement guidelines which, if followed, would have avoided the injury. To rebut such allegations it will be necessary to disclose documents relating to the process which led up to the decision not to promulgate or implement relevant guidelines. These may include the minutes of committee meetings, relevant Department of Health circulars, guidance from the relevant specialist organisations and any other documents taken into account (or, on the negative side, which should have been taken into account) in making the decision.

---

2   See cll 3.7–3.13 of the Protocol.

3   See, eg, cl 2.2 of the Protocol.

4   There is also a Protocol for Obtaining Hospital Medical Records, prepared by the Law Society's Civil Litigation Committee and approved by the Department of Health for use in NHS and Trust Hospitals: May 1998. Under the heading 'Records: What might be included', the Protocol states, *inter alia*:

> Reports on an 'adverse incident' and reports on the patient made for risk management and audit purposes may form part of the records and be discloseable: the exception will be any specific record or report made solely or mainly in connection with an actual or potential claim.

Clinical guidelines will often contain express provision for the collection of risk management and audit material, and sometimes the risk management/audit material will be incomprehensible without a reference to the guidelines under which it was collected. In such circumstances the guidelines themselves may be discloseable under the Protocol.

CAVEATS TO THE BASIC RULE OF DISCLOSURE

General

There are a number of these. They include legal professional privilege, the privilege against self incrimination, common interest privilege, public interest immunity (PII) and generally confidential communications.

Only two of these are likely to be of regular relevance to the disclosure of protocols. These are public interest immunity and confidential communications.

Public interest immunity

This type of immunity for disclosure has deep constitutional roots, which were traced by the House of Lords in *Conway v Rimmer*[5] and *Burmah Oil Co Ltd v Governor and Co of the Bank of England*.[6] The law surrounding the immunity has developed tremendously over the last few years, and has become much more flexible. There are some classes of documents which are deemed to attract the immunity: these are not relevant in this context. Generally, insofar as relevant here, documents will be judicially decreed to be privileged from disclosure (regardless of whether or not any party to the litigation asserts the privilege) if production would be injurious to the public interest, bearing in mind the balance between the public interest in the administration of justice and the public interest in concealment: see *Evans v Chief Constable of Surrey*.[7]

It is easy to see that documents evidencing the discussions which lie behind the formulation of protocols might sometimes, if disclosed, be injurious to the public interest themselves. And the courts will be aware, too, that to order disclosure of such documents might be more indirectly injurious to the public interest because the knowledge of the possibility of such disclosure might inhibit the desirable frankness of such discussions. Much medical material will be by its very nature confidential. Although there is no absolute protection of medical confidences in either criminal or civil litigation, the public interest in maintaining such confidence will sometimes cause courts to invoke PII in order to avoid the violation of confidences.[8] Probably the invocation of PII in such circumstances is unnecessary. It is generally legally possible, and legally neater, to achieve the same result by classifying the

---

5   *Conway v Rimmer* [1968] AC 910.

6   *Burmah Oil Co Ltd v Governor and Co of the Bank of England* [1980] AC 1090.

7   *Evans v Chief Constable of Surrey* [1989] 2 All ER 594.

8   See, eg, *DPP v Morrow* (1993) *The Independent*, 13 April. PII held to attach to documents held by an abortion clinic in relation to abortions carried out under the Abortion Act 1967.

information which should not be disclosed as confidential information, the disclosure of which would be oppressive: see below. But in order to take the 'merely confidential' route to non-disclosure it is necessary for a party to the litigation to object to disclosure. The judge of his own motion should, as the guardian of the public interest, forbid disclosure of documents subject to PII.

The CPR lay down the procedure for asserting PII.[9]

Generally confidential communications

It has always been possible to argue that otherwise discloseable documents should not be disclosed because disclosure would breach some sort of confidence and therefore be oppressive. This language is now likely to give way to the language of human rights.

Lots of medical disclosure is likely to involve, *prima facie*, a breach of Art 8 of the European Convention on Human Rights, which gives a right to respect for family life.[10] Some disclosure of the discussions which lie behind protocol formulation might include Art 8 breach of this type. Disclosure might also be withheld if it is necessary to withhold it to protect third party sources.[11] That, again, might sometimes apply to documents containing data considered by guideline-forming committees.

The discussions of Committees themselves will be *prima facie* confidential. There is a real public interest in maintaining that confidentiality, because confidentiality breeds candour, and candour breeds good guidelines. That argument can be put both in terms of simple confidentiality and of PII: see above.

The CPR lays down a procedure for asserting this head of quasi-privilege.[12]

THE USE THAT CAN BE MADE OF GUIDELINES AT TRIAL

Clinicians are worried about protocols because they think that failure to follow them will necessarily connote negligence.[13] This is nonsense. The *Bolam* test does not cease to apply simply because a protocol has been drafted.

---

9   CPR Pt 31.19.1. It may also be asserted in the same way as other types of privilege: see CPR Pt 31.19.3.

10 See *MS v Sweden* (1999) EHRR 313.

11 See *R v Mid Glamorgan Family Health Services ex p Martin* [1995] 1 WLR 110; *Gaskin v United Kingdom* (1990) 12 EHRR 36.

12 See CPR Pt 31.19.3.

13 For academic comment on these concerns, see Farmer, A, 'Medical practice guidelines: lessons from the United States' (1993) 307 BMJ 313–17; Kinney, ED and Wilder, MM, 'Medical standard setting in the current malpractice environment: problems and possibilities' (19891) 22 Univ of California at Davis L Rev 421.

The courts are, however, tending to regard clinical guidelines as indicators of accepted clinical practice. Of course they are not evidence in themselves of good or any practice. Procedurally they must be produced by an expert. If that expert relies on the protocol as summing up good practice, the expert will have to say so, and say why he says it. There cannot procedurally be mere trials by protocol.

In *Loveday v Renton*,[14] Stuart-Smith LJ, speaking about published contra-indications to pertussis vaccination, said:

> ... so far as the plaintiff seeks to rely on the contraindications as evidence of the opinions of experts not called as witnesses ... this evidence is inadmissible in law.[15] The reason for this is obvious; it is not known who holds the opinion or basis for it; and the evidence is not tested in cross-examination before the court. It is hearsay. But it is part of the medical literature in the case, experts are entitled to and have commented on it; and in particular have drawn inferences as to the incidence of the vaccine associated cases in relation to the observance or non-observance of the contraindications.[16]

He went on:

> ... the evidence contained in the contraindications against pertussis vaccination, published from time to time in this country by the DHSS and similar bodies in other countries, cannot be relied upon as though it was evidence of qualified experts not called as witnesses, that the vaccine in fact causes permanent brain damage.[17]

In *Ward v Ritz Hotel (London)*[18] the Court considered the relevance of the British Standards Institution recommendations in the context of an accident at work:

> ... [the British Standards] represent the consensus of professional opinion and practical experience as to the sensible safety precautions. How much weight they attach to them is shown by the words which I have quoted used in the laying down of the Standard. I would also accept and agree with the words used by HHJ Newey QC sitting as an Official Referee in *The Board of Governors for the Hospitals for Sick Children v McLaughlin & Harvey plc* 19 Con LR 25, 93:
>
>> British Standards Codes of Practice are not legal documents binding upon engineers or upon anyone else, but they reflect the knowledge and expertise of the profession at the date when they were issued. They are guides to the engineer and in my view they also provide strong evidence as to the standard of the competent engineer at the date when they were issued ...[19]

---

14 *Loveday v Renton* [1990] 1 Med LR 117.
15 The Civil Evidence Act 1995 now allows much freer admissibility of hearsay evidence.
16 *Loveday v Renton* [1990] 1 Med LR 117, p 130.
17 *Ibid*, p 182.
18 *Ward v Ritz Hotel (London)* [1992] PIQR 315.
19 *Ibid*, p 327.

The English courts' approach to clinical guidelines is illustrated well in the following three cases:[20]

Re C (A Minor) (Medical Treatment)[21]

The High Court considered the status of the guidance issued by the Royal College of Paediatrics and Child Health entitled *Withholding or Withdrawing Lifesaving Treatment in Children, a Framework for Practice*. It concluded:

> So it is clear that what is being proposed by the doctors has the support of the Royal College of Paediatrics and Child Health who considered the wide field of these matters in their meetings which led to the publication of that document.[22]

Early v Newham HA[23]

The High Court considered the status of locally issued guidelines relating to failed intubation, and concluded:

> It is, of course, common for attacks to be made against the medical profession but having heard Dr McAteer describing how, in relation to this procedure, it was put before the division of anaesthesia in the hospital, all consultants at Newham together, there are about ten of them there, seven or eight of whom are consultants who then decided that this was the proper procedure to follow and minutes of the discussion were kept. I find it somewhat unfortunate that Professor Robinson should suggest that those consultants and the drill that they adopted was nevertheless such that no reasonably competent medical authority could have adopted it.[24]

Airedale NHS Trust v Bland[25]

The House of Lords considered guidelines produced by the Medical Ethics Committee of the BMA regarding discontinuing artificial nutrition and hydration in PVS patients. Lord Goff said:

---

20 For an Australian example in a slightly different context, see *Cranley v Medical Board of Western Australia* [1992] 3 Med LR 94. D had prescribed injectable diazepam to heroin addicts. This was a deviation from the Australian National Methadone Guidelines, but his appeal against a finding of 'infamous and improper conduct' was allowed by the Supreme Court of Western Australia on the basis of evidence of a respectable, if minority, opinion which endorsed D's management of the addicts.

21 *Re C (A Minor) (Medical Treatment)* [1998] Lloyd's Rep Med 1.

22 *Ibid*, p 6.

23 *Early v Newham HA* [1994] 5 Med LR 214.

24 *Ibid*, p 216.

25 *Airedale NHS Trust v Bland* [1993] 4 Med LR 39.

... study of this document left me in no doubt that, if a doctor treating a PVS patient acts in accordance with the medical practice now being evolved by the Medical Ethics Committee of the BMA, he will be acting with the benefit of guidance from a responsible and competent body of relevant professional opinion, as required by the *Bolam* test.[26]

Note in *Bland*:

(1) that the conclusion that compliance with the BMA guidelines would constitute *Bolam*-defensible practice was a conclusion reached after 'study of [the] document'. The House did not presume that the fact that a protocol had been drawn up by an authoritative professional body necessarily meant that the protocol enshrined acceptable practice. In practice, however, it would be very difficult for a claimant to argue that a protocol drawn up by such a body after reasonable consideration does not represent conduct which would be (and has been) endorsed by a responsible body of medical opinion;

(2) that it was not compliance with the protocol *per se* which made the compliant practice reasonable. What made the practice reasonable as a matter of substantive law was that it was endorsed by a responsible body of medical opinion. Compliance with the protocol was evidence of the endorsement and the responsibility;

(3) although the House applauded the guidelines, it did not consider that the guidelines themselves should be the arbiter of professional rectitude, and considered that clinicians who proposed to withdraw nutrition and/or hydration from PVS patients should get the court to endorse that decision. This should not be taken to imply much about the way in which the courts will consider the relevance of guidelines in negligence actions. It implies lots of things, most of which are wholly irrelevant in this context, about the impact of public policy on withdrawal of nutrition/hydration cases, and the justifiable jealousy of the courts about their own supervisory role.

Generally, concordance with Department of Health or professional organisational standards[27] or reasonably well-considered local protocols is likely to exculpate. If a protocol does exist and it is not followed because a clinician has exercised independent clinical judgment and adopted an alternative method which would be *Bolam*-defensible, he will escape liability.[28]

---

26 *Airedale NHS Trust v Bland* [1993] 4 Med LR 39, p 61.

27 Note in *W v Egdell* [1990] Ch 359, which concerned an alleged breach of medical confidentiality, the Court of Appeal regarded compliance with the GMC's guidelines on confidentiality as compelling evidence that there had been no actionable breach of confidentiality.

28 For an example of the respect the courts have for clinical judgment, and the reluctance the courts have to put that judgment in the strait-jacket of inflexible protocols, see *Ratty v Haringey HA* [1994] 5 Med LR 413. Here, C had a stenosing lesion of the sigmoid colon. There was no histological evidence that this was malignant. The ... [cont]

Bolam recognises that there are often a number of professionally legitimate ways to skin a cat. If the failure to adhere to a protocol is not because there has been a responsibly taken decision to deviate from it, but simply because of some sort of slipshod practice, *Bolam* will not protect the slipshod clinician from a finding of breach of duty.

It may, though, give that clinician a causation defence. *Bolitho v City and Hackney HA*[29] concerned a paediatrician who, with incontestable negligence, had failed to attend the infant claimant, who was suffering apnoeic attacks. During one of those attacks the claimant suffered hypoxic brain damage. The evidence was that the only action which would have prevented the brain damage would have been immediate intubation. The paediatrician said that if she had attended she would not have intubated. That evidence was accepted. It was also accepted that there was a responsible body of paediatricians who would not have intubated in those circumstances. The House of Lords said that since the causation question ('Has damage been caused by negligence?') involved itself a question about negligence (which in English law is defined by the *Bolam* test), it inevitably followed that the *Bolam* test was relevant to causation. Accordingly, since this particular clinician would not have intubated, and failure to intubate would have been endorsed by a responsible body of paediatricians, the claimant failed to prove causation. The result would of course have been different if it had been proved that that particular clinician, had she attended, would have intubated.

The causation aspects of *Bolitho* might relate to a clinician who negligently failed to apprise himself of a protocol or attend to treat a patient whose treatment should, in the normal run of events, be according to that protocol. If following the protocol would have prevented the damage complained of, but the court accepts evidence from the clinician that he would, had he known of the protocol/attended, nonetheless decided to exercise his clinical judgment and adopt a *Bolam*-acceptable alternative which would not have avoided the damage, the claimant would have failed to establish causation.

Of course, and rightly, the courts will always be wary of assertions by clearly negligent clinicians that they would not have given the type of treatment which would have prevented the damage. They will tend to say of such assertions: 'Well, he would say that, wouldn't he?' Indeed, in *Bolitho* in the Court of Appeal, Simon Brown LJ, in a dissenting judgment which was

---

28 [cont] surgeon performed an abdomino-perineal resection, removing a huge mass. Later histology showed it to be non-malignant. The claimant sued, saying that the surgeon should not have done the resection. The claimant relied on 'Marnham's rule', a rule of thumb which asserts that there should be no abdomino-perineal resection without histological proof of cancer.

The Court of Appeal held that although Marnham's rule was a useful guideline, it was no more than this. Since there was evidence that responsible surgeons deviated from it for sensible clinical reasons, the surgeon here had not been negligent.

29 *Bolitho v City and Hackney HA* [1998] AC 232.

later given a good drubbing by the House of Lords, said that one should always presume that the clinician in those circumstances would give the treatment which is effective. The law does not go that far, but judges might quietly, in practice, do so. Where a protocol exists, there is likely to be a strong *de facto* presumption that, had it been known of/had the relevant doctor put himself in a position to follow it, it would have been followed.

Failure by para-medical personnel (who are not in the relevant clinical respects expected to exercise independent clinical judgment) to follow a protocol, which failure results in action or inaction which would be endorsed by some body of responsible medical opinion is for obvious reasons much more likely to lead to liability. The duty of personnel in that position is likely to be construed by the courts as simply a duty to carry out the protocol.[30] However, if the allegation of negligence is failure to carry out the protocol, and carrying out the protocol would have prevented the relevant damage, it may well be a *Bolitho* causation defence to assert that the clinician in overall charge of the patient would have required or endorsed (in a *Bolam*-defensible way), a departure from the protocol in a way which would still have allowed the damage to occur. Here, the position really is that the protocol relied on was not a protocol binding on that particular worker, and he was merely the *Bolam*-clean hands of the clinician, on whose behalf the *Bolitho* causation defence is asserted.

---

30 See, eg, *Sutton v Population Family Planning Programme Ltd* (1981) unreported (cited in Hurwitz, B, *Clinical Guidelines and the Law*, 1998, Radcliffe), where a nurse was found to have been negligent in failing to follow the procedure prescribed by the organisation which employed her for referring a patient with a breast lump.

CHAPTER 8

HUMAN RIGHTS AND CLINICAL GUIDELINES

NA Peacock

SYNOPSIS

The passing of the Human Rights Act 1998 (HRA 1998) represents the culmination of political pressure for the incorporation of human rights as set out in the European Convention on Human Rights (the Convention) by statute into UK law. The HRA 1998 will have an impact on virtually every area of law, but the impact on clinical negligence (and other medical) cases is perhaps less obvious, at least at first glance. The HRA 1998 sets out the mechanics by which human rights principles can be raised in UK courts. In particular:

(a) s 2 of the HRA 1998 requires UK courts and tribunals to 'take account of' the judgments, decisions, declarations, etc, of the various European legal institutions;

(b) s 6 of the HRA 1998 makes it unlawful for a public authority (including a court or tribunal, NHS Trusts and Health Authorities) to act, or propose to act, in a way which is incompatible with a Convention right.

The Convention is a living, breathing entity, which is capable of dynamic and creative interpretation and development: 'a living instrument which ... must be interpreted in the light of present-day conditions.'

The most important Convention Articles which may impact on clinical guidelines are:

(a) Art 2 (right to life), an absolute right, which is capable of affecting the very standard of clinical care which the law requires, as well as guidelines in respect of abortion, euthanasia and enforced treatment;

(b) Art 3 (prohibition against inhuman and degrading treatment), another absolute right;

(c) Art 8 (right to respect for private and family life), a qualified right, which has already been cited in cases about clinical confidentiality. To date UK courts have shown themselves to be relatively unwilling to entertain human rights arguments where a radical change in the common law is suggested.

INTRODUCTION

The European Convention on Human Rights – in full the Convention for the Protection of Human Rights and Fundamental Freedoms – (the Convention) was ratified by the British Government on 8 March 1951. The Convention came into force on 23 September 1953. At that time, there was no right of individual petition, nor would the UK accept the jurisdiction of the European Court of Human Rights in individual cases in UK courts. To date there have been some 50 judgments in UK cases in the European Court of Human Rights finding breaches of Convention rights. The passing of the Human Rights Act 1998 represents the culmination of political pressure (first voiced publicly in 1968) for the incorporation of Convention rights by statute into UK law.

So we are all human rights lawyers now. The HRA 1998 is capable of having an impact on virtually every area of law. We all need to learn new principles of law, new methods of interpretation and a whole new set of abbreviations for various law reports. It will no doubt assist to be able to speak a vast array of European (and world) languages, so we can have a greater knowledge and understanding of human rights decisions.

The impact on clinical negligence (and other medical) cases and, accordingly, on clinical guidelines, is perhaps less obvious, at least at first glance. It is necessary to have some understanding of the mechanics of the HRA 1998 before embarking on a tour of the Convention and some relevant European law.

THE HUMAN RIGHTS ACT 1998

Section 1 of the HRA 1998 provides that certain Convention rights (Arts 2–12 and 14 of the Convention, Arts 1–3 of the first protocol and Arts 1 and 2 of the sixth protocol, in each case read with Arts 16–18 of the Convention) are to be given (further) effect in domestic law. The word 'further' is merely a political sop – no UK politician could be heard to admit that UK law had no element of human rights before the HRA 1998 was enacted, hence 'further'.

Section 2 of the HRA 1998 requires UK courts and tribunals to take account of the judgments, decisions, declarations, etc, of the European Court of Human Rights, the European Commission on Human Rights (the Commission, or E Com HR, now disbanded) etc, so far as is relevant to the proceedings (see below on 'Interpretation'). UK courts are not bound to follow such judgments, etc. Again this is a political device to give the impression that UK parliamentary sovereignty, which was of course surrendered to Europe long ago, is in some way retained.

Section 3 of the HRA 1998 requires primary and subordinate legislation to be read and given effect in a way which is compatible with the Convention, wherever possible.

Section 4 of the HRA 1998 enables specified courts (higher courts) to make a declaration of incompatibility, where such a court is satisfied that legislation is incompatible with a Convention right.

Section 5 of the HRA 1998 entitles the Crown to intervene where a court is considering making a s 4 declaration.

Section 6 of the HRA 1998 makes it unlawful for a public authority to act in a way which is incompatible with a Convention right. It is an exception if: (a) the public authority, as a result of primary legislation, could not have acted differently; or (b) the public authority was giving effect to provisions of or under primary legislation. An act includes a failure to act.

A public authority includes a court or tribunal and any person some of whose functions are functions of a public nature, though a person is not a public authority if the nature of the act is private. Persons or organisations who may be challenged include: central government (excluding executive agencies), local government, the police, immigration officers, prisons, NHS trusts and health authorities. Perhaps curiously, when introducing the legislation in the House of Lords, the Lord Chancellor suggested that this would include doctors practising in the NHS, but not when practising privately.

Section 7 of the HRA 1998 identifies how a person may bring a claim before a domestic court or tribunal against a public authority alleged to be in breach of s 6 of the HRA. Such a person may bring proceedings in the appropriate court or tribunal or may rely on the Convention right(s) in any legal proceedings but must be a victim of the unlawful act. To be a victim, a person must be a victim for the purposes of Art 34 of the Convention (see below).

Section 8 of the HRA 1998 enables a court or tribunal to grant remedies where a public authority has acted (or proposes to act) in breach of a Convention right. A court or tribunal may in those circumstances grant such relief as it considers just and appropriate. Damages may only be awarded by a court or tribunal which has power to award damages (that is, civil courts only) and only if necessary to afford just satisfaction to the victim. There is no 'right' to compensation as such. This tallies with European human rights law, where the finding of a breach is often thought to be sufficient satisfaction to the victim, without the need to make an additional award of damages.

Section 9 of the HRA 1998 allows decisions of courts or tribunals to be challenged only by way of appeal (save where judicial review is available). Damages cannot be awarded in respect of a judicial act done in good faith (other than to compensate to the extent required by Art 5(5) of the Convention (arrest or detention in contravention of the Convention)).

Section 10 of the HRA 1998 enables speedy amendments to provisions which have been declared to be incompatible with the Convention by a court pursuant to s 4.

Section 11 of the HRA 1998 makes the rather obvious point that a person's reliance on a Convention right does not restrict any other right or freedom which UK law conferred on him anyway, and does nor prohibit him from making a claim or bringing proceedings which he could make or bring anyway.

Section 12 of the HRA 1998 ensures that courts will pay particular regard to the right to freedom of expression. There was no need (other than a political need) to include this section in the Act.

Section 13 of the HRA 1998 ensures that courts will pay particular regard to the right to freedom of thought, conscience and religion as exercised by religious organisations and their members. (This section is also, strictly, unnecessary – see above.)

Sections 14–17 of the HRA 1998 inclusive concern the technically specialised areas of derogations and reservations which the UK has to the Convention.

The remainder of the HRA 1998 (ss 18–22 inclusive) deals with the appointment of judges of the European Court of Human Rights, parliamentary procedure for declarations of incompatibility and various supplemental provisions.

INTERPRETATION

The Convention is a living, breathing entity, which is capable of dynamic and creative interpretation and development: 'a living instrument which ... must be interpreted in the light of present-day conditions.'[1] Where social mores change, so interpretation of Convention rights is capable of change. This is capable of producing a dramatic effect on the English common law doctrine of precedent (*stare decisis*). No such doctrine applies in Europe in any sense understood by an English lawyer, and English lawyers will just have to keep trying to persuade courts to review previous decisions where there are cogent reasons for doing so. The best explanation of the way in which the doctrine of precedent might be affected by the European human rights law is to be found at Appendix C to the Law Commission Consultation Paper (No 157) on 'Bail and the Human Rights Act 1998'.[2]

---

1 Application 5856/72, *Tyrer v UK* (1978) 2 EHRR 1.
2 Feldman, D, Dean of the Faculty of Law and Barber Professor of Jurisprudence, University of Birmingham, Appendix C to Law Commission Consultation Paper (No 157).

The Convention is supposed to guarantee practical and effective rights, not abstruse theoretical ones. It should ensure balance between the individual and the community. In particular the doctrine of proportionality requires that a restriction on any particular freedom guaranteed under the Convention must be 'proportionate to the legitimate aim pursued'.[3]

The doctrine of 'margin of appreciation' is particularly important: 'By reason of their direct and continuous contact with the vital forces of their countries, the national authorities are in principle better placed than an international court to evaluate local needs and conditions.'[4] Technically the doctrine will not apply to consideration of the Convention by domestic courts, but there may be circumstances where the court or tribunal will consider that the legislature and executive are better placed to balance the competing needs referred to above and will accordingly defer to the executive. Concern has been expressed about the possible conflation of this principle with the *Wednesbury* unreasonableness doctrine.

EUROPEAN CONVENTION ON HUMAN RIGHTS

UK lawyers are trained to interpret statutes and tend to look at the pronouncements of the judiciary as if they were statutes. The Convention sprang out of a Europe ravaged by years of war and uncertainty, and the derivation of many of the Articles is clearly understood in that context. For example, Art 3 (prohibition of torture, and of inhuman or degrading treatment or punishment) is a clear response to wartime atrocities. Notwithstanding the way in which the Convention came about, and the 'mischief' it was intended to prevent, the Articles have been interpreted in case law far beyond their original aim. This is either a tribute to the imagination of our European legal and judicial brethren or a cautionary tale of legal excess, depending on one's point of view.

This chapter seeks to examine the areas in which European human rights law may come to have an impact on medical law and, by necessary development, clinical guidelines. We have seen above that, following the enactment of the HRA 1998, wherever a public body (for which we can now read, for example, NHS Trust or health authority) acts or seeks to act in contravention of a person's (for which we can now read patient's) human rights, the law can intervene.

---

3   Application 5493/72, *Handyside v UK* (1976) 1 EHRR 737, p 754, para 49.
4   Application 20348/92, *Buckley v UK* (1996) 23 EHRR 101, p 129, para 75.

ARTICLE 2 – RIGHT TO LIFE

1   Everyone's right to life shall be protected by law. No one shall be deprived of his life intentionally save in the execution of a sentence of a court following his conviction of a crime for which this penalty is provided by law.

2   Deprivation of life shall not be regarded as inflicted in contravention of this Article when it results from the use of force, which is no more than absolutely necessary:

   (a) in defence of any person from unlawful violence;

   (b) in order to effect a lawful arrest or to prevent the escape of a person lawfully detained;

   (c) in action lawfully taken for the purpose of quelling a riot or insurrection.

This is an absolute right (it cannot be derogated from in time of war or other public emergency). Article 2 is likely to cover cases where injury has been sustained provided that loss of life was one possible consequence of the conduct complained of. Considered below are some areas where clinical guidelines exist and which might therefore be affected by European Human Rights law.

Medical care and attention

Article 2 imposes a positive obligation on the state, raising the question of the state's duty to provide the health care necessary to save life. This will include public authorities, including health authorities and NHS Trusts (as stated above, according to the Lord Chancellor it will include doctors treating NHS patients but not private patients). It is an oft-stated principle in the European Court that the concept that 'everyone's right to life shall be protected by law' enjoins the state not only to refrain from taking a person's life 'intentionally' but also to take appropriate steps to safeguard life.[5] The question for lawyers now is how far UK courts can develop that principle in the area of medical law and clinical guidelines.

Association X v UK[6]

The Association comprised parents whose children had suffered severe and lasting damage or had even died as a result of vaccinations. It adduced expert evidence to show that 15% of those children who suffered adverse reactions to vaccinations eventually died and that there was a causal connection between

---

5   Eg, Application 11604/85, *Naddaf v Germany* (1986) 50 DR 259.

6   Application 7154/75, *Association X v UK* (1978) 14 DR 31 Ecom HR.

the two. It further argued that, where the UK government knew that death was going to occur, there was an 'intention' (reluctant or otherwise) to inflict death. The alleged poor administration of the scheme failed to protect the children's right to life. The UK government argued that the vaccination/ immunisation scheme was carried out with the sole intention of protecting human life and that the scheme was assessed before and during its implementation. The Commission repeated the concept that 'everyone's right to life shall be protected by law' enjoins the state not only to refrain from taking life intentionally but, further, to take appropriate steps to safeguard life. However, the Commission was satisfied that where a small number of fatalities occur in the context of a vaccination scheme whose sole purpose was to protect the health of society by eliminating infectious diseases, it could not be said that there had been an intentional deprivation of life within the meaning of Art 2 nor that the state had failed to take adequate and appropriate steps to safeguard life. The fact that the UK government was aware of fatalities after adverse reactions did not mean that it intended such consequences. On the contrary, a large part of the scheme was concerned with the avoidance of such serious risks.

Comment: this is an interesting case in the context of present concerns about child vaccination programmes in the UK. Despite the oft-stated principle (repeated in the opening paragraph to this Article) that the right to life is absolute, this case perhaps shows otherwise. The Commission adopted a utilitarian view that the greater good outweighs the rare, but devastating, side effects of such vaccination programmes. There must be a sliding scale in such cases: there comes a point where the incidence of adverse outcomes cannot be justified by the greater good.

Negligence as understood by common lawyers will be a relevant factor. In *Buckley v UK*[7] the administration of drugs in circumstances leading to a patient's death did not disclose grounds for negligence in domestic (UK) law. The Commission found the Art 2 complaint to be manifestly ill-founded and inadmissible.

It is possible (though academic opinion is divided) to argue that the obligation in Art 2 can be extended to include the obligation to make adequate provision for medical care in all cases where the right to life of a patient would otherwise be endangered (which would of course include all surgery under general anaesthetic). The operative word is 'adequate' which appears to allow much less room for manoeuvre than the word 'reasonable'.[8]

---

7   Application 28323/95, *Buckley v UK* (1997) 23 EHRR CD 129.

8   See *NHS Trust A v M: NHS Trust B v H* [2000] MLC 272, in which the Family Division (Butler-Sloss P) held that there was no breach of Art 2 where, in the best interests of a PVS patient, life-sustaining treatment was withdrawn. The approach taken by the House of Lords in *Airedale NHS Trust v Bland* [1993] AC 789 was said to be Art 2 compliant.

This raises the following interesting issues for medical lawyers:

(1) there is scope for challenging the *Bolam* test, in that the obligation to provide adequate (or appropriate) care does not necessarily mean the same as the obligation to take reasonable care. At present this has not been argued in Europe nor in domestic cases. It is probable that UK courts would be loath to overturn the *Bolam* test on this basis, particularly where the European Court has not yet heard full argument on the matter. Indeed, the Court of Appeal (which recently suggested that lawyers had to have case law authority for any human rights point they wished to raise) is unlikely in the present climate even to entertain such an argument;

(2) lack of resources may provide no defence to an NHS Trust (if it still does anyway), though the doctrine of 'margin of appreciation' may apply here.[9] According to this argument, the obligation to provide adequate care is an absolute one, and one which simply cannot be avoided on the basis that there were insufficient funds available to meet the particular healthcare need concerned. It is this argument which coined the phrase 'postcode lottery'. The 'margin of appreciation' defence would be that the public authority concerned must have some freedom to allocate resources. One of the principal reasons why the National Institute for Clinical Excellence (NICE) was set up and given the task of producing clinical guidelines was to overcome the 'postcode lottery' problems of allocation of clinical treatment, in particular drug therapy;

(3) it may be possible to frame actions against the Department of Health for failure to provide adequate protection where death or injury may result[10] (though this was, in effect, the basis of the case of *Association X* (above)). Following on from the previous paragraph it is possible to envisage claims against NICE where a particular guideline prohibits a form of treatment which is expensive and of limited use but which assists the particular patient concerned.

LCB v UK[11]

While serving in the RAF, the applicant's father was present at Christmas Island during nuclear tests in 1957 and 1958. He also participated in the subsequent clean-up programme. The applicant was born in 1966. In 1970 she was diagnosed as having leukaemia. She brought a claim pursuant to Arts 2 and 3, complaining that she had not been warned of her father's exposure to radiation and that this had prevented pre-and post-natal monitoring which

---

9   See *R v Cambridgeshire HA ex p B* [1995] 1 WLR 898; cf *Robertson v Nottinghamshire HA* [1997] 8 Med LR 1, CA; esp *North West Lancashire HA v A, D & G* [1999] Lloyd's Rep Med 399, CA.

10 See, eg, Application 23143/94, *LCB v UK* (1999) 27 EHRR 212.

11 *Ibid.*

would have led to earlier diagnosis and treatment of her illness. The Court held unanimously that there had been no breach of Art 2 on the basis that the UK had done all that could have been required of it to prevent the applicant's life from being avoidably put at risk (note the test). The evidence suggested that the records of contemporaneous measurements of radiation did not indicate that radiation reached dangerous levels in the areas where ordinary servicemen were stationed. The Court was not satisfied of a causal link between the applicant's father's exposure to radiation and her own leukaemia, nor that earlier monitoring would have led to earlier diagnosis and treatment. Given the information available to the UK government at the time concerning the likelihood of the applicant's father having been exposed to dangerous levels of radiation and of this having created a risk to her health, the Court did not find it established that the UK government could have been expected to act of its own motion to notify her parents of these matters or to take any special action in relation to her.

Comment: it is often easy enough to predict the result of human rights cases: the import in this case however is not the result, but the fact that the tribunal, here the full Court, is prepared to listen to and analyse the argument. Someone soon will bring a case in the UK raising human rights points where UK law does not currently provide a remedy.

Unborn children (abortion) and enforced treatment

No consensus exists across Europe on the issue of abortion. A state is likely to have a broad margin of appreciation with regard to the Convention on the issue of abortion.[12] In *Paton v UK*[13] it was held that the termination of a 10-week foetus to protect the health of the mother did not breach Art 2, though the Commission left open the question of whether this was because the foetus was not included in the word 'everyone' or because, if included, its rights were not absolute and were subject to permissible limitations. The European Court of Human Rights has yet to decide whether 'everyone' includes an unborn child.[14]

Cases of enforced treatment (for example, sterilisation) where the patient lacks capacity to consent may be alleged to be a breach of this Article (see also Art 5 – right to liberty and security of person).

---

12 Application 17004/90, *H v Norway* (1992) 73 DR 155.

13 Application 8416/78, *Paton v UK* (1981) 3 EHRR 408, EcomHR.

14 See, eg, Applications 14234 and 5/88, *Open Door Counselling and Dublin Well Woman v Ireland* (1992) 15 EHRR 244, E Ct HR.

Euthanasia and prolonging life

Again, a state is likely to have a wide margin of appreciation, bearing in mind Art 3 (prohibition on inhuman and degrading treatment) and Art 8 (physical and moral integrity).[15] The Commission held in *Widmer v Switzerland*[16] that Art 2 does not require that passive euthanasia, by which a person is allowed to die by not being given treatment, is a crime. In *D v UK*[17] the European Court of Human Rights emphasised the importance (within the context of Art 3) of dying in dignity but declined to rule substantively on the Art 2 complaint. The position may be different where: (a) a positive act is concerned; or (b) where death is the express wish of the individual concerned. Clinical guidelines on the resuscitation of patients (DNR) must be considered in the light of Art 2. Provided that the patient (and, probably, his family) has been given full information about the repercussions of the decision, a DNR decision is unlikely to fall foul of Art 2 (indeed, there are circumstances when it could be argued that resuscitation in certain circumstances could amount to a breach of Art 3 – see below).

Summary

Article 2 is capable of having an effect on any clinical guideline where death (or possibly serious injury) is a possible (even if rare) outcome of the treatment concerned. At present this has had little impact on medical law in the UK. The rights protected by Art 2 are absolute; this may require UK law to be modified in certain areas where clinical guidelines exist.

ARTICLE 3 – PROHIBITION OF TORTURE, AND OF INHUMAN OR DEGRADING TREATMENT OR PUNISHMENT

No one shall be subjected to torture or to inhuman or degrading treatment or punishment.

As with Art 2, this is an absolute right (it cannot be derogated from in time of war or other public emergency).

Article 3 has been raised in the context of medical treatment. It is well established that there is an obligation under Art 3 to provide adequate

---

15 See *Re A (Children)* [2001] 1 FLR 1 (the 'Siamese twins case') and *NHS Trust A v Mrs M; NHS Trust B v Mrs H* [2000] MLC 272.

16 Application 20527/92, *Widmer v Switzerland* (1993) unreported.

17 Application 30240/96, *D v UK* (1997) 24 EHRR 423.

medical treatment for persons in detention[18] (a right which UK law also of course recognises).[19]

Measures taken out of therapeutic necessity cannot be regarded as inhuman or degrading treatment. Treatment will only be considered inhuman if it reaches a certain stage of gravity and, further, that treatment will not be degrading unless the victim has undergone humiliation or debasement attaining a minimum level of severity. The Commission stated in *Tanko v Finland*[20] that it 'does not exclude that a lack of proper medical care in a case where someone is suffering from a serious illness could in certain circumstances amount to treatment contrary to Article 3'.

Herczegfalvy v Austria[21]

The applicant was a Hungarian refugee who operated his own TV repair business in Austria. He was convicted of various criminal offences including acts of violence against his wife and children and business clients, fraud, extortion and resistance against officials. Whilst serving a sentence, new criminal proceedings were brought against him which involved seeking detention of the applicant in an institution for 'mentally deranged offenders'. He complained of numerous violations, including breaches of Art 3 (forcibly administering food and neuroleptics, isolation and attaching handcuffs to a security bed). The Court held that measures taken out of therapeutic necessity cannot be regarded as inhuman or degrading treatment. However, the Court must satisfy itself based on the evidence that the medical treatment had been convincingly shown to exist. In this case, according to psychiatric principles existing at the time, medical necessity justified the treatment in issue.

Comment: guidelines will plainly exist for the treatment of patients with mental illness. It is important to see these patients first of all as patients with a clinical need. The same is true of prisoners who require medical treatment. Elaborate guidelines and protocols exist for the clinical treatment of such patients, sometimes resulting in delay of unnecessary imposition. Until January 1996 female prisoners were handcuffed in hospital even whilst giving birth. This would now probably be actionable as a breach of Art 3.

X v Denmark[22]

The applicant was voluntarily admitted to a hospital to be sterilised, since she wished to avoid having further children. Prior to the surgical intervention, she

18   See, eg, Application 23636/94, *PM v Hungary* (1997) unreported.

19   See, eg, *Brooks v Home Office* (1999) unreported, 3 February, QBD (Garland J).

20   Application 23636/94, *Tanko v Finland* (1994) DR 77-A.

21   Application 10533/83, *Herczegfalvy v Austria* (1992) 15 EHRR 437.

22   Application 9974/82, *X v Denmark* (1983) 32 DR 282.

was informed that the result would be almost irreversible and she signed a declaration that she consented. The surgery took place by electric catheterisation of the oviducts, a method used for more than two years. However, the surgeon used a new model of pincers (in use for three months) which had the advantage, according to him, of preventing damage to adjacent areas. On leaving hospital the applicant was told that no contraceptive measures would be necessary. A few years later she became pregnant. She refused an abortion and gave birth to a baby boy. An official inquiry revealed that of 72 sterilsation operations carried out with pincers of that sort, 10 had failed. She brought an action for damages. Expert evidence at the trial accepted that there was a 1–2% risk of failure but it was not agreed that the new pincers produced a greater failure rate. The Commission restated the principle that treatment will only be considered inhuman if it reaches a certain stage of gravity and, further, that treatment will not be degrading unless the victim has undergone humiliation or debasement attaining a minimum level of severity. The Commission did state that medical treatment of an experimental character and without the consent of the patient may under certain circumstances be regarded as contrary to Art 3. In the present case, however, the Commission considered it obvious that the operation could not be considered a medical experiment as such.

Comment: this is an example of an argument being raised in an attempt to develop the Convention way beyond its original intention. However, the Commission did not completely close the door on this topic. Given the General Medical Council's publication 'Seeking patients' consent: the ethical considerations'[23] it is now possible to argue that full informed consent (that is, patient-centered information) now needs to be given before all intervention. If medical treatment results in the restriction of a previously enjoyed lifestyle, or in the inability to continue working in a much-loved career, it is possible that a complaint could be framed based on this case.

Notwithstanding *X v Denmark* (above), 'experimental' may mean no more than treatment which has not yet become properly established and absence of consent may be demonstrated where doctors have failed to notify the patient in advance that the treatment proposed is experimental. In addition, two areas of current concern in the UK are: (a) patients left on trolleys in hospital corridors for lengthy periods; and (b) incontinent (for example, elderly) ward patients who cannot be taken to the toilet in time because of inadequate levels of nursing staff. Both may conceivably raise complaints under Art 3.

---

23   GMC booklet 1999; available on the GMC website.

Summary

Guidelines for the treatment in particular of prisoners (but also of the vulnerable) need to be drafted consistently with retaining their dignity. The rights under Art 3 are absolute; this requires clinical guidelines to be drafted with Art 3 well in mind. There may be more scope for introducing Art 3 arguments in UK cases involving clinical guidelines than for Art 2 above.

ARTICLE 8 – RIGHT TO RESPECT FOR PRIVATE AND FAMILY LIFE, HOME AND CORRESPONDENCE

1 Everyone has the right to respect for his private and family life, his home and his correspondence.

2 There shall be no interference by a public authority with the exercise of this right except such as is in accordance with the law and is necessary in a democratic society in the interests of national security, public safety or the economic well-being of the country, for the prevention of disorder or crime, for the protection of health or morals, or for the protection of the rights and freedoms of others.

It should immediately be noticed that, unlike Arts 2 and 3 above, this is a qualified right. Its impact on English law may nonetheless be considerable. It is much broader than a protection of privacy alone. It includes the right to keep to oneself.

In *Guerra v Italy*[24] the applicants lived within a mile of a chemical factory classified as high risk in terms of hazards to the environment and to the local population. The European Court of Human Rights found a violation of Art 8 (right to respect for family life) in respect of the failure of the relevant authorities to provide the applicants with essential information relevant to their well-being, health and homes.

Of particular relevance to the drafting and implementation of clinical guidelines, the collection of medical data and the maintenance of medical records may now be affected by Art 8.

MS v Sweden[25]

The applicant was a Swedish citizen who was previously employed as a nursery school teacher. She suffered from a condition of the spine which was capable of causing chronic back pain. In October 1991 she slipped and fell at work, injuring her back. As she was pregnant at the time, she visited her

---

24 Application 14967/89, *Guerra v Italy* (1998) 26 EHRR 357.
25 Application 20837/92, *MS v Sweden* (1999) 28 EHRR 313.

doctor at the women's clinic. Following the accident, she was unable to resume work on a regular basis and was eventually granted a disability pension. She made a claim for compensation from the Social Insurance Office in respect of her fall at work. She subsequently discovered that, in response to a request for her records for the relevant period by the Social Insurance Office, and without consulting her, the women's clinic she attended had supplied copies of records dating from up to five years following the accident, which revealed details of an abortion she had had as a result of her back problem. Her claim for compensation was rejected on the basis that her sick leave had not been caused by the industrial injury (but by her pre-existing back problem). She complained to the Court of breaches of Art 8. The Court unanimously held that there had been no breach of Art 8: her medical data was communicated by one public institution to another in the context of an assessment of whether she satisfied the legal conditions for obtaining a benefit which she herself had requested. The Office had a legitimate need to check the information received from her against data in possession of the clinic.

Comment: Article 8 allows an interference with the right in certain clearly defined circumstances: this applicant's fraudulent claim might well have been a criminal offence. It was certainly in the interests of the economic well-being of the country that taxes were expended only where justified.

Z v Finland[26]

The applicant was a Swedish national married to X, whom she had met in Africa. During an investigation of X for a number of sexual offences, it was discovered that X was HIV positive. He was tried on several counts of attempted manslaughter. As it was not clear that he had knowledge of his medical condition at the time of commission of the offences, the issue at trial was when he might have acquired such knowledge. Z invoked her right not to give evidence, so orders were issued obliging the doctors treating both X and Z to give evidence. The Swedish Court of Appeal disclosed Z's identity and medical data in the course of its judgment, and ruled that the confidentiality of the proceedings should be maintained for 10 years (although all parties had requested a longer period). The applicant alleged breaches of Art 8 in relation to: (a) the orders requiring her doctors to give evidence; (b) the seizure of her medical records; (c) the decision to limit confidentiality in the proceedings to 10 years; and (d) the disclosure of her identity and medical data in the Court of Appeal judgment. Breaches were found in relation to the latter two aspects. However, the Court held that there was no breach in relation to the first two aspects, in particular in the context of an investigation and prosecution of crime.

---

26 Application 22009/93, *Z v Finland* (1998) 25 EHRR 371.

Comment: there may be an echo of Art 3 in this case – the publication of the confidential information which the Finnish courts allowed seems vindictive and unnecessary.

There may well be challenges to the use of covert video surveillance (common in large medical and personal injury cases) though the issue will be whether the use of such evidence is proportionate, and on the possible violation of Art 6 rights to fair trial if such evidence is excluded. The surveillance of employees whilst at work has already been successfully challenged.[27]

Clinical guidelines on the disclosure and use of health records will have been drafted for the purposes of the Data Protection Act 1998. In the healthcare world, this has meant the introduction of 'Caldicott guardians'. However, it is important that such guidelines are drafted not just with the DPA 1998 in mind, but also with one eye on the European Convention.

Summary

Together with another European-derived piece of legislation, the Data Protection Act 1998, Art 8 provides ample scope for changing UK medical law and clinical guidelines, particularly in the areas of the retention and use of healthcare records and medical information.

ARTICLE 12 – RIGHT TO MARRY

Men and women of marriageable age have the right to marry and to found a family, according to the national laws governing the exercise of this right.

Despite the apparent wording of the Article, the Court has stated that 'Article 12 is mainly concerned to protect marriage as the basis of the family'.[28]

Article 12 has been held to apply to prisoners marrying, where there is no ability to found a family.[29] It also confers the right to remarry for those whose previous marriage has ended as a matter of national law. It may now be arguable that a refusal by a public authority (for example, a health authority) to provide IVF would be in breach of Art 12,[30] though the issue has not yet been determined in Europe. This is no doubt an area in which NICE will be heavily involved (see also sections (2) and (3) on p 128).

---

27 Application 13710/88, *Niemitz v Germany* (1992) 16 EHRR 97; Application 20605/92, *Halford v UK* (1997) 24 EHRR 523. See also Application 27671/95, *Valanzuela Contreras v Spain* (1998) 28 EHRR 483.

28 Application 9532/81, *Rees v UK* (1986) 9 EHRR 56.

29 7114/75, *Hamer v UK* (1979) 24 DR 5.

30 See *R v HFEA ex p Blood* [1997] 2 All ER 687, CA.

ARTICLE 34 – VICTIMS

The Court may receive applications from any person, non-governmental organisations or group of individuals claiming to be the victim of a violation by one of the rights set forth in the Convention or the protocols thereto. The High Contracting Parties undertake not to hinder in any way the effective exercise of this right.

Broadly speaking, there is no general or hypothetical right to complain and the European Court of Human Rights will examine the concrete case before it. A person need not have had his rights actually infringed; he need only run the risk. An applicant may be an indirect victim (for example, family member or close relative). A trade union cannot claim to be a victim on the basis that it represents the interests of its members. A company may be the victim of a breach of its rights, for example, freedom of expression (but shareholders cannot usually claim to be victims because of infringements of the company's rights). A governmental organisation (for example, a local authority) cannot claim to be a victim.

THE ENGLISH APPROACH IN FUTURE

UK courts have so far shown themselves willing to consider relevant European principles but have sent warning shots across the bows of any lawyer who is too keen to raise a European point where UK law can solve the problem anyway.[31]

It will take some years before the full impact of the Convention starts to be seen in domestic UK law. What is already clear is that the Convention provides numerous areas in which medical law and clinical guidelines need to adapt.

---

31 Eg, *Daniels v Walker* [2000] 1 WLR 1382, CA and esp *North West Lancashire HA v A, D & G* [1999] Lloyd's Rep Med 399, CA.

CHAPTER 9

CLINICAL GUIDELINES IN THE UNITED STATES: PERSPECTIVES ON LAW AND LITIGATION

RP Solomon

SYNOPSIS

The development and use of clinical practice guidelines (CPGs) has proliferated in the US. Not surprisingly, attorneys have recognised the critical role that CPGs could play in setting the standards of care that govern medical malpractice litigation – both for inculpatory purposes (as a sword) and exculpatory purposes (as a shield). Healthcare professionals fear that the inculpatory use of CPGs in the courtroom would limit their professional discretion and stifle innovation in the practice of medicine. State legislatures wishing to reduce the cost of litigation have adopted demonstration projects that permit evidence of compliance with CPGs to constitute an affirmative defense in a medical malpractice action. However, the success of these legislative efforts has been difficult to measure.

In 1998, the US Government launched the National Guidelines Clearinghouse (NGC),[1] an Internet website intended to make evidence-based clinical practice guidelines and related abstract, summary, and comparison materials widely available to healthcare professionals. It is available on the World Wide Web at www.guideline.gov. The NGC database contains evidence-based CPGs as defined by the Institute of Medicine: 'Clinical practice guidelines are systematically developed statements to assist practitioner and patient decisions about appropriate health care for specific clinical circumstances.' Guidelines must meet minimum criteria in order to be included in the NGC.

CPGs are actually being used in US malpractice litigation as a sword and as a shield. From a litigation perspective, there may be evidentiary hurdles to overcome before a CPG is admitted into evidence and, if admitted, argument on the weight it should be accorded. There may, for example, be a need to qualify the CPG as one that is, in fact, sufficiently authoritative. The guidelines most often used were those issued by medical specialty societies, individual

---

1   See the National Guideline Clearinghouse www.guideline.gov for an internet-based web repository of over 1,000 guidelines (hereinafter referred to as 'NGC website'). See also ECRI's *Healthcare Standards Directory* 2001; Plymouth Meeting, PA, for listings of thousands of healthcare standards and guidelines and the issuing organisations.

hospitals, and the Joint Commission on Accreditation of Healthcare Organisations.

CPGs also play an influential role in the pre-trial negotiation. In Hyams' 1995 study, more than 27% of responding attorneys reported that a guideline influenced their decision to settle a case, 26% of claimant attorneys reported that CPGs influenced their decision to reject a case, and 31% were influenced to accept and file a suit.

CPGs are not likely to be a panacea for improving the costly, inefficient court systems for medical malpractice litigation in the US. However, the rapid proliferation of new guidelines and their widespread accessibility are making significant differences in the course, conduct, and outcome of litigation.

INTRODUCTION

Over the past two decades, the development and use of CPGs proliferated and the trend is likely to continue. There are literally thousands of CPGs with varying goals and objectives issued by a broad variety of public and private sector organisations.

Not surprisingly, CPGs have been touted as an opportunity to improve costly, inefficient court systems for medical malpractice litigation in the US: CPGs, it is argued, could set the standards of care that govern medical malpractice litigation, and thus inform healthcare professionals what the legal system expects of them. This, in turn, would motivate physicians to comply with CPGs and serve the twin goals of improving quality and reducing the overuse of certain procedures. Clearly articulated, evidence-based CPGs could help non-medically qualified judges and juries arbitrate otherwise conflicting medical expert testimony, some of which may embody bad science or opinions influenced by financial remuneration. On the surface, the idea of CPGs setting the legal standard of care seems like an appealing solution to a legal system that has long been recognised as a powerful contributor to the practice *of defensive medicine* – described as 'when doctors order tests, procedures, or visits, or avoid high-risk patients or procedures primarily (but not necessarily solely) to reduce their exposure to malpractice liability'.[2] Defensive medicine is said to be prevalent in the US, and while its true extent is immeasurable, it has been estimated to have an annual cost as high as 5% to 9% of the US health care budget – about $50 billion dollars.[3] This has

---

2   Office of Technology Assessment, US Congress, *Defensive Medicine and Medical Malpractice*, July 1994, publication OTA-H-602, Washington, DC.

3   Anderson, R, 'Billions for defense, the pervasive nature of defensive medicine' (1998) 159 J of the American Medical Association 20.

prompted state legislatures to enact various tort reform measures, one of which is to develop and adopt CPGs, and permit their use in litigation.

On the other hand, healthcare professionals fear that the inculpatory use of CPGs would unnecessarily limit their professional discretion and stifle innovation in the practice of medicine. Legal scholars have argued that increased reliance on CPGs to establish the legal standard of care would be deeply problematic if the CPGs were used in either an inculpatory or exculpatory fashion.[4] Legislated guidelines or CPGs may simply be out of line with the best medical practice, or they may be out of line with the customary practices that they are intended to supplant. Furthermore, the CPGs themselves may lack quality or credibility, and there may be competing or conflicting CPGs.[5]

Stakeholders have different perspectives on the primary need for and use of CPGs. Managed care organisations and other payers see them as a way to contain costs. They use CPGs in deciding whether to pay for a treatment or procedure, either as a class of technology or for a particular patient. Medical specialty societies see CPGs as a way to retain control over their professionalism and judgment. Such societies have become primary sources for guideline development and promulgation. State legislatures see CPGs as a way to reform the evils of uncurbed medical malpractice litigation and reduce the costs of defensive medicine. They have adopted schemes that permit evidence of compliance with CPGs to constitute an affirmative defense in a civil action. Courts are increasingly admitting CPGs as evidence of the standard of care in individual medical malpractice claims – both for inculpatory (the sword) and exculpatory (the shield) purposes – and this tendency is likely to grow in direct proportion to the rate of guideline development. While judicial use of CPGs may serve a public policy purpose of deterring substandard medicine, CPGs primarily affect individual parties to a lawsuit – the injured claimant and the alleged wrongdoers.

'Clinical practice guidelines' are defined by the Institute of Medicine (IOM) as 'systematically developed statements to assist practitioner and patient decisions about appropriate healthcare for specific clinical circumstances'.[6]

---

4   See Mello, MM, 'Of sword and shields: the role of clinical practice guidelines in medical malpractice litigation' (2001) 149 U of Penn L Rev 3.

5   See, eg, the Guideline Syntheses published on the NGC website, which point out areas of differences among competing guidelines issued by different organisations.

6   Institute of Medicine, in Field, MJ and Lohr, KN (eds), *Clinical Practice Guidelines: Directions for a New Program*, 1990, Washington, DC: National Academy Press, p 38.

LEGISLATED USE OF CLINICAL PRACTICE GUIDELINES

Several US states have in legislation defined acceptable standards of clinical care by reference to practice guidelines. Those guidelines help to establish a strategy for reducing healthcare costs while maintaining quality. Of these states, Maine and Florida have actually developed, implemented, and completed demonstration projects that test the strategy, allowing CPGs to be used as an affirmative defence in medical malpractice litigation. An affirmative defence is a 'defendant's assertion ... that, if true, will defeat the plaintiff's or prosecution's claim, even if all allegations in the complaint are true'.[7]

This section examines the experiences of Maine and Florida, and then more briefly, initiatives taken by other states.

THE MAINE LIABILITY DEMONSTRATION PROJECT

On 21 April 1990 the Maine legislature established the Medical Liability Demonstration Project.[8] The Maine project was the first state legislative initiative in the US to establish CPGs that could be used as an affirmative defence in medical malpractice litigation. The project aimed to reduce the practice of defensive medicine – that is, ordering unnecessary diagnostic tests and performing excessive therapy primarily to reduce exposure to medical malpractice liability – and, thus, lower healthcare costs by reducing payments for unnecessary tests and procedures. The Maine project has been widely discussed in scholarly legal and health policy journals (which have extensively debated questions of constitutionality and fundamental fairness), and also in medical specialty society journals and trade journals.[9] Despite all the analysis and attention, the project generated little evidence of practical effectiveness and was not extended beyond its scheduled termination date in 2000.

Under the Maine scheme, a physician's compliance with the state-established guidelines would represent a rebuttable presumption in medical malpractice litigation that a physician had met the standards of care for the patient. The guidelines could be raised by a physician defendant in a medical

---

7 *Black's Law Dictionary* 430, 7th edn.

8 Maine Public Law 1990, Chapter 931; subsequently amended on 17 June 1991 at Maine Public Law 1991, Chapter 319.

9 See, eg, Begel, M, 'Maine physician practice guidelines: implication for medical malpractice litigation' (1995) 47 Med L Rev 69; Morton, JR, 'Using practice parameters as an affirmative defense', August 1995, Bull Am Coll Surg (8):30-3; Kuc, GW, 'Practice parameters as a shield against physician liability' (Spring 1994) J Contemp Health Law Policy 10: 439–68.

malpractice lawsuit as representing an acceptable standard of care without the need for accompanying medical expert testimony. The scheme was notable in that it created a 'one way street' for CPGs – it permitted their exculpatory use by defendants but prohibited their inculpatory use by claimants. The claimant could, however, challenge the applicability of the specific CPG to the clinical situation at issue in the litigation and the compliance of the physician with the CPG.

The legislation provided for the participation of four medical specialties: anesthesiology, emergency medicine, radiology, and obstetrics/gynaecology. The legislature chose those four specialties because it believed that they were highly affected by costly malpractice claims that resulted in the practice of defensive medicine. Specialty advisory committees were established, made up of physicians and non-physician representatives, to develop practice guidelines for the four specialties. These committees developed 20 guidelines as follows:

Documentation of anesthaesia care

Anaesthesia monitoring standards

Post anaesthesia care

Requirements for pre-operative testing

Cervical spine x-ray

Patient transfer

Caesarean delivery when labour is not progressing normally

Assessment of foetal maturity before repeat caesarean or elective induction of labour

Surgical removal of the uterus

Inhibition of premature labour

Extrauterine pregnancy

Infant in other than head-first position during labour

Herpes-simplex virus infections before and after birth

Foetal distress during delivery

Management of prolonged pregnancy

Screening mammography

Ultrasound to assess foetal development

Outpatient assessment of blood vessel disorders

Examination of the lower intestine

The Maine project was premised upon the belief that physicians would change their practice of performing medically unnecessary tests and procedures if their fear of malpractice suits could be removed. The legislation provided this protection by allowing participating physicians to assert compliance with the guidelines as constituting an affirmative defence in a malpractice suit by statute. Patients could not use a physician's non-compliance with the guidelines as evidence of negligence unless the physician had already admitted the guidelines as evidence.

Medical malpractice attorneys have stated that the guidelines would be likely to have an impact in the pre-trial litigation stage because, under Maine law, medical malpractice litigants must submit their case to a pre-trial screening panel that issues findings regarding the legal merits of the claim. A unanimous finding by the panel would be admissible in any subsequent malpractice trial of the claim. Thus, a unanimous finding by the panel that the physician followed the state guidelines and therefore acted within the applicable standard of care would be likely to discourage claimants from taking their claims to trial.

The project had participation requirements. The guidelines were to be available as a legal defence only if at least 50% of the physicians in each of the four specialties agreed to participate. Majority participation was achieved, despite advice to the contrary from officials of the Maine Medical Mutual Insurance Company, a leading medical malpractice insurer in Maine, which sent a letter to its insured physicians expressing reservations about the project. The highest rate of participation was achieved among emergency physicians: 111 of 121 (92%) of eligible specialists chose to participate. The lowest rate was achieved among radiologists: 59 of 69 (87%) of eligible specialists chose to participate.

Impact on defensive medicine

The success of the Maine project has been difficult to measure. In 1995, the US General Accounting Office (GAO) issued a report describing the factors that contributed to the difficulty.[10] First, there were numerous data related problems. There were no reliable data available from managed care and other health plans to show whether the number of defensive medicine practices actually decreased. Secondly, even if adequate data were available, there were changes in the healthcare marketplace that would have made it difficult to determine whether any reduction in the number of defensive medicine procedures, if measurable, was influenced by the legislation. For example, one of the radiology standards covers performance of adult barium enema

10 United States General Accounting Office, *Maine Practice Guidelines*, 1995, GAO/HEHS–95–118R 20548, Washington, DC.

examinations because missed colon carcinomas are the leading cause of malpractice claims for radiologists. However, internists and gastroenterologists, rather than radiologists, typically determine whether a barium enema or a colonoscopy is done and thus it is possible that the main guideline would have no affect on the number of procedures done because the guideline applies only to radiologists.

FLORIDA'S CAESAREAN DEMONSTRATION PROJECT

Florida, like Maine, established a demonstration project to evaluate the effectiveness of practice parameters with regard to the costs of defensive medicine and professional liability insurance.

In 1992, the state legislature directed Florida's Agency for Health Care Administration to adopt practice parameters with standards of practice designed to avoid liability claims and to increase the defensibility of claims, thereby reducing the need for physicians to practise defensive medicine.[11] Physicians participating in the project named as a defendant in an action could introduce evidence of compliance with the practice parameters as an affirmative defence to a liability claim. However, unlike Maine, the Florida statute did not prohibit a claimant from introducing CPGs into evidence in a malpractice case – there was not a 'one way street' – but such use would not conclusively establish the standard of care.

Florida's Caesarean Demonstration Project began in the summer of 1994 and was statutorily authorised through to 1 October 1998. Caesarean section was the most common surgical procedure performed in Florida hospitals. In 1996, there were 41,212 caesarean deliveries, accounting for 140,000 hospital days and over $347 million in hospital charges. One explanation for the high rate of caesarean deliveries was that some were performed for defensive medicine purposes – that is, to reduce malpractice liability exposure by reducing a perceived risk of adverse birth outcomes. A total of 281 physicians and 34 hospitals volunteered to participate in the project by complying with the state guidelines, establishing a peer review committee to examine all caesarean deliveries, and submitting documentation to the Agency for Health Care Administration.

In 1998, the Agency evaluated the project and made recommendations to the Florida legislature on the results of the demonstration project.[12] It concluded:

---

11   Florida Statutes Title XXIX (1992) Chapter 408.02(9).
12   Agency for Health Care Administration, 'Practice Guidelines as affirmative defense: the Cesarean Demonstration Project Report', January 1998, State Center for Health Statistics, Tallahassee, FL.

(a) that the use of CPGs in litigation, either by claimants or defendants, was not well established (there was no known use of a CPG in court as an affirmative defence);

(b) that use of a CPG as an affirmative defence was insufficient incentive to induce substantial physician participation (only 20% of eligible physicians participated);

(c) that there was weak evidence that project participation was motivated by a need for protection from medical malpractice claims;

(d) that participating physicians were already more aggressive in their management of labour and delivery (that is, they were less likely to use caesarean delivery) prior to the start of the project;

(e) that if all physicians complied with the CPG, the caesarean rate would go down;

(f) that the amount of defensive medicine, as measured by caesarean deliveries without a sufficient documented reason, was at most 8% (this could also have been the result of inadequate record keeping);

(g) that the use of the CPG did not have any apparent detrimental impact on newborn outcomes.

It was unable to make any findings on the relationship between the use of the CPG and malpractice premiums or the frequency of malpractice claims.

Although the project was not extended beyond its original expiration date, Florida has adopted other legislation by which the Agency for Health Care Administration is required to:

> … co-ordinate the development, endorsement, implementation, and evaluation of scientifically sound, clinically relevant practice parameters in order to reduce unwarranted variation in the delivery of medical treatment, improve the quality of medical care, and promote the appropriate utilisation of health care services.

Florida hospitals are required to forward to the state agency a description of any practice guideline that has been adopted by the medical staff, as well as outcome data for persons treated according to such a practice guideline. The Agency, in turn, is required to summarise and report on the hospital outcome data and work with other state agencies and state specialty societies to develop state practice parameters, or to adopt nationally developed practice guidelines. Practice parameters may be adopted by state law, but in any event they shall not be grounds for any administrative action. The Agency was also directed to develop practice parameters for services provided by diagnostic-imaging centers, radiation therapy services, clinical laboratory services, physical therapy services, comprehensive rehabilitative services, and mammography services.[13]

---

13 Florida Statutes Title XXIX (2000) Chapter 408.02 (1)–(8).

OTHER STATE AND FEDERAL EFFORTS

In addition to Maine and Florida, other states have developed programmes that allow physicians to use CPGs in some form as a legal defence in a malpractice case.[14] In 1993, Maryland, for example, created an Advisory Committee on Practice Parameters in order to study the development of practice parameters for medical specialties and to provide information for and make ... recommendations on the adoption and use of practice parameters. The Committee was to propose practice parameters that 'are consistent with the appropriate standards of care ... and are designed to discourage inappropriate utilisation'. Thus, like Maine, Maryland embraced a two-fold approach that sought to improve quality and contain costs. It also incorporated a risk management approach in that the Committee was required to develop practice parameters for 'individual procedures or diseases that are subject to a significant amount of medical malpractice litigation'. However, any such practice parameters were, by statute, precluded from being admissible as evidence in any legal proceedings in Maryland as evidence of the standard of acceptable care.[15]

In Kentucky, the State Workers' Compensation statute requires the state to develop or adopt practice parameters or CPGs for use by providers of medical care. It also provides that medical care providers following such practice parameters or CPGs shall be presumed to have met the legal standard of care in medical malpractice cases regardless of any anticipated complication that may thereafter develop or be discovered.[16] Interestingly, there is no such presumptive effect for non-workers' compensation cases, which may encourage the application of different standards of care for the same treatment or procedures depending on whether the underlying injury was work-related or not.

In 1996, the Oklahoma Health Care Authority was required by state statute to submit recommendations to the governor and the legislature that contained 'a plan for facilitating the use of practice parameters based upon outcomes research'.[17] In 1994, Utah established the Utah Health Policy Commission to investigate, among other things, the feasibility of a statewide repository for gathering statistical information on practice parameters.[18]

On the national level, the Agency for Health Care Policy and Research (now the Agency for Healthcare Research and Quality (AHRQ) briefly

---

14 Fla Stat Ch 408.02; KY ref Stat Ann s 342.0235; ME ref Stat Ann Title 24 s 2971–79; MD code ann, health-jen I s 19–1602.

15 MD Health-General Code Ann s 19–1602 *et seq*.

16 KRS s 342.035 (8)(a)(b) (2000).

17 63 Okl Stat s 5012 (4) (1993).

18 Utah Code Ann s 63C–104(1)(a)(vii)(1994).

developed national practice guidelines. However, that effort has been supplanted by a new initiative, the National Guidelines Clearinghouse, which is described below. The US Federal Government supports the development of CPGs through AHCPR, the National Institutes of Health (NIH), the Centers for Disease Control and Prevention (CDC) and the US Preventative Service Task Force (USPSTF).

THE NATIONAL GUIDELINES CLEARINGHOUSE

In 1998, the US Government launched the National Guidelines Clearinghouse (NGC), an Internet website intended to make evidence-based clinical practice guidelines and related abstract, summary, and comparison materials widely available to healthcare professionals. The NGC, which can be found at www.guideline.gov, is operated by the US Department of Health and Human Services, The Agency for Healthcare Research and Quality (AHRQ) (formerly the Agency for Health Care Policy and Research (AHCPR) in partnership with the American Medical Association (AMA), and the American Association of Health Plans (AAHP). All of the technical work for the site is performed by ECRI. This consists of identifying, gathering, analysing, summarising, and comparing guidelines and making them available via the Internet.

The NGC supports specific statutory mandates promulgated by the US Congress: (1) to support research designed to improve the quality of healthcare, reduce its cost, and broaden access to essential services; and (2) to develop and disseminate evidence-based information to increase the scientific knowledge needed to enhance patient and clinical decision-making, improve healthcare quality, and promote efficiency in the organisation of public and private systems of health care delivery.

The NGC database contains evidence-based CPGs as defined by the Institute of Medicine: 'Clinical practice guidelines are systematically developed statements to assist practitioner and patient decisions about appropriate health care for specific clinical circumstances.' These guidelines are not fixed protocols that must be followed, but are intended for healthcare professionals and providers to consider. While they identify and describe generally recommended courses of intervention, they are not presented as a substitute for the advice of a physician or other knowledgeable healthcare professional or provider. Individual patients may require different treatments from those specified in a given guideline. Guidelines are not entirely inclusive or exclusive of all methods of reasonable care that can obtain/produce the same results. While guidelines can be written that take into account variations in clinical settings, resources, or common patient characteristics, they cannot address the unique needs of each patient nor the combination of resources available to a particular community or healthcare professional or provider.

Deviations from CPGs may be justified by individual circumstances. Thus, CPGs must be applied based on individual patient needs using professional judgment.

The NGC has adopted minimum criteria for inclusion on the website. All of the criteria below must be met for a clinical practice guideline to be included in NGC:

- The clinical practice guideline contains systematically developed statements that include recommendations, strategies, or information that assists physicians and/or other healthcare practitioners and patients make decisions about appropriate health care for specific clinical circumstances.

- The clinical practice guideline was produced under the auspices of medical specialty associations, relevant professional societies, public or private organisations, government agencies at the Federal, state, or local level, or healthcare organisations or plans. A clinical practice guideline developed and issued by an individual not officially sponsored or supported by one of the above types of organisations does not meet the inclusion criteria for NGC.

- Corroborating documentation can be produced and verified, confirming that a systematic literature search and review of existing scientific evidence published in peer reviewed journals was performed during the guideline development. A guideline is not excluded from NGC if corroborating documentation can be produced and verified detailing specific gaps in scientific evidence for some of the guideline's recommendations.

- The guideline is in the English language, current, and the most recent version produced. Documented evidence can be produced or verified that the guideline was developed, reviewed, or revised within the last five years.

JUDICIAL USE OF CLINICAL PRACTICE GUIDELINES

There are many more private CPGs than legislative ones. They have been formulated by a variety of organisations, such as medical specialty societies, physician organisations, private research organisations, and even medical malpractice liability insurers. They are also developed commercially by private companies, who sell them to managed care and other payer organisations. While non-governmental guidelines do not have the official legal status of providing an official legal defence, as in Maine, their overall impact in medical malpractice litigation has been far greater than guidelines grafted into legislation. This is because they are being admitted at trial as evidence of the standard of care that should be followed in a particular medical malpractice case.

The introduction of CPGs into medical malpractice litigation is not new. The standards developed by medical specialty societies, such as the American Society of Anaesthesiologists and the American College of Obstetrics and Gynaecologists, have been introduced in court as evidence for over two decades.[19, 20, 21] For a variety of reasons, many CPGs would not be useful in medical malpractice litigation; they may, for example, be geared toward utilisation review rather than patient care, or be too vague to be of use. In this regard, it is important to understand the genesis of a particular CPG and whether it was intended to point the way toward higher quality care, or toward more cost-effective care. While these two goals are not always mutually exclusive, they often present competing interests that shape the content and format of a CPG. Brennan has pointed out the distinctions between *appropriateness* guidelines and *standard of care guidelines*.[22] Appropriateness guidelines were initially developed in the aftermath of health services research studies identifying striking variations in medical practice in the same state or region. This included the overuse of medical technologies or interventions for which there was not a reliable evidence base. Appropriateness guidelines focus on care that is not indicated, and have evolved to define appropriateness and thus reduce the rates of various procedures. Standard of care guidelines generally aim to reduce medical injury and help to ensure that physicians reach a certain standard of care consistent with patient safety. Patient safety rather than cost is the driving element.

By way of example, Brennan contrasts guidelines such as those issued by the RAND Corporation for cardiac catheterisations (an appropriateness guideline) with the American Society of Anaesthesiologists (ASA) guidelines mandating the use of pulse oximetry and end tidal CO_2 monitoring (a standard of care guideline): the former is intended to reduce inappropriate catheterisation procedures, while the latter is intended to reduce the number of injuries resulting from the administration of general anaesthesia. If cost effectiveness or cost containment is the primary goal of a CPG, a court may be sceptical about introducing it as evidence of the standard of care.

Indeed, medical malpractice litigation itself was the initial force behind the ASA standards. The standards were initially developed by Harvard University after conducting studies of anaesthesia malpractice closed claims

---

19 *Washington v Washington Medical Center*, ASA monitoring standards introduced in a case alleging hospital negligence for failure to provide pulse oximetry to detect hypoxia.

20 *James v Woolley*, 523 so2d 110 (Ala 1998). ACOG guidelines on recommendations for caesarean deliveries for babies estimated to weigh more than 4,000 grams.

21 *Pollard v Goldsmith*, 572 P 2d 1201 (Ariz Ct of App 1977). ACS Guideline on Prophylaxis Against Tetanus and Wound Management were introduced in a case alleging that the physician should have administered human immune globulin.

22 Brennan, TA, 'Methods for setting priorities for guidelines development: medical malpractice', in Field, MJ (ed), *Setting Priorities for Clinical Practice Guidelines*, 1995, Institute of Medicine, Washington, DC: National Academy Press.

records, in which the researchers concluded that a high percentage of hypoxic accidents might have been prevented by the use of certain equipment, such as pulse oximetry, and by effective equipment maintenance. The Controlled Risk Insurance Company, a self-insurance programme that underwrites medical malpractice insurance and provides risk management services for Harvard-affiliated medical institutions, began to mandate the use of the new technologies as a condition to insurance coverage. As a result, the number of anaesthesia-related injuries dropped, and so did the anaesthesiologists' insurance premiums. Despite the success of this intervention, the development of or mandated use of CPGs by medical malpractice insurance companies is unusual,[23] probably because of the potential conflicts that could arise in the event of a suit being based on the guideline contents.

In any event, most commentators agree that, over time, the distinctions between cost-based CPGs and quality-based CPGs will become less and less clear as the health care system responds to a more cost-constrained environment. Future legal challenges will increasingly involve claims related to withholding or denying care, not just providing care in a negligent manner.[24]

THE STANDARD OF CARE IN MEDICAL MALPRACTICE CASES

Although the law pertaining to medical malpractice liability in the US has been developed by individual states and may differ from state to state, there are similarities in how courts apply them. As in UK law, a medical malpractice claimant has the burden of proving four elements:

(1) the physician or other health care provider must owe a duty of care to the injured claimant;

(2) there must have been a breach of the applicable standard of care expected of the health care provider;

(3) the breach of the standard of care must have been the legal cause (the proximate cause) of the claimants injury; and

(4) the claimant must have suffered injury of a type that is legally compensable by damages.[25]

---

23 The COPIC Insurance Company in Colorado has promulgated guidelines on obstetrics, anaesthesia monitoring, and other areas as part of its Participatory Risk Management Programme. Insured physicians must sign an agreement stating intention to comply with the guidelines. See, in general, www.copic.com.

24 Rosoff, AJ, 'Clinical Practice Guidelines: how the law will affect their development and use', in ECRI *Healthcare Risk Control* 1999, Risk and Quality Management Strategies 12, Plymouth Meeting, PA USA.

25 *Restatement of the Law*, Second, Torts 2d section 328A (1965).

Thus, the applicable standard of care must be defined in each and every medical malpractice case. While the medical profession itself (in practice, if not legal theory) sets the standard of care in most cases through expert testimony, CPGs may provide a definition of the standard of care in certain cases and thus are of interest to medical malpractice litigants – for inculpatory purposes, 'the sword' by claimants, and for exculpatory purposes, 'the shield' by defendants.

How are CPGs used in malpractice litigation? A claimant in a malpractice case has the burden of proving that he or she was injured by care or treatment that failed to reach the standard of care reasonably expected of the medical practitioner. Therefore, it would follow that a physician who complied with CPGs incorporating a standard of care could have a very good defence in a malpractice case; that is, a physician could use the guideline as a shield. The strength of the shield could vary, ranging from being grounds for summary judgment being a dubious ground for defending at trial against a specific allegation of negligence. On the other hand, a physician's failure to comply with a clinical practice guideline could be used as evidence of negligence in a malpractice case; that is, the claimant could use the guidelines as a sword. Again, the strength or value of the guideline in the particular case might range from utter irrelevance, through to providing an inference of negligence, to providing conclusive evidence of negligence.

From a litigation perspective, key questions are whether CPGs will be admitted into evidence and, if so, the weight they will be accorded. In the past, US courts have been unwilling to adopt broad exceptions to the hearsay rule and have thus refused to admit CPGs into evidence in malpractice and other tort cases. The hearsay rule limits the admissibility of out-of-court statements where the author or person making the statement is not sworn in as a witness and available for cross-examination. Over the years, the courts have developed exceptions to the hearsay rule that accommodate the use of authoritative materials such as CPGs and other 'learned treatises'.

There may be a need to qualify the CPG as one that is, in fact, authoritative and the authors properly qualified, much in the way that an expert witness must be qualified to render an opinion. Some courts require an expert to testify as to the authority of the specific clinical practice guideline;[26] others are willing to admit CPGs as evidence without expert testimony. A 1993 US Supreme Court decision, which created stricter standards for the judicial evaluation of the reliability and authoritativeness of proffered scientific evidence,[27] may encourage judges to scrutinise the process by which CPGs were developed, as well as the credentials and motivations of the issuing

---

26 *Frakes v Cardiology Consultants* (1997) Tenn App LEXIS 597, regarding the admissibility of the American College of Cardiology's 'Exercise test parameters associated with poor prognosis and/or increased severity of CAD'.

27 *Daubert v Merrell Dow Pharmaceuticals, Inc*, 509 US 579 (1993).

organisation. The NGC inclusion criteria, described above, may provide an example of the type of minimum credentialing criteria that should be required for admissibility of a reliable and authoritative CPG. The rules of admissibility are still being tested. Last year, a federal appeals court issued an opinion on whether a videotape on managing shoulder dystocia sponsored by ACOG should be admitted into evidence in an obstetrical malpractice case.[28] The court held that the video did qualify for admission under the 'learned treatise' rule, and that it was sufficiently authoritative.

If CPGs are admissible, what weight will they be given? The same as an expert witness? And, if the litigants rely on conflicting guidelines, will both be treated equally – or are some more equal than others? In the obstetrics case mentioned above, the court acknowledged that the video was 'highly probative evidence' that there was no breach of the standard of care, since it indicated that a limited or appropriate amount of traction on the baby's head was an acceptable medical practice – which conflicted with the claimant's assertion of what the standard of care should be. The video, then, was an effective shield. Of interest is the court's comment that ACOG's legend stating 'this video does not define a standard of care' should have been redacted as it might prejudice a jury to think that a claimant was merely being litigious.

LITIGATION ANALYSES

The legal literature is rife with scholarly articles on the role that CPGs should play in malpractice litigation, but there have been very few studies that examine their actual use. Andrew L Hyams and his colleagues have performed two studies that are very instructive on the frequency and nature of the use of guidelines in litigation, the frequency of the use of guidelines by attorneys in the pre-trial stage, and the impact that guidelines had on the outcome of the litigation.[29]

Hyams' 1995 study reviewed 259 open and closed claims of two professional liability insurance companies to investigate the use of practice guidelines.[30] A large sample was requested for anaesthesia and obstetrics claims, since it was believed that guidelines would play an important role in those claims. The reviewers searched for references to guidelines in various legal documents, such as briefs, interrogatories, depositions, and other

---

28 *Constantino v Herzog*, 203 F 3d 164 (2d Cir), 2000 US App LEXIS 2085.

29 Hyams, A, Brandenburg, J, Lipsitz, S, Shapiro, D and Brennan, T, 'Practice guidelines and malpractice litigation: a two-way street' (1995) 122 Ann Intern Med (Mar): 450–55; Hyams, A, Shapiro, DW and Brennan, TA, 'Medical Practice Guidelines in malpractice litigation: an early retrospective' (1996) 21(2) J Health Polit Policy Law (Summer), 289–313.

30 Hyams, A, Brandenburg, J, Lipsitz, S, Shapiro, D and Brennan, T, 'Practice Guidelines and malpractice litigation: a two-way street' (1995) 122 Ann Intern Med (Mar): 450–55.

materials. They noted specific uses to which the guidelines were put and the parties invoking the guidelines – that is, the claimants or the defendants – and they assessed the weight of the guidelines in the litigation. The reviewers classified a claim as involving a practice guideline if, in their judgment, the guideline was relevant to and played a pivotal role in the proof of negligence. Only 17 of 259 claims involved the use of practice guidelines (6.6%), of those 17, 12 were cases in which the guidelines were used for inculpatory purposes, four were used for exculpatory purposes, and one was indeterminate (see Figure 9.1). The guidelines most often used were those issued by medical specialty societies (especially the American College of Obstetricians and Gynaecologists), individual hospitals, and the Joint Commission for Accreditation of Healthcare Organisations (JCAHO).

Figure 9.1: Litigation file review

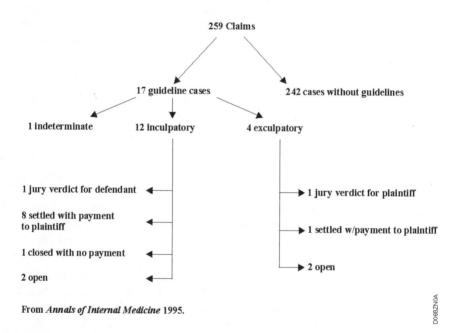

From *Annals of Internal Medicine* 1995.

Reprinted with permission.

Hyams' study also surveyed attorneys who litigate malpractice cases to assess their views on the role of guidelines. The attorney's survey involved a four-page questionnaire that was mailed to 980 attorneys from all 50 states in the US. Of 399 responses, 48% had at least one case per year in which CPGs played a role; however, only 36% had one case per year in which CPGs played an important role (see Figure 9.2). More than 27% of attorneys reported that a guideline influenced their decision to settle a case, and 22% stated that a guideline had influenced the judge or jury in a case in the previous year.

Interestingly, 26% of claimant attorneys reported that CPGs influenced their decision to reject a case, and 31% were influenced to accept and file a suit.

Figure 9.2:   Attorney estimates of cases in which guidelines play a role*

Estimate *n(%)*	Attorney Response	
Average number of cases per year in which guidelines played any role		
0	207	(52.0)
1	58	(14.5)
2-5	96	(24.0)
>5	38	(9.6)
Average number of cases per year in which guidelines played an important role		
0	255	(64.0)
1	58	(14.5)
2-5	63	(15.8)
>5	23	(5.7)

* Based on 399 responses.

From Ann Intern Med 1995. Reprinted with permission.

The authors found that CPGs were used as both sword and shield, but they were used for inculpatory purposes more than twice as often as they were used for exculpatory purposes. This two-way street is a stark contrast to the one-way use of guidelines in the Maine Project, which prohibits claimants from using CPGs for inculpatory purposes. The authors also speculate that the availability of clinical practice guidelines may, in effect, increase the number of medical malpractice cases by providing previously unavailable information resources to attorneys – that is, attorneys may get smarter about which cases are meritorious and which are not. The authors also noted that their study might underestimate the use of CPGs since the claims they studied were filed in the late 1980s, arising out of care provided in the mid-1980s, which preceded the issuance of many newly formulated CPGs.

MEDICAL MALPRACTICE CASES

CPGs used as a sword

The Hyams study pointed out that claimants have successfully used CPGs as a sword, both in the pre-trial and trial stage of litigation. There are several examples in the reported decisions. The standards of the American Society for Anaesthesiologists (ASA) have been cited in several court opinions. In one, an appeals court upheld a jury verdict for over $4 million dollars against a hospital that failed to provide an end-tidal carbon dioxide monitor (capnograph) in 1987 to a patient undergoing general anaesthesia during elective surgery. The device, which is used to detect hypoxia, would have identified the oesophageal intubation that led to the patient's serious injury. At trial, the claimant's expert relied on the ASA *Standards for Basic Intraoperative Monitoring*, which recommended the use of capnography for all patients undergoing general anaesthesia. In upholding the lower court decision, the court rejected the application of a 'locality' standard, stating that a national standard is proper when it comes to the provision of medical equipment. It also specifically rejected the hospital's assertion that the ASA standards were 'emerging', not mandatory.[31]

CPGs rejected as a sword

In response to the clinical practice guideline introduced by a claimant, defendants often respond that guidelines are just that – *guidelines* – and are not mandated standards. In one case, for example, the claimants argued that an emergency department physician arbitrarily deviated from the American Heart Association's guidelines for advanced cardiac life support by administering the drug atropine rather than epinephrine. In response, the defendant said that the AHA guidelines are not mandatory and may be altered by the physician. In this case, the court affirmed the lower court's ruling of summary judgment in favor of the defendant and, thus, did not see the general AHA guidelines as more significant or persuasive than the particular facts of the case.[32] Of special interest is a case alleging a failure to diagnose breast cancer, in which the claimant sought admissibility of a physician malpractice carrier's risk management guidelines for breast cancer. The court refused to admit the guidelines on the basis that they were promulgated by a private insurance company as part of an insurance contract, and did not represent standard medical practice.[33]

---

31 *Washington v Washington Hospital Center*, 579 A 2d 177 (DC1990).
32 *Lowry v Henry Mayo Newhall Memorial Hospital*, 229 Cal Rptr 620 (1986).
33 *Quigley v Jobe*, 851 P 2d 236 (Colo Ct App 1992).

CPGs used as a shield

A 1997 case of first impression in the Court of Appeals of Tennessee rested solely on the propriety of giving to the jury during its deliberations a CPG which had not formally been admitted on the evidence before the jury retired.[34] A cardiologist failed to admit the patient into the hospital despite the fact that the claimant exhibited significant chest pain symptoms during a treadmill ECG test. He died after arriving back at home. The defendant's attorney cross-examined the claimant's expert regarding the parameters on the interpretation of treadmill tests issued by the American College of Cardiology and American Heart Association, 'Exercise Test Parameters Associated With Poor Prognosis and/or Increased Severity of CAD'. Other defence experts testified that the CPG represented the recognised standard of care. The court ruled that the CPG was admissible because two of the three experts testified that it represented the standard of care, and the court upheld the jury's verdict in favour of the defendant physician. The concurring opinion underscored the importance of CPGs in litigation, extolling the potential benefits in assisting courts, yet cautioning that they should not be given conclusive weight as the standard of care.

The Hyams study identified six cases in which defendants successfully used guidelines and standards to show that there was no breach of their duty of care. However, the article cogently points out that a search of the case law is unreliable in determining the actual extent to which guidelines exceed in being used as a shield because of the influential role they can play in pre-trial negotiation and activities.

CPGs rejected as a shield

Many courts acknowledge that guidelines are relevant and admissible on the issue of whether or not a breach of duty has occurred but, with the exception of Maine (*supra*), do not regard compliance with a guideline as necessarily exculpating, or failure to comply with a guideline necessarily inculpating. CPGs are therefore just one source of information which will be considered together with many other sources, such as expert testimony, drug package inserts, manufacturer instructions, accreditation standards, the hospital's own policies and procedures, and other 'voluntary' standards.[35] This is obviously different from CPGs, which by a statute or regulation that has the force of law make a particular practice mandatory. In the courts of states which do not treat CPGs as legally mandatory, CPGs function much like expert testimony in that they help to inform the court about the nature of existing practice. The

---

34 *Frakes v Cardiology Consultants* (1997) Tenn App LEXIS 597, fn 26, above.

35 *Denton Regional Medical Center v Lacroix*, 947 SW 2d 941 (Tex App 1997).

guidelines are not evidence *per se* nor are they binding on the fact finder, but they shed light on existing or customary practice. Unlike the Maine project practice guidelines, the claimant would not be prohibited from introducing a CPG into evidence in a medical malpractice case – that is, it could be used offensively and well as defensively. And unlike the Maine project, privately promulgated CPGs would not be binding on courts; however, they might be useful in providing courts with professional consensus and thus reduce their reliance on potentially partisan expert testimony.

COMPETING OR CONFLICTING CPGS

As noted earlier, CPGs are issued by a variety of organisations. Sometimes, one type of medical condition or treatment is the subject of guidelines issued by many organisations, with significant differences in approach. This is illustrated on the NGC website feature called 'Guideline Syntheses', which provides comparative analysis of competing and/or conflicting guidelines. For example, the guideline synthesis on *Screening for Colorectal Cancer*, points out differences between the specific types of screening tests that are recommended in the CPGs issued by three different organisations. This suggests that one defence to a CPG 'sword' would be to raise another CPG that conflicts with the one raised by the claimant. A 1992 case involved conflicting guidelines on mammography screening: the recommendations of the American Cancer Society were raised by the claimant's expert witness, and those of the American College of Obstetricians and Gynaecologists were raised by the physician-defendant's expert witness. The court permitted the use of the ACOG guidelines as a shield based on the two schools of thought doctrine, which acknowledges that competent medical authority may differ, and a physician should not be held responsible for the exercise of judgment that is based on the view of a considerable number of recognised and respected professionals.[36]

CPGS AS A FLOOR

Even if a defendant provider can show that he complied with the CPG, the claimant can argue that the CPG represents a minimum standard of care, and that care and treatment beyond the minimal is necessary in order to comply with the applicable standard of care. In such circumstances the CPG establishes a floor for acceptable professional practice – it defines what courts regard as necessary, but not necessarily sufficient under the circumstances. A

---

36 *Levine v Rosen*, 616 A 2d 623 (Pa 1992).

CPG in such circumstances will generally condemn substandard care, but unlike the Maine guidelines, would not necessarily absolve a defendant of liability. This rationale applied in an obstetrical malpractice case alleging that a failure to monitor during labour resulted in the child's death. On appeal from a directed verdict in favour of the obstetrician, the claimant's expert conceded that there was no violation of the standards of care issued by the American College of Obstetricians and Gynaecologists, but that the care was nevertheless negligent because ACOG standards 'are the minimal accepted standards for his specialty'. The court accepted this approach and sent the case back to the jury to determine negligence.[37]

COMPLIANCE WITH CPG DOES NOT NECESSARILY EXCULPATE

Judicial deference to customary medical practice is not absolute. An extreme example of a court rejecting a customary practice standard is found in the controversial case of *Helling v Carey*[38] in which the claimant appealed from a judgment in favour of an ophthalmologist, arguing that the trial court erred in failing to instruct the jury that adherence to the widely acceptable medical custom of not giving routine glaucoma pressure tests to persons under the age of 40 was not determinative of reasonableness. The claimant argued that the customary standards *themselves* were inadequate and thus unreasonable. The Washington Supreme Court found in favour of the claimant. The court held that even though the defendant ophthalmologists had complied with the professional standard, they still would be held negligent because 'as a matter of law, that the reasonable standard of care that should have been followed under the undisputed facts of this case was the timely giving of this simple, harmless pressure test'. This is one of the very few cases in which a court has refused to be bound by what the profession itself believes to be appropriate.

Most US courts reject the Washington court's approach of establishing a standard of care as a matter of law, but the case demonstrates that compliance with a widely endorsed CPG will not necessarily exculpate. It is trite law that industry custom is not necessarily determinative of the standard of care: a claimant can thus argue that the customary standard is itself negligent or unreasonable. This would support an approach in which courts looked at a clinical practice guideline as providing some evidence of the applicable standard of care, although not absolute evidence. What is customary is not necessarily what is reasonable. Indeed, an entire industry may be seen as

---

37 *Jewett v Our Lady of Mercy Hospital*, 82 Ohio App 3d 428; 612 NE2d 724 (Ohio 1992); 1992 Ohio App LEXIS 19.
38 519 P 2d 981 (Wash 1974).

acting below a reasonable standard of care. It is interesting to note that some attorneys have used the tactic of labelling a clinical guideline issued by a medical specialty society as less than credible evidence because it is self-serving to the physician members of the society.

CPG DEVELOPMENT PROCESS INADEQUATE

A claimant or defendant could impeach the credibility or authority of a CPG by demonstrating that the process used to develop a CPG was ineffective and should therefore preclude its use in court as a standard of care. This raises interesting notions of what criteria should be used to measure the appropriateness of a CPG, such as evidence-based research, expert review, updating, etc. The NGC has developed minimal inclusion criteria that CPGs must meet in order to participate in NGC, and attorneys may argue that these constitute minimal requirements for admission into evidence in a medical malpractice case. Such criteria could be said to be the minimum required to establish the authority (and therefore the admissibility at trial of CPGs), in much the same way that expert witnesses themselves must meet certain requirements in order to render an admissible opinion in a malpractice case. The use of such criteria would also encourage a policy that aims to reduce the use of 'junk science', and would assist judges in determining whether science meets the *Daubert* test.

THE RISK MANAGEMENT VALUE OF CPGS

A variation of the Hyams study approach was performed in 1997 by the Physician Insurers Association of America (PIAA) and the American College of Radiology (ACR). Twenty-eight malpractice insurance carriers participated in the Practice Standards Claim Survey by evaluating claims experience since the inception of practice standards issued by the American College of Radiology. Questionnaires were designed to examine the claims and suits that specifically related to selected ACR standards, such as mammography, adult barium enema examinations, antipartum obstetrical ultrasound, and communication. The ACR's Medical Legal Committee had identified these standards as being most frequently in issue in litigation. The study did not look at the role of practice guidelines in malpractice litigation, but rather at the frequency and severity of those malpractice claims which related specifically to departures from published standards – even if these standards were not specifically noted in the report of litigation. Nevertheless, the ACR standard on communication was specifically referred to in many claims. The communication standard requires generation of a written report after any examination or procedure. In the 20 claims in which the standard was a factor, it was asserted by the claimant 13 times but was successfully asserted in only four claims.

In a commentary on the ACR/PIAA claims survey, the authors concluded that if the four ACR standards had been followed in the claims reviewed, significantly fewer litigation problems would have ensued. That is, the standards can be used as effective risk management tools to avoid patient injuries as well as malpractice actions.[39]

CONCLUSION

Whether CPGs will play a significant role in simplifying the current messy and uncertain US medical malpractice litigation system is unknown. None of the state-based demonstration projects has yielded enough experience to conclude that the use of CPGs as an affirmative defence can accomplish such a heroic task, and court approaches are too varied and infrequent to glean a clear message. Some argue that a 'battle of the guidelines' would be just as messy as the 'battle of the experts' is in determining the standard of care. One author has attempted to explain that CPGs will never be universally or even substantially decisive in the day-to-day practice of actual malpractice cases because there is a fundamental mismatch in orientation. He points out that the rationale behind, and the scientific underpinnings of, CPGs conflict with the rationale and goals underpinning the legal concept of proximate cause: clinical decision-making is inherently prospective in orientation, that is, it relates to the probability of injury occurring in the future based upon action that is taken. This is in direct conflict with legal concepts applied in medical malpractice cases in which courts retrospectively review a specific injury sustained by a particular individual. Scientific constructs of probabilistic association do not easily meld into the legal framework of proximate causation.[40]

39 Branner, RJ, Lucey, L, Smith, J and Saunders, R, 'Radiology and medical malpractice claims: a report on the Practice Standards Claim Survey of the Physicians' Insurers Association of America and the American College of Radiology' AJR: 171, July 1998: 19:22.

40 Matthews, JR, 'Practice guidelines and tort reform: the legal system confronts the technocratic wish' (April 1999) 24 J of Health Politics, Policy and Law 2: 275–3 4.

CHAPTER 10

CLINICAL GUIDELINES: HEALTHCARE RATIONING AND ACCOUNTABILITY FOR REASONABLENESS

OF Norheim

SYNOPSIS

The chapter starts by explaining the somewhat unfamiliar idea of guidelines as tools for rationing. Healthcare rationing is an issue being increasingly discussed within the field of ethical theory. The conflict between the rights of individuals, clinical autonomy and the recommendations given by guidelines is illustrated by a clinical example: the case of guidelines for reducing the risks of cardiovascular disease. Such guidelines have the potential for improving practice and saving lives, but current guidelines typically also exclude some patient groups from such benefits. Next, the ethical implications of implementing coverage exclusions through clinical guidelines are examined. Coverage exclusions might violate some fundamental principles of medical ethics and health law. In particular, coverage exclusions limit personal autonomy (for the patient), clinical autonomy (for the health carer), and they might be in conflict with rights to health care, either seen as moral or legal rights as enacted in many countries' healthcare laws. Next, the chapter includes a broader perspective. From the perspective of distributive justice – within systems with an acknowledged obligation to provide universal access to healthcare for all its citizens (such as the NHS) – exclusion of marginal benefits may be required in order to secure access to more important services for others. From this perspective, rationing might be seen as fair, even if this implies some infringements of individual autonomy and rights. The challenge is how to evaluate practices from a normative and political perspective: the use of guidelines as rationing tools must exclude only benefits of very low priority – and such practices must be perceived as fair by the general public. This raises the issues of legitimacy and accountability. The ethical framework of Accountability for Reasonableness, developed by Norman Daniels and James Sabin, is explained in detail, and its relevance for guidelines is outlined. Finally, the practical implications of applying this ethical framework for the design and development of practice policies are illustrated with reference to the work of the National Institute for Clinical Excellence (NICE). It is argued that guidelines used as tools for excluding marginally beneficial treatment are only legitimate if the criteria for exclusion are made explicit, reasons for exclusion are given, and a reasonable and transparent process decides the threshold of exclusion.

Clinical guidelines are designed to reduce inappropriate clinical practice.[1] Clinical guidelines can also be seen as tools for rationing.[2] Guidelines advise on the appropriate selection criteria for identifying those patients that can benefit most from an intervention, whether it is a diagnostic procedure or some form of treatment. The flip side of the coin is that they also can be used to exclude individual patients for which only a small benefit can be expected. The chapter explores the problems associated with this potential implication of the use of guidelines, and in addition argues that they can be used for improving the rationing process itself towards a goal of fair and ethically acceptable rationing. This can be achieved if the criteria for exclusion are made explicit, reasons for exclusion are given, and a reasonable and transparent process decides the threshold of exclusion. Achieving such a goal is formidable because the practice of rationing involves so many stakeholders and often conflicting and competing demands. Even an institution as theoretically powerful as NICE is likely to move only very slowly towards such a goal.

Norman Daniels and James Sabin have recently developed 'Accountability for Reasonableness', an ethical framework for assessing rationing procedures.[3] This framework has been applied to assess coverage exclusions by institutions such as managed care organisations in the US,[4] public agencies in Canada,[5] and most recently, decisions made by such institutions as NICE.[6] Healthcare rationing is an issue being increasingly discussed within the field of ethical theory.[7] Building upon this framework, this chapter argues that

1   Hayward, RS, Wilson, MC, Tunis, SR, Bass EB and Guyatt, G, 'Users' guides to the medical literature: VIII. How to use clinical practice guidelines: A. Are the recommendations valid?', The Evidence-Based Medicine Working Group (1995) 274(7) JAMA 570–74. Naylor, CD and Guyatt, GH, 'Users' guides to the medical literature: X. How to use an article reporting variations in the outcomes of health services', The Evidence-Based Medicine Working Group (1996) 275(7) JAMA 554–58. Wilson, MC, Hayward, RS, Tunis, SR, Bass, EB and Guyatt, G, 'Users' guides to the Medical Literature: VIII. How to use clinical practice guidelines: B. What are the recommendations and will they help you in caring for your patients?', The Evidence-Based Medicine Working Group (1995) 274(20) JAMA 1630–32.

2   Norheim, OF, 'Healthcare rationing – are additional criteria needed for assessing evidence based clinical practice guidelines?' (1999) 319 BMJ 1426–29.

3   Daniels, N and Sabin, J, 'Closure, fair procedures, and setting limits within managed care organizations' (1998) 46(3) J Am Geriatr Soc 351–54. Daniels, N and Sabin, J, 'Last chance therapies and managed care. Pluralism, fair procedures, and legitimacy' (1998) 28(2) Hastings Center Rep 27–41. Daniels, N and Sabin, J, 'Limits to health care: fair procedures, democratic deliberation, and the legitimacy problem for insurers' (1997)(4) Philosophy & Public Affairs 303–50.

4   Daniels, N and Sabin, J, 'Limits to health care: fair procedures, democratic deliberation, and the legitimacy problem for insurers'(1997)(4) Philosophy & Public Affairs 303–50.

5   Singer, P, Martin, D, Giacomini, M and Purdy, L, 'Priority setting for new technologies in medicine: qualitative case study' (2000) 321 BMJ 1316–18.

6   International study on priority setting. Reports to be published (2001) in a collection of articles edited by Chris Ham (OUP).

7   McKneally, M, Dickens, B, Meslin, E and Singer, P, 'Bioethics for clinicians: 13. Resource allocation' (1997) 157 CMAJ 163–67.

Accountability for Reasonableness provides a promising framework for assessing and improving the development of guidelines as rationing tools.

SECTION 1:
CLINICAL GUIDELINES
AS TOOLS FOR RATIONING

It is now widely recognised that most health care systems are rationing potentially beneficial health care by more or less explicit mechanisms.[8] To see the intricate relation between rationing and clinical practice guidelines, it is useful to distinguish between the levels of decision-making. Levels of resource allocation involve, according to Klein, decisions about:

(a) the size of the *total budget*;

(b) the allocation of *resources* to broad sectors or client groups;

(c) the allocation of *resources* to specific forms of organisational provision and treatment within such broad categories;

(d) the priority to be given to particular types of *patients* when determining access to the available services and facilities; and finally

(e) the *level of service* to be provided to individual patients once access has been achieved.[9]

Clinical practice guidelines aim to describe the content, quality and terms of access for the management of a particular condition. They can thus be seen as 'precise' recommendations for rationing at the 'meso-level' of decision-making, answering such questions as: What medical and personal characteristics identify the type of patients that should have access to a particular treatment, service or facility? What level of service should be provided, once the person is selected for the service?[10] The development of guidelines could be seen as the formalisation of the informal rules defining access to and exclusion from health services.[11] The use of formal and informal clinical 'indications' for referral, investigation and prescription, is probably one of the most influential mechanisms of cost containment and rationing.

Practice policies or clinical guidelines can be thought of as 'generic decisions – recommendations intended for a collection of patients rather than

8   Ham, C (editorial), 'Health care rationing' (1995) 310 BMJ 1483–84. Mechanic, D, 'Dilemmas in rationing health care services: the case for implicit rationing' (1995) 310 BMJ 1655–59.

9   Klein, R, 'Rationality and rationing: diffused or concentrated decision-making?', in Tunbridge, T (ed), *Rationing of Health Care in Medicine*, 1993, London: Royal College of Physicians of London, pp 73–82.

10   *Ibid*.

11   Mechanic, D, 'Dilemmas in rationing health care services: the case for implicit rationing' (1995) 310 BMJ 1655–59.

for a single patient'.[12] Sackett and his colleagues define clinical practice guidelines as 'user-friendly statements' for a collection of patients, based on the best external evidence.[13] Eddy defines a clinical practice policy as follows:

> [T]he purpose of a practice policy is to modify the behaviour of practitioners to steer their decisions toward actions that the policy-makers consider desirable.[14]

This definition introduces other and legitimate stakeholders in the development of guidelines. It goes without saying that there are conflicting views about what actions are desirable among them.

Grimshaw and Hutchinson argue directly that guidelines should play a role in the rationing process:

> Since the rationing of scarce resources requires a targeting of those resources to obtain best value for money, it is important to have mechanisms for assuring effective health care. Clinical practice guidelines offer an opportunity for introducing evidence-based health care into local practice and for influencing the commissioning of effective health care.[15]

The goal of effective service-provision can be achieved, the authors argue, by evidence-based clinical practice guidelines used as tools for rationing. The problem is that guidelines might end up as instruments for unjustified and covert rationing disguised as expert recommendations.

SECTION 2: CLINICAL EXAMPLE: PREVENTIVE CARDIOLOGY

This article defines rationing as the withholding of potentially beneficial healthcare through financial or organisational features of the healthcare system in question. The definition is broad enough to encompass the view that withholding of treatment perceived to be beneficial should be seen as a question of rationing. Even when the methods of evidence-based medicine are applied, there remain abundant grey zones with uncertain indications for treatment.[16] Setting limits within this area should not be separated from the issue of rationing. It is in these grey zones of decision-making that clinical

---

12 Eddy, DM, 'Clinical decision making: from theory to practice. Designing a practice policy. Standards, guidelines, and options' (1990) 263 JAMA 3077, 3081, 3084.

13 Sackett, DL, Richardson, WS, Rosenberg, W and Haynes, RB, *Evidence-based Medicine. How to Practice and Teach EBM*, 1997, New York: Churchill Livingstone.

14 Eddy, DM, 'Clinical decision making: from theory to practice. Guidelines for policy statements: the explicit approach' (1990) 263 JAMA 2239–40, 2243.

15 Grimshaw, JM and Hutchinson, A, 'Clinical practice guidelines – do they enhance value for money in health care?' (1995) 51(4) Br Med Bull 927–40.

16 Naylor, CD, 'Grey zones of clinical practice: some limits to evidence-based medicine' (1995) 345(8953) The Lancet 840–42.

guidelines have the potential of changing the pattern of practice and shift resource allocation in a more or less just direction.

Consider the following example. A general practitioner is examining a 60-year-old male non-smoking patient with no previous indications of a cardiovascular disease. After repeated testing, the practitioner has found that the patient has several risk factors for cardiovascular disease in the future. The systolic blood pressure is 158 mmHg, the total serum cholesterol level is 7.0 mmol/l, HDL cholesterol is 2 mmol/l, the serum glucose level is normal and the electrocardiogram shows no sign of left ventricular hypertrophy. Amongst this information are several commonly acknowledged predicators of future risk.

The practitioner knows that the most recent clinical guidelines recommend that the appropriate choice of treatment should be chosen according to the patient's total risk. He uses one of the software programs that are in use for the calculation of total risk for a cardiovascular event. These programs are based on rigorous research into known risk factors. He estimates the 5-year total risk for a cardiovascular event to be about 9–10%. Next he consults a clinical guideline, the Joint British Recommendations for the appropriate treatment of coronary disease,[17] assuming that proper preventive measures, in addition to advice on lifestyle changes, could include some anti-hypertensive drug, and probably also a cholesterol-lowering drug. He then realises, however, that the guideline – authorised and recommended in his practice by the primary care group he belongs to – advises that medical treatment should only be prescribed for patients with 5-year total cardiovascular risk of above 10% (equivalent to 10-year risk of 20%). This is explicitly stated in the recommendations:

> High risk individuals are defined as those whose 10 year risk of coronary heart disease exceeds 15% (*equivalent to a cardiovascular risk of 20% over the same period*). As a minimum, those at highest risk (30%); ... should be targeted and treated now, and as resources allow others with a risk of >15% ... should be progressively targeted. (Emphasis added.)[18]

What to do with patients with a cardiovascular risk of less then 10% is not mentioned explicitly, but standard guidance is to suggest non-medical measures such as diet and lifestyle changes. Note that no explicit reasons for setting this threshold are mentioned, but available 'resources' are alluded to indirectly.

Leaving this clinical scenario for a moment, it should also be noted that this threshold is recommended in several recent guidelines in various

---

17 British Cardiac Society, British Hyperlipidaemia Association, British Hypertension Society, Association BD, 'Joint British recommendations on prevention of coronary heart disease in clinical practice: summary' (2000) 320 BMJ 705–08.

18 In the following the threshold of 10% five-year risk for cardiovascular disease is used as reference point. Observe that this is different from the risk of coronary heart disease (excluding stroke).

countries.[19] The underlying reasons might be, to frame them in the language of rationing, that the benefits of medical interventions for low-risk patients are low compared to the cost. It can be calculated (see below) that the benefit assessed in terms of the absolute risk reduction (ARR) over five years, is about 3.2%. This means that the number of patients needed to avoid one cardiovascular event is 31 (the inverse of ARR). The costs of treating everyone with drugs for risk levels below 10%, in terms of NHS economic resources and use of personnel time, have been shown to be significant. Prevention with drugs for low-risk patients is simply not cost-effective.

In general terms, this underlying reasoning can be described by referring to the well-known law of diminishing returns.

Figure 10.1: The law of diminishing returns

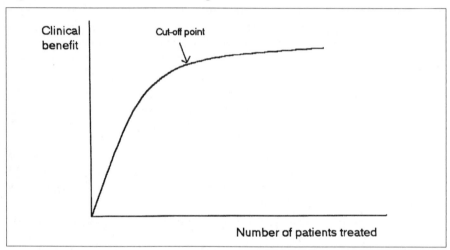

The figure can be read as follows. The x-axis shows number of patients treated. Assume that patients are ranked according to absolute risk for a cardiovascular event, so that those with highest risks are to the left, and that the patients with lowest risk are to the right. The y-axis shows the magnitude of clinical benefit (say, total number of cardiovascular events averted). The curve is a function of number of patients treated. The first patients treated will add more clinical benefits to the total, while including patients with low risk will add only marginal benefits. By setting a cut-off at 10% 5-year absolute total risk (as indicated by the arrow), only those to the left of that threshold will be treated. Including more patients (moving the cut-off point to the right) will add some benefit, but only marginally so.

In a population of patients with risk for cardiovascular disease; some have high risks, others have lower risks. By treating high-risk patients, large

---

19 Jackson, R, 'Guidelines on preventing cardiovascular disease in clinical practice' (2000) 320(7236) BMJ 659–61.

benefits are gained. By treating low-risk patients, only marginal additional benefits are gained. Setting a cut-off at, say 10% of ARR over five years will ensure that those with highest benefits will be helped. Including more patients will be costly, and the returns (measured as clinical benefit) will diminish. This is elementary economic reasoning and a standard argument within the theory of healthcare rationing.[20]

If the cut-off point discussed above expresses a practice policy endorsed by the NHS, one needs to assess whether the threshold set in the guidelines is fair and acceptable to the public. Why exactly 10%? And what are the reasons for rationing this intervention? As discussed above, the reasons might be given with reference to some notion of distributive justice. But before turning to principles of distributive justice, the practice of coverage exclusion through guidelines must be considered with respect to other ethical principles.

SECTION 3: HEALTHCARE RATIONING AND ETHICS

Coverage exclusions might violate some fundamental principles of medical ethics.[21] First, coverage exclusions limit personal autonomy for the patient. Let us return to the patient in our clinical scenario. In the case of preventive cardiology, there is evidence available showing that medical intervention for low-risk patients is also beneficial (the WOSCOP study). The patient in our clinical scenario might prefer to have an intervention with a five-year risk reduction of 3.2% than no treatment at all. If the doctor fails to mention this possible benefit, and not offer the choice to the patient, this could be seen to be a problematic departure from the ideals of patient autonomy and shared decision-making. British citizens tend to expect that the NHS provides all interventions that are proven to be effective. At least, they generally expect to be informed about this form of coverage exclusion. Failing to take this consideration seriously would be insensitive to traditional professional ethics endorsed by most medical associations. Good reasons are needed to depart from the patient's right to choose the level of beneficial care.

Secondly, coverage exclusions limit clinical autonomy for the health carer. Should practitioners not recommend and prescribe medical treatment with a proven benefit to the patient? Some practitioners might prefer to inform the patient and leave the choice to him, deviating deliberately from the recommendations in the guidelines. They could choose to be their patients' 'advocates'. Or they could choose the role as 'gate-keeper' and act with the concerns of the common good in mind. The question remains, therefore, what status the recommendations given in the Joint British Recommendations have.

---

20 Drummond, M, Stoddart, G and Torrance, G, *Methods for the Economic Evaluation of Health Care Programmes*, 1987/97, Oxford: OUP.
21 Beauchamp, TL and Childress, JF, *Principles of Biomedical Ethics*, 2nd edn, 1983, New York: OUP.

Do they express a practice policy endorsed by the NHS? Should the reasons for setting the threshold high be given in the guideline, so that doctors have an informed choice of what role to adopt? And should the reasons be given to the patient?

Thirdly, coverage exclusions might be in conflict with rights to health care, either seen as moral rights or as legal rights as enacted in many countries' healthcare laws. Space does not allow going into this difficult issue here, but two points should be noted. Healthcare rights involve both to be informed about the options available for treatment (in order to make informed choice), and the substantial right to health care itself.

In the latter case, healthcare rights in many countries prohibit discrimination on the basis of race, ethnicity, place of origin, religion, age, sex, social status, sexual orientation and physical or mental disability. This should be seen as unjustified discrimination or inequality before the law. In addition, many countries have formulated general rights to 'appropriate' or 'necessary' care. In some countries, the legal system is gradually developing precedents for the proper interpretation of such notions as appropriate or necessary care. In other countries, the courts have been reluctant to specify the appropriate level of care, leaving the final decisions to the medical system itself. It therefore remains an open question whether the patient in our clinical scenario could invoke the right to health care in order to claim treatment below the risk level given in the Joint British Recommendations.

The right to information is firmly established in medical ethics.[22] In most jurisdictions it is also, to some degree, established in law (particularly firmly in relation to information which must be disclosed in order to render consent to treatment valid). To be informed about potentially beneficial treatment (even if the value of this treatment is considered low by some) is a precondition for individual choice.

Summing up, the kind of recommendations discussed in the clinical example might imply coverage exclusions that clearly limit patient autonomy and clinical autonomy. This should be recognised, but need not render the coverage exclusions ethically unacceptable. This is so because in medical ethics there are also other principles that need to be balanced against the principle of autonomy. The issue of distributive justice is of particular importance here, especially in public healthcare systems such as the NHS. Principles of distributive justice order claims or rights for groups of individuals. If there is a limited amount of resources available for the distribution of health benefits, some claims might end up not being satisfied. Resource scarcity therefore introduces the need for recognising the limits to individual (and clinical) autonomy. In a setting with competing interests, the

22 McKneally, M, Dickens, B, Meslin, E and Singer, P, 'Bioethics for clinicians: 13. Resource allocation' (1997) 157 CMAJ 163–67.

claims from one patient must be compared to other patients. The right to autonomous choice of treatment (when treatment is financed from a common 'pool' of resources) holds only insofar as this right does not limit other people's rights. Within this perspective it would be unethical not to take a broader set of patients into account. Society ultimately has to make an ethical judgment as to whether limited resources should be deployed helping people at a small risk of cardiovascular disease, or in helping (for example) people at the relatively higher risk of mental illness.

The next section turns to principles of distributive justice, and examines how these principles might order the strength of claims from different individuals with competing needs. It should be noted, however, that no principles of distributive justice allow that individuals are denied effective treatment without being informed and without being given a justification for such a decision (see section 5).

SECTION 4: DISTRIBUTIVE JUSTICE

Principles of distributive justice order claims or rights for groups of individuals. Bill New, on behalf of the Rationing Agenda Group in UK, has reviewed a large literature on theories and approaches to healthcare rationing. Among the topics he considered was how to describe the characteristics of people which are candidates for discriminating between competing claims for resources. He said:

> It is ... possible to outline criteria – all based in some way on characteristics of people (including the effects of health care interventions on them) – which are generally considered to be candidates for discriminating between competing claims for resources. ... The NHS can concentrate on improving the health of the following possible groups:
>
> The whole population as much as possible (based on cost effectiveness measures)
>
> People most in need – those with the greatest illness or ill health deficit (for example, triage)
>
> Particular disadvantaged groups (for example, ethnic minority communities)
>
> People on whom others depend (for example, those with dependent children)
>
> People whose contribution to society is highly valued (for example, an eminent scientist)
>
> People who 'deserve' it (for example, those who avoid unhealthy lifestyles)
>
> People who have been waiting the longest
>
> Particular age groups (for example, people who have most of their lives still before them)

Which of these criteria (and the objectives with which they are associated) are ethically defensible and which are not? Can we assign weights to those that are defensible?[23]

Needless to say, some of these suggestions reveal the controversial aspects of developing proper criteria and general principles ordering the criteria. New concludes that, as for now, there is no consensus on these principles.

Earlier developments in medical ethics have focused on finding general principles for selecting appropriate claims and resolving the conflicts between such appropriate but competing claims for resources. One such account is Norman Daniels' 'fair equality of opportunity' approach.[24] The idea is that health is an all-purpose substantial good that is a necessary condition for achieving fair equality of opportunities to develop, form and revise a rational life plan. Disease, defined as departure from art-specific normal functioning, restricts the range of opportunities open to an individual. Health care that can maintain or improve health-related opportunities should thus be distributed equally.

Another principled approach derives from the ethical framework of consequentialism in general and utilitarianism in particular. Various variants are found in the literature on healthcare rationing, but in its general form the principle of utility maximisation is recommended for resolving the conflicts between competing claims for resources.[25] Utility can be defined in terms of, for example, Disability Adjusted Life Years or Quality Adjusted Life Years.[26] This approach can be operationalised into the principle of giving highest priority to interventions with the best cost-utility ratio (where utility can be measured as, for example, QALYs).

23 New, B, 'The rationing agenda in the NHS. Rationing Agenda Group' (1996) 312(7046) BMJ 1593–601.

24 Daniels, N, *Just Health Care: Studies in Philosophy and Health Policy*, 1985, New York: CUP. Daniels, N, 'Principles for national health care reform' (1994) 24 Hastings Center Rep 8–9. Daniels, N, 'Four unsolved rationing problems. A challenge' (1994) 24(4) Hastings Center Rep 27–29.

25 Broome, J, 'QALYs' (1993) 50 J of Public Economics 149–67. Gerard, K and Mooney, G, *QALY League Tables. Handle with Care*, 2nd edn, 1993. Mooney, G and Olsen, JA, 'QALYs. Where next?', in McGurie, A *et al* (eds), *Providing Health Care. The Economics of Alternative Systems of Finance and Delivery*, 1991, Oxford: OUP. Wagstaff, A, 'QALYs and the equity-efficiency trade-off' (1991) 10 J of Health Economics 21–41. Williams, A, 'QALYS and ethics: a health economist's perspective' (1996) 43(12) Soc Sci Med 1795–804. Nord, E, 'The QALY – a measure of social value rather than individual utility?' (1994) 3(2) Health Econ 89–93. Cubbon, J, 'The principle of QALY maximisation as the basis for allocating health care' (1991) 17 J of Medical Ethics 181. Nord, E, Pinto, JL, Richardson, J, Menzel, P and Ubel, P, 'Incorporating societal concerns for fairness in numerical valuations of health programmes' (1999) 8(1) Health Econ 25–39. Singer, P, McKie, J, Kuhse, H and Richardson, J, 'Double jeopardy and the use of QALYs in health care allocation' (Review) (1995) 21 J of Med Ethics 144–50.

26 Williams, A, 'Economics of coronary artery bypass grafting' (1985) 291 BMJ 326–29.

Recent debates on healthcare rationing have increasingly acknowledged the difficulties, observed by New, involved in this task of developing criteria for priority setting. In empirical studies, strong disagreement about the proper principles for priority setting has been found.[27] At a theoretical level, the ethical justifications for the different principles are also diverging, and no consensus on acceptable first principles has developed.

Daniels suggests there are four problems or cluster of problems that current theories have failed to address directly and adequately:

> Faced with limited resources, medical providers and planners often ask bioethicists how to limit or ration the delivery of beneficial services in a fair or just way. What advice should we give them? To focus our thinking on the problem they face, I offer a friendly challenge to the field: solve the four rationing problems described here.[28]

These rationing dilemmas are:

(a) The best-outcome problem: how much should we favour producing the best outcome with our limited resources?

(b) The priorities problem: how much priority should we give to treating the sickest or most disabled patients?

(c) The aggregation problem: when should we allow an aggregation of modest benefits to larger numbers of people to outweigh more significant benefits to fewer people?

(d) The democracy problem: when must we rely on a fair and democratic process as the only way to determine what constitutes a fair rationing outcome?

Daniels (and others) have concluded that it is hard to find principles that can guide us in solving these rationing dilemmas.[29] Instead, he argues that decision-makers must turn to fair processes:

> In pluralist societies we are likely to find reasonable disagreement about principles that should govern priority setting. For example, some will want to

---

27 Nord, E, Pinto, JL, Richardson, J, Menzel, P and Ubel, P, 'Incorporating societal concerns for fairness in numerical valuations of health programmes' (1999) 8(1) Health Econ 25–39. Nord, E, Richardson, J, Street, A, Kuhse, H and Singer, P, 'Maximizing health benefits vs egalitarianism: an Australian survey of health issues' (1995) 41(10) Soc Sci Med 1429–37.

28 Daniels, N, 'Four unsolved rationing problems. A challenge' (1994) 24(4) Hastings Center Rep 27–29.

29 *Ibid*. Singer, P, Martin, D, Giacomini, M and Purdy, L, 'Priority setting for new technologies in medicine: qualitative case study' (2000) 321 BMJ 1316–18. McKneally, M, Dickens, B, Meslin, E and Singer, P, 'Bioethics for clinicians: 13. Resource allocation' (1997) 157 CMAJ 163–67. Daniels, N and Sabin, JE, 'The yin and yang of health care system reform. Professional and political strategies for setting limits' (1995) 4 Archives of Family Medicine 67–71. Daniels, N, Light, D and Caplan, RL, *Benchmarks of Fairness for Health Care Reform*, 1996, New York: OUP. Holm, S, 'The second phase of priority setting. Goodbye to the simple solutions: the second phase of priority setting in health care' (1998) 317(7164) BMJ 1000–02.

give more priority to the worst off, some less; some will be willing to aggregate benefits in ways that others are not. In the absence of consensus on principles, a fair process allows us to agree on what is legitimate and fair.[30]

Although this debate in medical ethics indicates that there is no overarching theory of justice to balance competing claims, it should be noted that there are some reasons for rationing that every theory of resource allocation in health care would accept.

For example, most theories of distributive justice in healthcare focus on a specific set of information. Based on recent literature on principles for priority setting,[31] there emerges an overlapping consensus on a minimal information set. This set can form a basis of developing relevant reasons for rationing. Accordingly, the priority of a given condition and its intervention should be assessed in terms of:

1   The burden of disease, if untreated

2   The benefit from the intervention

3   Treatment costs

4   The quality of evidence on 1–3

This information can in particular cases be formulated in terms of characteristics of the patient and the condition and treatment in question. There is general consensus that individual characteristics such as race, ethnicity, place of origin, religion, age, sex, social status, sexual orientation and physical or mental disability should be irrelevant in devising rationing criteria.[32]

Building upon the consensus on what kind of information is necessary to assign priorities and what information is considered normatively irrelevant, one could focus on low-level principles and criteria which everyone could have reasons to accept, despite disagreement over first, or mid-level principles.[33] A possible list, then, of reasons for rationing in particular cases could be the following:

•   The burden of disease, if untreated, is not important enough.

•   The expected benefit from treatment is not important enough.

30   Daniels, N, 'Accountability for reasonableness' (2000) 321 BMJ 1300–01.

31   Ham, C, 'Synthesis: what can we learn from international experience?' (1995) 51(4) Br Med Bull 819–30. Ham, C and Locock, L, *International Approaches To Priority Setting In Health Care: An Annotated Listing Of Official And Semi-Official Publications. With A Selection Of Key Academic References*, 1998, Birmingham: University of Birmingham. Ham, C and Coulter, A, 'Where are we now?', in Coulter, A and Ham, C (eds), *The Global Challenge of Health Care Rationing*, 2000, London: OUP.

32   McKneally, M, Dickens, B, Meslin, E and Singer, P, 'Bioethics for clinicians: 13. Resource allocation' (1997) 157 CMAJ 163–67.

33   Scanlon, TM, 'Contractualism and utilitarianism', in Sen, AK and Williams, B (eds), *Utilitarianism and Beyond*, 1982, Cambridge: CUP, pp 103–28. Scanlon, TM, *What We Owe to Each Other*, 1998, Cambridge, Mass: The Belknap Press of Harvard UP.

- The costs are too high compared to the benefit.
- The costs can be born by the patient himself.
- Evidence is inconclusive.

By careful examination of the cases in question, such reasons can be explored and discussed; evidence can be consulted and thus make it possible to test evidence against arguments and against conflicting systems of norms.[34] These reasons for rationing are explored further in section 6.

It should be noted, however, that reasonable disagreement is to be expected also over the application of such criteria. How are they to be interpreted? What is important enough? Disagreement over the proper judgements on issues of this kind is precisely the reason for turning to fair procedures.

SECTION 5: ACCOUNTABILITY FOR REASONABLENESS

We are now able to tie the various strands of the argument together. Section 1 argued that clinical guidelines could be seen as tools for rationing. The clinical example examined in section 2 shows how, and section 3 explored the possible conflict between coverage exclusions through guidelines and the principles of autonomy. This conflict can be resolved by appeal to principles of distributive justice, and section 4 suggests some minimal criteria that could be used to order competing claims. This section turns to the question of legitimacy. When can we expect that coverage exclusions be perceived as fair and acceptable by all those affected by such a decision?[35]

It can be argued that the Joint British Recommendations for prevention of cardiovascular disease do not provide reasons for the threshold of exclusion. Why should doctors or patients comply with these thresholds? In the following, the framework of Accountability for Reasonableness is explained, and its application for the assessment of guidelines is outlined.

The framework is developed from the theory of deliberative democracy, that is, the idea that legitimate democracy issues from the public deliberation of citizens.[36] One important element in this theory is the idea of accountability

---

34 Klein, R, 'Dimensions of rationing: who should do what?' (1993) 307(6899) BMJ 309–11.

35 Daniels, N and Sabin, J, 'Closure, fair procedures, and setting limits within managed care organizations' (1998) 46(3) J Am Geriatr Soc 351–54.

36 *Ibid*. Eddy, DM, 'Clinical decision making: from theory to practice. Designing a practice policy. Standards, guidelines, and options' (1990) 263 JAMA 3077, 3081, 3084. New, B, 'The rationing agenda in the NHS', Rationing Agenda Group (1996) 312(7046) BMJ 1593–601. *Op cit*, Klein, fn 34. Elster, J (ed), *Deliberative Democracy*, 1998, Cambridge: CUP. Gutman, A and Thompson, D, *Democracy and Disagreement*, 1996, Cambridge, Mass: The Belknap Press of Harvard UP. Ezekiel, JE and Ezekiel, LL, 'What is Accountability in Health Care?' (1996) 124(2) Ann Intern Med 229–39.

for reasonableness. Rationing decisions satisfy the requirements of accountability if all relevant reasons for the decisions are given by those responsible for it to those who are affected by it.[37]

Daniels and Sabin have proposed four conditions that need to be met to ensure accountability for reasonableness:[38]

Publicity condition: decisions regarding coverage for new technologies (and other limit setting decisions) and their rationales must be publicly accessible.

Relevance condition: these rationales must rest on evidence, reasons, and principles that all fair minded parties (managers, clinicians, patients, and consumers in general) can agree are relevant to deciding how to meet the diverse needs of a covered population under necessary resource constraints.

Appeals condition: there is a mechanism for challenge and dispute resolution regarding limit setting decisions, including the opportunity for revising decisions in light of further evidence or arguments.

Enforcement condition: there is either voluntary or public regulation of the process to ensure that the first three conditions are met.

As mentioned in the Introduction, this framework has been used to assess coverage exclusions by institutions, such as managed care organisations, public agencies and clinical practitioners. If this framework should also be applied to assess clinical guidelines as rationing tools, several points need to be considered.

First, the publicity condition, that is, that decisions regarding coverage for new technologies should be accessible to the public, is met when a guideline is written and published. The second part of the condition, that is, that the rationales for coverage decisions must be publicly accessible is equally important. This requirement is not met for instance in the Joint British Recommendations. The threshold for exclusion is given without proper justification.

Secondly, the relevance condition states that these rationales must rest on evidence, reasons, and principles that all fair minded parties can agree are relevant to deciding how to meet the diverse needs of a covered population under necessary resource constraints. Building upon recent developments in medical ethics, the minimal reasons for rationing, stated at the end of section 4, could be seen as such relevant reasons.

Thirdly, the appeals condition is not straightforward in this context. It could apply both to the decisions concerning identified patients, and to the more general decision concerning the threshold for exclusion. In this context, the latter interpretation is most relevant. If precise coverage exclusions are

---

37 Gutman, A and Thompson, D, *Democracy and Disagreement*, 1996, Cambridge, Mass: The Belknap Press of Harvard UP.

38 *Op cit*, Daniels and Sabin, fn 35.

recommended by guidelines there should explicitly be a mechanism for challenge and dispute resolution regarding this choice, including the opportunity to revise decisions in light of further evidence or arguments.

Fourthly, institutions responsible for guideline development should regulate the process to ensure that the first three conditions are met. Until recently, no institution responsible for developing guidelines has regulated the process as suggested by this ethical framework. Summing up, one could conclude that if all four conditions are met, coverage exclusions through the use of clinical guidelines as rationing tools could be conceived as legitimate.

SECTION 6: IMPLICATIONS FOR DEVELOPING CLINICAL POLICIES

It is well established that the quality of guidelines varies, both with respect to the evidence they rest on, and the procedures used for their development. One of the most encouraging developments within this field is the establishment of NICE. NICE is part of the NHS, and its role is to provide patients, health professionals and the public with authoritative, robust and reliable guidance on current 'best practice' (www.nice.org.uk).

NICE plans to issue guidelines on several topics, and some are already published and disseminated. According to NICE's own definition:

Clinical Guidelines are produced to help health professionals and patients make the right decisions about health care in specific clinical circumstances. Research has shown that if properly developed, communicated and implemented, guidelines can improve patient care (www.nice.org.uk).

They also explicitly include considerations of cost-effectiveness, as well as procedures for public consultation:

NICE guidelines are based on the best available research evidence and expert professional advice. They take into account both clinical effectiveness and cost effectiveness, and must be practical and affordable. In developing guidelines, NICE involves the clinical professions, the NHS and those who speak for patients (www.nice.org.uk).

Glen Robert has recently evaluated the policies of NICE according to the framework of Accountability for Reasonableness, and concludes that it appears to 'broadly meet all of the requirements'.[39] Richard Smith, editor of the BMJ, has recently argued that NICE has failed in one respect:

Despite the protestations of its boss, the National Institute for Clinical Excellence (NICE) is an instrument for rationing health care ... One failing of NICE is that it's living a double lie. The first lie – which is as Orwellian as its

---

39 Robert, G, 'Country report UK', 2001, unpublished paper.

name – is to deny that it's about rationing health care, which might be defined as 'denying effective interventions'. Denying ineffective interventions is not rationing; rather it's what the Americans call a 'no brainer'. The population is smart enough both to know that NICE is rationing health care and that rationing of health care is inevitable. The second, and related, lie is to give the impression that if the evidence supports a treatment then it's made available and if it doesn't it isn't. In other words, the whole messy problem of deciding which interventions to make available can be decided with some data and a computer. It's a technical problem. This lie corrupts the concept of evidence based medicine, which the BMJ has long championed. The evidence supports decision making, but the evidence can't make the decision. The values of the patient or the community must be part of the decision.[40]

Without taking side in the debate between the friends and critics of NICE, I would like to end this chapter by suggesting how the work of NICE on guideline development could be improved and help to achieve the goal of fair and legitimate rationing. Based on the reasoning in previous sections, I suggest how the threshold for exclusion can be made explicit, what reasons for exclusion can be given, and how the threshold of exclusion can be decided by a fair and transparent process.

Part of NICE's programme plan is to modify already 'inherited' guidelines from the Department of Health. Let us now, for the sake of argument, assume that NICE would like to modify the Joint British Recommendations for preventing cardiovascular disease. The first thing to do would be to make explicit the threshold for exclusion. This can be done in the following way. Part of the package in the Joint British Recommendations is a software program that practitioners can install in their computers and use to calculate total risk for cardiovascular disease. There exist several such programmes. One of them is a cardiovascular risk calculator for Excel developed by Rodney Jackson (based on Framingham data), and supplied with the guidelines developed in New Zealand.[41] The physician can insert all relevant patient characteristics, and the program calculates five-year risk and the excepted risk reduction from treatment. This program can easily be modified so that a threshold (based on five-year risk) is directly incorporated in the recommendations. For example, if the risk is below 10%, the program assigns 'Priority: No' to the patient.

40   Smith, R, 'The failings of NICE' (2000) 321 BMJ 1363–64.
41   Downloadable from www.nzgg.org.nz.

Figure 10.2: Cardiac risk calculator

Enter Patient Information Below			Calculated Cardiac Risk	
Gender	m	m=male, f=female	5 yr probability of CVD	9,8%
Age	60	years	Absolute Risk Reduction	3,2%
SBP	157	mmHg	Number needed to treat	31
Smoker	n	y=smokes now or anytime in last year, n=no	**Priority**	**NO**
Total Cholestoral	7	mmol/L		
HDL Cholestoral	2	mmol/L		
Diabetes	n	y-yes, n=no		
ECG LVH	n	y=yes, n=no		

Notes: The calculation if for 5 year risk, with relative risk reduction of 33%. ECG LVH is not the same as echo LVH which is a lesser risk factor, echo is a more sensitive but less specific test for LVH.

CVD includes the following fatal and non-fatal events: MI, angina, coronary insufficiency, sudden and non-sudden coronary death stroke, TIA, PVD (claudication), LVF (symptomatic).

(Adapted for use in New Zealand by Dr Rodney Jackson, Associate Professor of Epidemiology, Dept of Community Health, School of Medicine, University of Auckland, New Zealand, rt.jackson@auckland.ac.nz. Modified by Ole F Norheim, 2001.)

Characteristics for a male patient with low risks are calculated. The expected benefit from preventive measures is clinically significant (absolute risk reduction is 8,9%, numbers needed to treat is 31), but the patient is below the threshold for priority treatment. The programme is modified so that it assigns 'no priority' if 5-year absolute risk is below 10%.

If the risk is above 10%, 'Priority: Yes' is assigned.

Figure 10.3: Cardiac risk calculator

Enter Patient Information Below				Calculated Cardiac Risk	
Gender	m	m=male, f=female	5 yr probability of CVD		27,0%
Age	60	years	Absolute Risk Reduction		8,9%
SBP	174	mmHg	Number needed to treat		11
Smoker	n	y=smokes now or anytime in last year, n=no	**Priority**		**YES**
Total Cholestoral	9	mmol/L			
HDL Cholestoral	1,5	mmol/L			
Diabetes	y	y-yes, n=no			
ECG LVH	n	y=yes, n=no			

Notes: The calculation if for 5 year risk, with relative risk reduction of 33%. ECG LVH is not the same as echo LVH which is a lesser risk factor, echo is a more sensitive but less specific test for LVH.

CVD includes the following fatal and non-fatal events: MI, angina, coronary insufficiency, sudden and non-sudden coronary death stroke, TIA, PVD (claudication), LVF (symptomatic).

(Adapted for Use in New Zealand by Dr Rodney Jackson, Associate Professor of Epidemiology, Dept of Community Health, School of Medicine, University of Auckland, New Zealand, rt.jackson@auckland.ac.nz. Modified by Ole F Norheim, 2001.)

Characteristics for a male patient with high risk are calculated. The expected benefit from preventive measures is clinically significant (absolute risk reduction is 8,9%, numbers needed to treat is 11), and the patient is above the threshold for priority treatment.

In this way, the practitioner is instantly made aware of what the guideline developers recommend.

Space for clinical discretion should of course still be allowed for in exceptional cases, as also noted in the Joint British Recommendations:

The estimates of risk from the chart are based on groups of people, and in managing an individual patient the doctor also has to use clinical judgment in deciding how intensively to intervene on lifestyle and whether or not to use drug treatment.[42]

---

42 British Cardiac Society, British Hyperlipidaemia Association, British Hypertension Society, Association BD, 'Joint British recommendations on prevention of coronary heart disease in clinical practice: summary' (2000) 320 BMJ 705–08.

I have modified Rodney Jackson's calculator in such a way that the threshold is set to 10%, but this can easily be adjusted according to the decisions made by the guideline developers. The use of such calculators highlights the possibility of being explicit on thresholds – if that is desirable.

Next, reasons for exclusion below the threshold ought to be given by NICE, according to the ethical framework. The following is a suggestion:

- The risk of disease, if untreated, is not important enough to justify funding from public money through the NHS. Given other competing needs, an absolute five-year risk below 10% is comparatively small.
- The expected benefit from treatment is not important enough. The absolute risk reduction for, for example, a male patient with a total risk of 9.8% is only 3.2%. Put differently, 31 patients must be treated with drugs in five years to avoid one cardiovascular event (see Figure 10.2).
- The costs are too high compared to the benefit. There is good evidence from cost-effectiveness studies that the drugs in question, for example, anti-hypertension drugs, statins, and others have an unfavourable cost-effectiveness ratio.
- The costs can be borne by the patient himself. Even if the NHS is not willing to fund this treatment, patients are free to purchase the drug themselves if they believe that the expected benefit is of high importance to them. Practitioners should inform their patients about this possibility.
- Evidence is inconclusive. The benefit for low risk patients without established cardiovascular disease is calculated from a few randomised clinical trials, and there is some disagreement among specialists about the quality of this evidence.
- The evidence on burden of disease if untreated, the benefit for high-risk patients, and the cost-effectiveness of the interventions are, on the other hand, conclusive.

Framed in this way, the reasons for rationing can be made explicit by NICE so that 'all fair minded parties' can consider whether they are 'relevant to deciding how to meet the diverse needs of a covered population under necessary resource constraints'.

Needless to say, different stakeholders might disagree about the exact threshold and the reasons given. Some might disagree about the assessment of the evidence, or some might consider the benefit of 3.2% risk reduction over five years as so valuable that the NHS should fund it. The threshold of exclusion should be decided by a due process. This can easily be achieved because NICE has already incorporated mechanisms that secure that stakeholders are heard in the final development of a guideline. As part of their validation process the Guideline Development Group sends the first and second draft guideline to stakeholders for consultation:

The Institute wants stakeholders to contribute to the development of the guidelines as they bring their own perspective to the clinical area that is being addressed. For a NICE clinical guideline development, stakeholders are the:

- national organisations that represent those patients and carers whose care is described in the guideline;

- national organisations that represent health professionals directly providing those services;

- manufacturers with products in the clinical area covered by the scope of the guideline whose interests are likely to be significantly affected by the guideline (A Guide to Stakeholder Involvement in Guidelines Development).

Advice on the proper threshold could easily be obtained by this method. Of course NICE, as part of the NHS, must have the final authority to decide the exact threshold of exclusion, but this decision could be considered legitimate if developed through a due process. Put differently, a guideline should not be implemented if the impact on key stakeholders is not perceived to be acceptable for those affected by it.

SECTION 7: CONCLUDING REMARKS

This chapter has argued that clinical guidelines are at risk of being used as tools for unacceptable and covert rationing disguised as expert recommendations. While it is problematic to generalise from only one case (preventive cardiology), the case illustrates many of the dilemmas of healthcare rationing. It can, therefore, be used as a model for understanding how rationing might occur, and ultimately for how the processes of such forms of rationing could be improved through the use of the ethical framework of Accountability for Reasonableness. Achieving such a goal is, however, formidable because the practice of rationing involves so many stakeholders and often conflicting and competing demands. It is, therefore, encouraging that such an institution as NICE has incorporated so many of the tools and mechanisms necessary for fair priority setting. What remains is to see whether it, and other institutions, dare to use them.

CHAPTER 11

THE ECONOMICS OF CLINICAL GUIDELINES

S Heasell

SYNOPSIS

The perspective of an economist is used in this chapter to consider clinical guidelines in the context of allocating scarce resources for healthcare. Allocation is the unavoidable issue of deciding to which particular use various versatile resources (not just money but what it can buy) will be committed. Sometimes, clinical guidelines might be part of an attempt to influence decisions of this kind but, in any case, their introduction might have that effect.

This chapter begins with an explanation of why clinical guidelines can never be regarded merely as statements of good practice if the purpose is to identify their impact on resource allocation. The economic perspective is also inherently a social one which recognises that the material interests of different individuals might conflict to some extent, or else appear to those individuals to do so. It is suggested that material incentives, introduced with a particular set of guidelines, could determine whether or not those guidelines fulfil the healthcare objectives set for them. Material, usually financial, incentives are one alternative to a reliance on the threat of crude force to impose guidelines. The economic perspective underlines the case for evaluating any guidelines regime in terms of its cost-effectiveness in achieving the objectives set for it, not merely whether it has some effect (possibly at a wastefully high cost).

The dynamic and risky aspects of health care are identified as reasons why the consequences of clinical guidelines might be complex and their cost-effectiveness difficult to predict, although the adoption of an economic perspective does at least make it possible to be more aware of some plausibly possible costs and effects and take them into account when making decisions about the adoption of clinical guidelines. The relationship between guidelines and the law is considered as an economic issue in terms of how clinical rights and responsibilities (for resources) are allocated and upheld between clinicians and others in society.

The second part of the chapter illustrates the economic perspective of clinical guidelines in general by considering in more detail the particular case of the NHS in the UK at and around the time of writing. The singular institutional and organisational setting of health care in the UK serves as a reminder that there are limits to the generalisations that can be made about clinical guidelines, but also that systematic application of an economic perspective can offer a short-cut to some insights about clinical guidelines across a range of settings, mainly because the underlying problem about allocation decisions is common to all. Hence, the details of attempts by the Labour Government in Britain to refine and extend the use of clinical guidelines reflect conflicting pressures on resource use and indicate that differences of opinion on what constitutes good clinical practice are not necessarily the only obstacles to full compliance. Some of the social institutions, in the sense of accepted ways of doing things, that help to give the NHS its distinctive character are also ways in which the allocation of resources to it and within it are resolved. The interaction of the NHS with the law and with institutions of national government are seen to supplement the process. It is possible to predict some of the consequences for resource allocation of these particular institutions, or at least to identify some of the characteristics of their influence. New NHS-related organisations such as the National Institute for Clinical Excellence (NICE) and the Commission for Health Improvement (CHI) can be seen as part of an attempt to modify the accepted ways of doing things in health care, specifically in deciding the allocation of resources. If it takes hold as the Labour Government has advocated, clinical allocation decisions made by reference to an explicit common evidence base and an explicit allocation of responsibility for co-operative clinical governance within the NHS would be a shift in decision-making culture as well as a new set of guidelines.

The overall message of the chapter is that, since clinical guidelines cannot in practice be disassociated from potential conflict about the allocation of resources for healthcare, their introduction in prospect and their evaluation in retrospect should both be considered by integrating the economic and social dimension of the issue with the clinical dimension.

INTRODUCTION

This chapter includes, first, an account of why an economic perspective is integral to a full understanding of the application of clinical guidelines (CGs) in healthcare. Having established that there are risks of over-generalisation when thinking about guidelines beyond one particular context, the chapter continues by way of illustration with an economic perspective on the development of CGs in the dynamic context of the NHS in the UK around the turn of the millennium.

GUIDELINES AND RESOURCE ALLOCATION

It might seem that CGs need have nothing to do with resources or resource allocation. Notionally, at least, they might merely be indicators of the clinical characteristics of one or more clinical services. Many people, perhaps, wish that this would remain so. Nevertheless, scarce resources and their implications are cited frequently in discussions about CGs.[1] It has been suggested that increasing pressures to use up more resources for health care services, or else the wish to respond to those pressures, helps to explain attempts to devise, implement and respond to guidelines.

The logic of scarcity seems inexorable because the resources made available each year for healthcare, as for other purposes, will never be limitless. Decisions about what to do and not to do with those resources that are available will continue to be made. CGs, in their devising and dissemination, use up resources that are thereby denied, at least temporarily, to any other alternative use.

In addition, if they are at all effective, the guidelines will cause some activity that is somewhat different from what would otherwise have occurred without them, perhaps because they are supported by other tools of governance in healthcare that seek to influence their impact on individual or organisational practice. If so, then the impact of guidelines on resource allocation will be the greater, although it might not be wholly of an expected kind. The economics of CGs are not identical with the economics of clinical services themselves, but it is impossible to understand the one without some reference to the other.

It would be possible, in principle if not in practice, to confine the information contained in CGs to clinical characteristics and not attempt to include any influence on that information of the impact on resource pressures which particular clinical services would have. Such an omission, of course, would leave the impact on resource allocation to be influenced and assimilated in other ways, systematically or otherwise. Any indication within the guidelines that particular clinical characteristics are good or bad, better or worse, however, might well influence the adoption of one clinical service instead of another and hence influence the pattern of resource allocation for healthcare services.

It is conceivable that the allocation of resources occasioned by guidelines would leave everyone feeling sufficiently better off to produce a consensus in favour of it and a commitment to make it happen. This is highly unlikely to occur, because of a technical lack of expertise to accomplish such an ambitious outcome and also, perhaps, because of insufficient commitment by enough

---

1   Woolf, SH, Grol, R, Hutchinson, A, Eccles, M and Grimshaw, J, 'Clinical guidelines: the potential benefits, limitations and harms of clinical guidelines' (1999) 318 BMJ 527–30.

people. Some individuals may feel that they, or those they care most about, would be better off from allocating resources in a way which would create some losers as well as some gainers. It can be expected that various individuals and organisations will each try to secure as much of the benefits of CGs and as little of their costs as possible. Distribution of costs and benefits will be an active issue alongside any attempt to maximize the overall net benefits. Only some of those people affected would be patients of clinical services. Others would find their prospective lives or livelihoods changed, possibly in terms of income or job satisfaction, or just by feeling at risk of being adversely affected in some way.

It would not be surprising, then, if CGs in prospect or in operation tended to be contentious, much as an explicit decision to direct scarce health service resources to the provision of one clinical service or one set of patients instead of another can be contentious. Consensus is unlikely, either in favour of CGs, or on targets for CGs to achieve, or about which CGs are to be adopted to achieve them. In the circumstances, the exercise of some power by the protagonists for CGs may be required to ensure that they are effective. The exercise of power over resource allocation is unlikely to be costless even to the powerful. The greater and more widespread is the consent to comply with the guidelines, however, the lower are likely to be the costs of successful implementation. Contentiousness is likely to persist also because of genuine uncertainties about the evidence base on which guidelines are developed. By no means all indicators of the comparative effectiveness and cost effectiveness of different ways to respond to a given clinical condition are as yet sound or subtle enough to quash variations in clinical opinion based on long standing professional experience and expertise.

CGs are more likely to have a distinctive impact on clinical services if the information they contain is accompanied by some relevant and powerful incentives which persuade potential users of the guidelines to reallocate resources they have available, or to allocate additional ones that become available, to produce a distinctive effect. Effective incentives might be attractive ones (carrots) or unpleasant ones (sticks), from the perspective of each potential user.

APPRAISAL OF GUIDELINES IN FULL CONTEXT

Rigorous evaluations of the clinical effectiveness of one or more programmes of guidelines can provide potentially very useful information.[2] They are incomplete, however, as indicators of whether resource commitments to a

---

2   Grimshaw, JM and Russell, IT, 'Effect of clinical guidelines on medical practice: a systematic review of rigorous evaluations' (1993) 342 The Lancet 1317–22.

programme are worthwhile unless they are integrated within an equally rigorous evaluation of cost effectiveness. An implication of scarcity is that resources could be combined and used in various mutually exclusive ways, so an element of deliberate choice is possible. Whatever the benefits associated with one programme of CGs, it is impossible to be reasonably confident whether or not it is worthwhile without some systematic consideration of alternative uses for the same resources.

The range of alternatives could include pursuing the same objectives by alternative means, including other programmes of CGs. They could also include pursuing alternative objectives, either by CGs or otherwise. For example, an objective of fewer errors in surgery might be pursued by changes in legal liability for error or by incentive payments to clinicians without any use or revision of CGs. Equally, the effective alternatives might include different mixtures of all these elements.

The full influence of CGs could be understood only if the full physical and social context of their application were to be taken into account. That context includes an economic aspect insofar as the physical environment and people, or their capabilities, are among the resources to be allocated if CGs are devised and applied. Full understanding may anyway be a technically or practically over-ambitious aspiration, but even a workably reliable one would surely require some attention to matters beyond the purely clinical. It might be more reliable to do so by integrating the consideration of these other aspects systematically with that of the clinical dimension than to consider them entirely separately and as an afterthought.

There may be some features which link prospective or actual CGs in different physical, social, organisational or temporal settings. Comparable pressures on the use of resources might be one characteristic link in some cases. It would be risky, however, to assume that details of a set of guidelines which are applied in one context, with whatever apparent degree of success, can be transposed successfully elsewhere. In designing CGs, there is a balance to be struck between making them relevant in some specific setting (not too vague as to be ineffective) and making them relevant across various different cases. They could be defined so narrowly as to be too rarely effective. They could, instead, require the development of so complex a set of guidelines for all the relevant possibilities as to be prohibitively difficult and costly to devise or operate adequately well.

It will be important to consider the dynamic resource context of CGs rather than be tempted, for reasons of simplification, to dwell entirely on their implications at one fixed point in time. Changes will affect the context in which CGs are applied, at various times and at various rates. The CGs themselves and the associated programme of organisational arrangements will have to be sufficiently flexible and also up-dated from time to time to remain relevant and cost effective as the context of healthcare services develops. Even in the absence of other changes, responses to the existing CGs will develop over time as both instigators and users learn to use them to better advantage as each of them sees it. Hence, the cost and effectiveness of the information and incentives created may well be modified over time.

Another aspect of the dynamic context is the fluidity of objectives against which guidelines are to be assessed. A standard cost effectiveness analysis presumes one readily identifiable set of objectives throughout but it might well be that they (or interpretations of them) emerge and evolve as part of the process of working with guidelines.

GUIDELINES AND RESOURCE IMPLICATIONS OF RISK

A recurring theme in the literature on CGs is the attempt not only to improve performance but, in doing so, to reduce variations in performance which cause it to fall below an acceptable minimum. Guidelines directed to that purpose are presented as setting particular standards of service, explicitly or implicitly, which all should seek to uphold consistently.

For numerous reasons, it would be counter-productive to eliminate all variation in clinical practice, even for apparently similar clinical conditions. Variety of cases, variety of expertise (where it is not inferior expertise) and the existence of only imperfect evidence of what constitutes best practice are among the reasons why complete homogeneity of practice cannot, and should not, be expected. More appropriate targets for reform are those variations in practice which constitute unnecessarily poor clinical service. A full assessment of which dips in service are unnecessary would take into account the resource costs of eliminating them, resources which might otherwise be used to improve performance in other ways. Equally, the efficient feasible reform programme could be one which, on occasion, deters beneficial variations in practice if the cost or technical difficulty of formulating an operational programme with a perfectly sensitive and subtle filter would be excessive.

The minimum standards to be upheld might be regarded by clinicians as higher or lower than those they currently achieve but, in any case, the guidelines could require or suggest differences from current practice. If they are at all effective, they are likely to imply some constraint on current practice by some individual clinicians.

If new guidelines are fully effective, there will be a degree of greater conformity of practice among the currently less successful practitioners. It is possible that the characteristics of a particular regime of CGs would also push up levels of performance among the more successful practitioners, or it might expand the range and variety of performance among them. In contrast, less successful new regimes could prompt some more capable practitioners to regress their performance towards the average, fearing the consequences for them of breaching the guidelines by chance were they to engage in bolder decision-making. Clinicians will decide how much risk of non-compliance with guidelines they are prepared to run and the CGs themselves might indicate that it is appropriate to take more chances or, perhaps more often, fewer chances than a clinician would otherwise have chosen to take.

Regimes which have the effect of curbing variations in performance, or which are designed to do so, are exercises in clinical risk management, although the risk can take various forms. Performance can vary from place to place, person to person, organisation to organisation and from time to time. The variations might be systematic and predictable or less so. They might be controllable and avoidable or less so. Decisions about committing resources to clinical services if performance varies around its average level might well differ from decisions taken if performance never strayed from the same average level. Efficient risk management, whether by patients and clinicians individually or by health service organisations, would take into account not only the characteristics of the risk but also the attitudes to risk held by influential decision-makers.

For example, the more that clinicians prefer to avoid bearing adverse risk, the greater are the incentives required to persuade them to comply with a regime of CGs that would increase such risks. In some CG regimes, a requirement to exercise professional judgement about when or how to depart from explicit guidelines in the cause of best practice for the specific local circumstances of a particular case could itself add to the risk borne by the clinician. Smaller incentives to clinicians, or none, would be required if they can use guidelines to help to reduce the burden which risk imposes upon them.

GUIDELINES AND RESOURCE IMPLICATIONS OF THE LAW

A CG regime might include an element of regulation of clinical practice by health service organisations. Regulations will of necessity take into account any legal institutions that are constituted beyond the organisation and any laws to which it is expected to conform. The resource implications of CGs depend partly on their relationship with the law.

In some respects, legal institutions might support the regulatory regime within a health service organisation that includes CGs. Indeed, the CGs may have the force of law. Ultimately, however, these are two alternative ways to allocate clinical rights and responsibilities. Health service organisations and their internal institutions nevertheless are usually subject to the law and no understanding of the resource implications of CGs would be complete without considering its potential influence systematically.

The law, and legal institutions in any jurisdiction more generally, can be regarded as a way to allocate the ownership of rights and responsibilities where resources are concerned, if ownership is subject to a dispute involving particular organisations or individuals.[3] In that perspective, an assault by one individual on the person of another would be in a set of special cases, albeit among the more important cases, alongside disputes about interference with inanimate property whose ownership is claimed by others. Legal institutions might be used as a contribution towards an efficient allocation of resources, although criteria other than efficiency such as notions of equity (fairness) or justice in distributing rights and responsibilities might well also affect the pattern of institutions or how they are used.

Clinicians and others can be expected to allocate resources at their command to reflect their understanding of how their professional rights and responsibilities would be enforced if under pressure. For example, if clinicians believe themselves to be legally liable for clinical error to any extent, then we can expect that they will allocate some of the resources at their command in an attempt to manage that liability cost effectively in accordance with their own objectives. If so, it follows that in a jurisdiction where compliance with CGs might be used as evidence to support a clinician in a dispute about liability for unsatisfactory clinical service, it is predictable that clinicians would allocate more resources apparently to comply with CGs than they would if the guidelines are always disregarded for legal purposes. Equally, short of legal liability, it is to be expected that clinicians will use more of the resources they command apparently to comply with CGs if there is a credible threat that health service organisations will enforce effective sanctions on those who do not do so.

The efficiency of the resulting allocation of resources by clinicians will then depend partly on the allocation of liability, hence costs between clinicians and others who might bear the burden instead. It could be cost effective overall, at least in some contexts, for clinicians individually to face full liability, including all financial costs for all clinical practice that harms patients. Considerations of fairness or justice, however, might indicate otherwise and, in any case, no one is surprised that clinicians struggle to avoid such an imposition. The effectiveness of that struggle, and the resources used up to support it or resist the burdens, add to the calculations required to identify the cost effective allocation of liability. In practice, these calculations are refined, continually but implicitly, as the social mix of legal and other institutions that influence clinical practice within health service organisations continues to evolve.

---

3   Dnes, AW, *The Economics of Law*, 1996, London: International Thomson Business Press. Posner, R, *Economic Analysis of Law*, 4th edn, 1992, Boston: Little Brown & Co.

GUIDELINES IN THE NHS

The term clinical guidelines had already been applied to developments in the NHS before 1997.[4] It was the incoming Labour government of that year, however, which began to consolidate the role and function of CGs within a framework for a new system of NHS governance.[5] The National Institute of Clinical Excellence (NICE) was established as part of the new system and it formally began work in April 1999.[6]

Clinical governance for the NHS has been described as a framework requiring a systematic set of mechanisms, for supporting an organisational environment in which excellent and improving quality of clinical services will flourish.[7] Governance in this case can also be regarded as a set of social institutions (patterns of ways of doing things, perhaps partly governed by rules), involving distinctive processes with supporting organisational structures. The NICE was envisaged as a supporting structure largely to provide information, with other elements of governance being used to supply the incentives for individuals and organisations to pursue consistently excellent quality of service. For example, the Commission for Health Improvement, or CHI (informally soon known as 'nasty' in contrast with NICE), was set up as a central organisational structure to investigate evidence of unsatisfactory local clinical performance, to recommend changes if necessary, and to press for improvement.

The main remit of the NICE was threefold but, initially, the considerable task of distilling and disseminating reliable evidence-based appraisals of new clinical technologies assumed the highest priority. Its other main categories of activity were to be those of issuing or kite marking CGs and of encouraging clinical audit nationwide.[8] Initially, a sharp distinction was drawn between information about individual clinical products or services (from NICE appraisals) and information about providing services in general for a particular health condition (in CGs endorsed by the NICE). The inclusion of cost effectiveness criteria in the appraisal process, as well as clinical effectiveness criteria, is notable and will affect the characteristics of CGs increasingly if and as the results of appraisal are assimilated into them.

---

4 Humphris, D, 'Clinical guidelines: an industry for growth' (1994) 90(40) Nursing Times 46–47. Sims, J, 'Be flexible with clinical guidelines', May 1995, Health Care Management, 8–10.

5 NHS Executive, *A First Class Service: Quality in the New NHS*, Health Service Circular HSC113/98', 1998, HMSO.

6 Department of Health, 'The New National Institute for Clinical Excellence Opens for Business', 31 March 1999, Press Release 0193.

7 *Op cit*, NHS Executive, fn 5.

8 Smith, R, 'NICE: A Panacea for the NHS?', Editorial (1999) 318 BMJ 823–24.

More generally, an economic perspective on healthcare services was prominent, though not dominant, in early statements about the rationale for establishing the NICE. In a series of introductory pages on the organisation's website, we were told that the NICE was set up 'to help health professionals in the NHS give patients the best possible health care within the resources available'[9] by, among other things 'focusing on the most cost-effective treatments'. Elsewhere in the same series, we were told that NICE was needed because, among other things, 'the demand for health care ... is greater than the financial and human resources available' and that health professionals have sometimes chosen technologies, clinical management programmes or methods without adequate evidence about (cost) effectiveness or value for money.[10]

DEVELOPING AN ECONOMIC DIMENSION TO NHS GUIDELINES

However strong the case for integrating an economic dimension within a regime of CGs for the NHS, it is not proving easy to do so systematically and convincingly. The problems are not unique to CG development. Systematic use by clinicians of cost effectiveness appraisals and their systematic management of limited resources for clinical services was not fully ingrained and endemic in NHS practice or culture when the latest CG proposals were introduced from 1997. It is implied, therefore, that all these developments will proceed simultaneously from now, so that increasing success of each of them presupposes an increasing success of the others.

As recently as 1995, a leading health economist in the UK still felt it necessary to put the case in favour of using information on cost effectiveness to influence clinical practice.[11] It is by no means clear, even now, that the case has ceased to be contentious within the NHS, especially among clinicians whose wholehearted compliance will be essential if CGs with a cost effectiveness dimension are going to be fully successful. Even if the principle of taking account of cost and cost effectiveness within the CGs is gradually gaining ground, there is still less of a consensus on how to do it. A particular worry among health economists in the context of CGs,[12] and more widely, is

9   National Institute of Clinical Excellence, *About NICE. Frequently Asked Questions 12: Why is NICE Needed?*, 2000, Section 2, http://www.nice.org.uk.

10 *Ibid*, Section 12.

11 Williams, A, 'The measurement and validation of health: a chronical', Discussion Paper 136, 1995b, University of York Centre for Health Economics, York: University of York.

12 Mason, J, Eccles, M, Freemantle, N and Drummond, M, 'A NICE start? Economic analysis within evidence based clinical practice guidelines', in Smith, P (ed), *Reforming Markets in Health Care*, 2000, Buckingham: OU Press, Chapter 10, pp 211–46.

that cost will continue to be seen by clinicians merely as a separate extra consideration, to be bolted on after the strictly clinical matters have been decided. To do so risks failure to recognise (wilfully or otherwise) that the economic dimension is integral to the context of clinical services. For particular pragmatic or organisational reasons, it might be better in some cases to achieve integration of the economic dimension beyond the CGs themselves, but the provision for this must be clear in any discussion of CGs. To bolt on a cost analysis almost as an appendix to a set of guidelines would be possibly the worst kind of compromise between integration and alternative development of the economic dimension of clinical services. Such a cost analysis is likely to be misleading because it is not fully integrated with the evidence of benefits to yield indicators of cost effective practice. It also might seem to lend credence to the fears expressed by clinicians and others that CGs are but one more attempt to emphasise mere cost containment in the NHS.

It would be disappointing if the expertise which health economists can bring to the development of CGs as envisaged for the NHS were to be devoted exclusively to the improvement of the cost effectiveness appraisal information base, essential though that task and that expertise is to such a development. It is equally essential to resolve issues of institutional and organisational development that have an economic dimension. Promotion of appropriate cost effectiveness appraisal has been a long standing project among a substantial proportion of health economists in the UK. The opportunities and the formidable problems associated with the development of appraisals systematically throughout the NHS and beyond help to explain why so much scarce effort has been devoted to that activity. Much of it is extremely detailed technical work but it is also laden with questions of broad principle, conflicting interests and simple applicability.

Protagonists among health economists for cost effectiveness appraisal in the NHS acknowledge, perhaps more explicitly now, that a technocratic blueprint alone will not necessarily be successful within a particular social, organisational and cultural context. They also acknowledge explicitly that active, systematic co-operation if not empathy is required among many participants, including clinicians, to stand the best chance of success. In addition, the best health economists also recognise that professional economic expertise does not automatically make the economist an expert in the politics or other aspects of the NHS.

An appreciation of the technical and other problems of cost effectiveness appraisal can perhaps be had by considering a textbook version of such an analysis. An archetypal cost effectiveness appraisal, conforming with principles suggested by economists, would measure and total in standard money terms all the incremental costs borne by anyone through the use of resources in particular ways to effect a chosen category of benefit (for example, improvements in health). There are long standing conventional methods for doing so. The chosen category of benefits also would be measured and totalled for each prospective use. This part of the exercise is done not usually in money terms, but nevertheless by just one index number which, like money, can be compared directly between one way and another of achieving that category of benefits. Various attempts have been made to design an index of numbers based on a standard unit of measurement for this purpose in healthcare, including the Quality Adjusted Life Year, or QALY.[13]

Health economists and others tend to regard a lot of the standard methods for cost measurement as established conventions, even where they recognise some scope for significant improvement.[14] The methods or conventions for measuring effectiveness are less firmly established, perhaps especially not in healthcare. Health economists recognise that the attempt to get widespread agreement to the measurement of any improvement in health by just one index of numbers is extremely ambitious. They should also acknowledge, however, that similar apprehensions may be appropriate to some extent about measurement of all costs of resources by just one index of numbers, where that index is in standard monetary units. This may be especially so in a context such as that of the NHS, where market forces as a way to allocate resources have partly and deliberately been suspended.

It is not helpful to allow the perfect to be the enemy of the merely very good, or to deter attempts at improvement. The awesome task of achieving even one archetypal cost effectiveness appraisal need not provoke a council of despair. Robust and simplified methods of appraisal may well be practical and also cost effective for healthcare, compared with no systematic appraisal of cost effectiveness at all. Equally, it might well be cost effective for economists to contribute to the development of systems of cost effective support for CGs rather than devote all their energies to one more refinement of appraisal methods.

CLINICAL FREEDOM IN THE NHS: AN ECONOMIC DIMENSION

A particular concern with CGs that has been expressed among clinicians employed by the NHS is the apparent threat to their clinical freedom to decide

---

13   Williams, A, 'How should information of cost-effectiveness influence practice?', in Delamothe (ed), *Outcomes in Clinical Practice*, 1995, London: BMJ.

14   Sugden, R and Williams, A, *The Principles of Practical Cost Benefit Analysis*, 1979, Oxford: Blackwell. Drummond, MF, O'Brien, B, Stoddart, GL and Torrance, GW, *Methods for the Economic Evaluation of Health Care Programmes*, 2nd edn, 1997, Oxford: OUP.

what services to provide for individual patients.[15] The concern did not originate with the recent CG proposals. It has been current at least since the development of the general management function with decentralised responsibility for limited budgets in local NHS organisations from the 1980s.[16]

The emergence of a cohesive body of health service managers has been seen as a countervailing source of power over use of resources in the NHS to balance that exercised by clinicians, individually or as a group. Clinicians may associate health service managers with efforts to ensure that CGs are followed in practice. If the guidelines effectively constrain how some clinicians practise, with effects on how they allocate resources, then cries of clinical freedom being lost in the name of cost containment might be heard from them.

The contribution that clinical freedoms make towards ensuring best clinical practice is largely an empirical question, but one which depends not least on how those freedoms affect pressures on demand for resources and on the willing supply of services by clinicians as one set of resources. The contribution made by clinical freedom also depends on which particular criteria of good practice are adopted. Furthermore, it depends on whether or not the relationship of individual patient with clinician is the only appropriate reference point for judging good practice. At least at the level of the local or national NHS as a whole, limited resources will be inevitably allocated among and between many services for many potential patients. The allocation will be made not wholly by reference to the preparedness to pay an explicit market price for those services.

NHS GUIDELINES, RISK AND RESOURCES

A feature of the objectives announced initially for the NICE was the promotion not only of examples of excellent quality clinical services but a more consistently good quality, special attention being given to alleged geographical inconsistencies in the services currently offered. An implied objective, therefore, is to change the pattern of risk in clinical services and, in particular, to reduce the adverse risk associated with poor clinical services. Ironically, an existing proliferation of CGs of variable quality was said to contribute to this risk.[17]

---

15 Woolf, SH, Grol, R, Hutchinson, A, Eccles, M and Grimshaw, J, 'Clinical guidelines: the potential benefits, limitations and harms of clinical guidelines' (1999) 318 BMJ 527–30. Hurwitz, B, 'Legal and political considerations of clinical practice guidelines' (1999) 318 BMJ 661–64.

16 Klein, R, *The New Politics of the NHS*, 3rd edn, 1995, London: Longman.

17 NHS Executive, *A First Class Service: Quality in the New NHS*, Health Service Circular HSC113/98', 1998, HMSO.

If it usually takes more resources to offer good quality clinical services than poor quality ones, a NICE programme of trying to level up the quality of service towards the best quality ever available in the NHS will put further upward pressure on the use of resources. Unsurprisingly, there has been no suggestion from the NHS Executive of an intention to pursue a levelling down where quality is currently regarded as the best available, although there might be some scope in those places for attention to cost effectiveness. In other words, the NICE seems to be offering to identify the cost effective means of achieving an objective that is more ambitious and resource intensive than one of maintaining the currently variable levels of quality in clinical services across the NHS. If the NICE restricts itself to issuing information only when the evidence suggests that quality can be improved simultaneously with less resource use (and no loss of quality elsewhere) then its output may be meagre because only a limited number of examples will be found. The implication for the NHS as a whole seems to be that the NICE and CGs will generate an extra reason to press central government to allocate extra funding for the organisation each year.

An objective of reducing adverse risk also means that since this adversity by definition is less than certain to occur, at least from an individual's point of view, individual commitment to the objective might be so much the weaker. If so, then its achievement might well require reinforcement of incentives to commit scarce resources to pursue it, given other pressures on local resources, even if information on how to do so is reliable, clear and available at low cost to the user. Equally by overstating particular risks or their consequences, at least compared with others, more resources than necessary might be allocated to attempts to reduce them.

THE LAW, RESOURCES AND NHS GUIDELINES

There are many ways in which plans for the NHS by the 1997 Labour Government in the UK might have affected the relationship between that organisation and the law, or might yet do so. New clinical guidelines, or governance more generally, could be causes of such a change.

Various authorities seem to suggest, however, that little has changed since 1997 so far as the formal allocation of legal liability for adverse consequences of clinical events is concerned.[18] The so called *Bolam* test[19] is still used as a test of whether or not a health professional's practice is acceptable for the purpose of determining, under English law, whether or not clinical negligence has

---

18 McClarey, M and Thompson, J, 'Clinical guidelines and the Law, Health Care Risk Report', April 2000, 19–21.

19 *Bolam v Friern Hospital Management Committee* [1957] 1 WLR 582 (QBD).

occurred. Clinical practice passes the *Bolam* test if it would be endorsed by a responsible body of clinicians practising in the relevant discipline. Statements by professional peers are used as evidence in applying the test to particular examples of practice. The implementation of the *Bolam* test seems to imply that responsibility and professional accountability for clinical decision-making remains with the individual health professional (clinician or manager) who takes the decision. Currently, NHS CGs are explicitly not mandatory; if this were to change, then responsibility could reside with those who impose guidelines as mandatory restrictions on the ability of others to take decisions.[20]

Formally, liability for negligence may not have changed but we can expect reference to be made on occasion to NHS CGs in connection with the law, and guidelines might influence various decisions as a result. If so, then they could still be instrumental in affecting the allocation of resources for health services in the UK, and also the consequences of such an allocation. As yet, however, no reliable evidence has been presented that such has systematically been the case.[21]

Uncertainty remains about the effect of NHS CGs on the law in practice, so attempts to use them in support of a claim for negligence, or in support of a defence against such a claim, might yet be made. If such attempts are made, some scarce resources will be allocated to doing so. Slavish adherence to explicit clinical guidelines, where it would be legally appropriate to do otherwise, would not necessarily prevent a finding of clinical negligence. Nevertheless, a belief that contravening explicit guidelines without a legally acceptable reason could be used as evidence of negligence seems likely to influence resource allocation by NHS decision-makers. Resource allocation by or for patients who are dissatisfied with the clinical service they receive could also be affected by the same belief about CGs, even though contravention of guidelines will not always be legally acceptable evidence of negligence, let alone sufficient to secure a claim for negligence.

INCENTIVES TO USE NHS GUIDELINES

The establishment of the CHI ('nasty') seems to indicate that the Labour government recognised an imperative to create incentives, as well as CG information, to ensure that local NHS organisations would commit resources available to them in such a way as to achieve relentless improvement to the quality of clinical services and its consistency. The incentives created might be

20 Mann, T, *Clinical Guidelines – Using Clinical Guidelines to Improve Patient Care Within the NHS*, 1996, Department of Health.
21 Feenan, D, *Clinical Resources and Audit Group: Legal Implications in Clinical Practice*, 1993, Scottish Office, Dundee.

regarded by decision-makers in each relevant local organisation either as carrots or as sticks or as a mixed blessing. In any case, however, designing and implementing them adds to the overall cost of making the CGs effective. These additional costs will be borne in some proportions among the various individuals and organisations affected, NHS ones and others.

Various types of incentives could be created, differing in the levels and distributions of cost and effectiveness. The set of incentives created for the NHS from 1997, associated with the initiatives on clinical governance and CGs, offered a particular mixture between central direction and local discretion that was presented as a contrast to what had gone before it. The 1980s and 1990s had seen an attempt by successive Conservative governments to establish, within a central NHS management framework, a system of incentives arising from limited competition between local NHS organisations with local budget management in which contracting for clinical services was routine.

The change of government in 1997 brought with it a rhetoric for the NHS which suggested that local competition would be replaced by local co-operation or partnership towards a common overall objective, and that fragmented short term contracting for services would be replaced by integrated longer term service agreements. The inclusion of the NICE and especially the CHI in the initiatives associated with clinical governance also suggested a shift from de-centralised quasi-market incentives in which local negotiations about contract prices were prominent. Instead, there would be a greater emphasis on incentives applied by pressures from the centre of the NHS. These pressures might be merely implicit where local motivation and performance seem satisfactory, as judged from the centre, but would be explicit if that were not so.

It has proved difficult and contentious to establish reliable evidence about the costs and effectiveness of the incentives applied in the complex quasi-market context of the NHS and hence to compare them with anything that follows them. To do so requires, among other things, that the consequences of local contracting (most prominent before 1997) be compared with the consequences of requiring information and incentives to be managed from the centre of the NHS (perhaps more so after 1997). Both regimes might contribute towards desirable effectiveness but, more certainly, both are costly in terms of using up scarce resources. The term 'bureaucracy' has sometimes been misapplied to describe with disapproval some of the organisational consequences associated with both features, in particular the staff time and delay involved in organising the delivery of clinical services.

Financial interests and incentives clearly played a part in the quasi-market for clinical services, but could also be encouraged to do so under a more centralised regime. Apportionment of the overall NHS budget allocation each year among local NHS organisations could be made to depend partly on indications of compliance with CGs, although centrally managed performance related payment systems in organisations such as the NHS tend to be fraught with costly problems in identifying reliable evidence of the kind of performance sought.

The costs of incentives to comply with NHS CGs will be the greater if the guidelines themselves do not gain the respect of those NHS decision-makers who are expected to implement them. Among those decision-makers will be some who are convinced that to do so would compromise the objectives set for the NHS, including perhaps the very ones that were cited when initially setting up the guidelines.

The efficient balance between allowing local discretion and insisting on compliance with rigid centrally imposed CGs would allow for the possibility that local improvisation and innovation will sometimes produce the least inefficient ways to achieve the set of objectives desired by the centre or more generally. Centrally imposed guidelines inevitably are limited by a more remote and less detailed, if broader, conception of the local context in which the guidelines are to be applied. Strict compliance with an imperfect programme of guidelines, together with the costs of securing it, is to be compared with achieving a cost effective degree of compliance consistent with achieving desirable objectives.

APPRAISAL OF NHS GUIDELINES

CGs for the NHS will be effective if they contribute towards a demonstrable improvement in clinical services. They will also be cost effective if those improvements in clinical services could not have been achieved in any other way that would have used up less valuable resources. The CGs will also be worthwhile if the resources used up could not have been used effectively in a more valuable way instead.

CGs alone cannot secure cost effective clinical services for the NHS, although they might well be a contribution towards cost effectiveness. A valid guideline that incorporates an economic dimension would be one that, if used, resulted in the benefits and costs predicted by it. In that sense, a guideline might be valid yet not worthwhile, if the cost outweighs the benefits or if the cost of ensuring a valid guideline outweighs the benefits net of costs that valid guideline generates.

It remains rather too early to pronounce with any reasonable confidence on whether or not the post-1997 NHS programme that has included CGs has been a worthwhile commitment of scarce resources, or even about whether those CGs have been part of the cost effective way to achieve any stated set of objectives. It is unlikely that the potential peak of performance of those CGs has yet been reached in respect of the quality and consistency of clinical services. There is some possibility, however, that they will later prove to have been too sclerotic to cope at all efficiently with changes to come in a dynamic context as extensive, as complex and as contentious as that of the NHS. An extensive early account of the possibilities of and constraints on CG development in the context of the NICE and from an economic perspective has set the scene.[22] The chances that the CG programme for the NHS will ever reach its potential peak of performance could turn on political decision-making which may or may not be dominated by a reasonable appraisal of the evidence about the contribution of the programme to the quality and consistency of clinical services.

---

22 Williams, A, 'The measurement and validation of health: a chronicle', Discussion Paper 136, 1995, University of York Centre for Health Economics, York: University of York.

INDEX